# Civil War Justice

## Union Army Executions under Lincoln

*by*
*Robert I. Alotta*

*White Mane Publishing Co., Inc.*

This White Mane Publishing Company, Inc. publication
was printed by
Beidel Printing House, Inc.
63 West Burd Street
Shippensburg, PA 17257

In respect to the scholarship contained herein, the acid-free paper used in this book meets the guidelines for permanence and durability of the Committee on Production Guidelines for Book Longevity of the Council on Library Resources.

For a complete list of available publications
please write
White Mane Publishing Company, Inc.
P.O. Box 152
Shippensburg, PA 17257

Library of Congress Cataloging-in-Publication Data

Alotta, Robert I.
    Civil War Justice: Union Army executions under Lincoln / by Robert I. Alotta.
       p.    cm.
    Bibliography: p.
    Includes index.
    ISBN 0-942597-10-9 (alk. paper) : $24.95
    1. Military offenses--United States--History--19th century.
  2. United States--Armed Forces--History--Civil War, 1861-1865.
  3. United States--History--Civil War, 1861-1865. 4. Executions and executioners --United States--History--19th century.    I. Title.
E491.A43    1989
973.7'41--dc19                                        88-36680
                                                          CIP

PRINTED IN THE UNITED STATES OF AMERICA

*Dedication:*
*To the Conspiracy, plus one.*

# Table of Contents

# PREFACE

Each year, in the advent of his birthday, Abraham Lincoln is cited by a number of American historians as one of the most outstanding presidents in the history of this nation.

The recognition, they say, is justified because the tall, gaunt Lincoln preserved the Union. But when asked if Lincoln's abuse of presidential powers and constitutional authority did not diminish his stellar qualities, the answer is a resounding NO! One historian indicated that Lincoln's goal was to preserve the Union at any cost; how he did it didn't really matter. In other words, we are to believe the ends justify the means — at least in Lincoln's case. Despite his abuse of power, Lincoln's image is still cloaked in sainthood.

This book, before you get the wrong idea, is not *another* biography of Lincoln; neither is it a revisionist history of the Civil War period. Rather it is a factual account of how Lincoln's lack of management skills, his vacillation in regard to military justice decisions, and his complete disregard for the Constitution caused the deaths of many Union soldiers . . . off the battlefield. At the same time, it is a glimpse — perhaps the first — into the real world of the Union soldier. It is a frightening account of justice denied to hundreds of poor, uneducated soldiers who were tried, convicted, and executed for military offenses, sometimes trivial. It is also the account of a major government "cover up" of the actual number of men who were executed by court-martial order.

This is the first book to deal with the court-martial system during the Civil War and the effect of this system on the common soldier. Perhaps as the reader gains insights into what happened over one hundred years ago, he will be able to see that serving one's country can be hazardous in more ways than one.

*The Author*

# INTRODUCTION

Death, a soldier's constant companion, does not discriminate against rank, age, color, or creed. Whenever a young man enters the service of his country, the possibility of his not returning to his loved ones exists.

When a nation is engaged in an armed conflict, be it a war, police action or rebellion, the odds increase that men will die. As soldiers enter a combat zone, possibility approaches probability. There has never been an armed conflict without casualties. Soldiers recognize this fact and, as many believe, the goals and objectives of a state or nation cannot be served without sacrifice.

In retrospect, there was a greater possibility for death in the military during the American Civil War than in any other conflict in which the United States participated. In that war, fourteen out of every 100 men [359,528 deaths out of an aggregate of 2,494,592 United States soldiers] died in the service of the Union.[1] Though the number of deaths is impressive because of the large number of men in combat, the majority of deaths were not combat-related, but were due to sickness and disease.[2]

To many histories, these figures have opened up areas of intriguing research — from tales of heroics to the horrors of primitive sanitation and medical technology. One set of figures that has escaped close scrutiny has been the fairly small number of soldiers who were executed by Union authorities during the war and slightly thereafter. Perhaps the acknowledged number of 276 seems minuscule in contrast to all of the heroic and tragic deaths. Less than one percent of all Union deaths were due to executions. When viewed over the entire Army, the number appears insignificant [.011%]. However, in the history of the United States military, the number has great significance. From 1776 to 1965, 474 men were executed by the armed forces; 56.4 percent of them during the Civil War. [See Chart 1]

There had to be a reason why more men were executed during the Civil War than in all other United States conflicts combined. This question has not been addressed until now. The answer is not a pleasant one.

It is our purpose to explore the concept of military justice as it existed at the outbreak of the Civil War and to examine how this code was interpreted by field commanders in their practice of discipline. Further, it is our intention to expose the reader to actual case historians of the men whose lives were considered so insignificant that as a group they warrant nothing more than a footnote in most history texts.

Because the general subject of military executions has not been addressed by historians[3], this study leans heavily on primary sources, many of which have not been touched by others.

## CHART 1: MILITARY EXECUTIONS

| PERIOD | ARMY | NAVY | AIR FORCE | TOTAL |
|--------|------|------|-----------|-------|
| 1776-1860 | 1 | 5 | n/a | 6 |
| 1861-1867 | 267 | 0 | n/a | 267 |
| 1868-1913 | 3 | 0 | n/a | 3 |
| 1914-1918 | 35 | 1 | n/a | 36 |
| 1919-1941 | 3 | 0 | n/a | 3 |
| 1942-1948 | 146 | 0 | n/a | 146 |
| 1949-1950 | 0 | 0 | 3 | 3 |
| 1951-1953 | 8 | 0 | 0 | 8 |
| 1954-1965 | 2 | 0 | 0 | 2 |
| Total | 465 | 6 | 3 | 474[4] |

The execution of Union soldiers during the Civil War is not one of the brightest pages in the annals of American history. A study of this period, however, points out deficiencies in the military justice system — some of which are perpetuated in today's all-volunteer forces. An awareness of where we went wrong is the first step toward correcting our path.

# ENDNOTES TO INTRODUCTION

1.        Frederick H. Dyer, *A Compendium of the War of the Rebellion* [2 vols., Dayton, Ohio, 1979 reprint], pp. 11-12.

2.        *Ibid.*, p. 12. Total deaths of Union soldiers, as reported by the Adjutant General's Office, are estimated at 359,528, including 110,070 combat deaths or as the result of combat [30.6%]; 199,720 deaths while prisoners — whether due to sickness, combat-related injuries, mistreatment or execution by the Confederates [6.9%]; 9,058 accidental deaths [2.5%]; and 15,814 deaths from all other causes [4.4%]. Though the author presents these figures — those accepted for more than a century, he has strong reservations about their accuracy. Unless someone with the drive and determination of a Frederick H. Dyer can devote his or her life to the monumental task of researching each and every military service file at the National Archives, and create a new statistical base, we will never have a true and accurate picture of the Civil War.

3.        The focus of study on military executions has been on individual cases, rather than on the events and delivery — or miscarriage — of justice.

4.        Judge Advocate General's Office, "Death Sentences Imposed — US Armed Forces," undated photocopy. Though these numbers have been used as reference by the government, they are incomplete, e.g., there is no breakdown of executions by charge until the 1868-1913 period, and a complete itemization is not available until the World War II period. The accepted Civil War data, though inaccurate and incomplete, has been available since 1885.

# CHAPTER ONE

## RULES AND REGULATIONS

For any society to function efficiently, it must establish rules and regulations to which every member must adhere. Individuals are expected to learn and abide by a specific code of conduct. The military, like society in general, has a set of rules and regulations that governs its members. Many, but not all, of the military codes of discipline are based on common sense, and easily understood by the civilian; others are unique and incomprehensible to the non-military population.

A Union soldier, though in service to defend the Constitution, was denied many of the rights available to him under the document he was defending. In particular, Union soldiers were denied the rights of free speech [First Amendment], immunity from search and seizure [Fourth], double jeopardy [Fifth], a speedy and public trial, confrontation of prosecution witnesses, processes for obtaining witnesses in their own behalf, and the assistance of counsel [Sixth], trial by jury, according to the rules of the common law [Seventh], avoidance of cruel and unusual punishment [Eighth], and other basic personal rights [Ninth].

The question of the Constitution versus military codes, as viewed during the Civil War, was examined by Chief Justice Salmon P. Chase [Ex parte Milligan, 71 U.S. 2, 141 (1866)]: '' There is no law for the government of the citizen, the armies, or the navy of the United States which is not contained in or derived from the Constitution.''[1] The Chief Justice's perception, however, ran contrary to much judicial opinion of the Civil War.

The Civil War stands out as an "eccentric period," as James G. Randall calls it,

> a period when specious arguments and legal fictions were
> put forth to excuse extraordinary measures. It was a

*1*

period during which the line was blurred between executive, legislative, and judicial functions; between State
and Federal powers; and between military and civil
procedures.[2]

There was no precedent for the Civil War in the American judicial system.
Military men, just like those steeped in the law, were unprepared for the ad-
justment to wartime reality. And, there apparently was no desire — at least
on the part of the military — to come to grips with the situation. Though legal
advisor to the War Department, Columbia University political theorist Francis
Lieber suggested a course be taught at West Point on the laws of war; the
academy commandant resisted, stating his curriculum was too crowded.[3] To
have introduced such a course, even to such a small group of potential officers,
might have prevented a few injustices from being perpetrated during the war.
If commissioned officers, especially the elite from West Point, had gained an
awareness of the Articles of War, they might have been able to exercise their
commands in line with established rules of conduct. Military discipline which
is drawn from these Articles would have improved. Lieber's codification of the
laws of war, however, were later formalized in General Order 100.

Chase's contention was dropped and theory was brought into confor-
mance with reality in 1953 by the United States Supreme Court [346 U.S. 137,
140], when the Court declared that "Military law, like state law, is a
jurisprudence which exists separate and apart from the law which governs in
our federal judicial establishment. The Court has played no role in its development; we have exerted no supervisory power over the courts which enforce
it . . . ."[4]

Modified in 1776, 1786 and 1806[5], the Articles of War that governed
the military during the Civil War were substantially the same as the ones first
approved in 1775.

The first American Articles of War, enacted by the Continental Congress, were copied from the eighteenth century British Articles of War which
had evolved from the seventeenth century rules of Gustavus Adolphus.[6]
Gustavus Adolphus' code was not an innovation but an adaptation of centuries
of refinement of military discipline and justice.

As early as 2000 BC, the Egyptians and Sumerians waged war according to rules. Sun Tzu, in his fourth century BC *The Art of War,* speaks of rules
and norms of war. The Hindu *Book of Manu* regulated rules of land warfare.
With the birth of Christ and the advent of Christianity, rules of conduct were
adjusted to comply with Christian beliefs. In fact, from the sixth through the
twelfth centuries, the Roman Church required combatants to prepare themselves
for death by receiving the sacraments before battle — and to confess and do
penance following combat for any killings in which they might have been
involved.[7]

The Greeks and Romans had detailed systems of military justice. The Romans employed a "camp police" to enforce order and military regulations, similar to the latter-day provost guard and military police.[8]

In the Roman legions, "the general was at liberty to behead any man serving in his camp, and to scourge with rods the staff officers as well as the common soldier . . . ."[9]

Medieval military law had its roots in the laws and customs of the Germanic tribes, sharing the Roman idea of the unlimited power of command in disciplining troops.[10] The crusaders had a relatively formalized code. In his Ordinance of 1190, Richard Coeur de Lion dictated that offenders would be subject to punishment "with the common consent of fit and proper men."[11]

Various European nations developed formalized codes, based on the king as the chief executive and commander-in-chief. The Statute of Westminster of 1279 asserted royal power to punish soldiers according to the law and custom of the realm. In the comprehensive Articles of War of 1385, Richard II stipulated offenses with penalties.

It was not until the late sixteenth and early seventeenth centuries that a regular judicial process emerged for the determination of guilt and the awarding of punishment, in the Articles of War of the Free Netherlands of 1590 and the Gustavus Alolphus Articles of War of 1621.

Gustavus Adolphus' material was translated into English in 1639 and served as a model for royalists and rebels alike. The former promulgated Articles of War in 1639; Parliament, in 1642. Forty-seven years later, Parliament passed the original Mutiny Act, and established a standing army with provisions for its discipline. It must be noted, however, that the 1689 rules applied only to regulars; the militia was excepted.[12]

On 30 June 1775, the Continental Congress adopted a set of Articles of War which were based on the British military code, the direct descendent of Gustavus Adolphus', and on the colonial Massachusetts Articles of War.

Unhappy with British ideology and striving for their own independence, Americans nevertheless adhered to the strict codes of the British. During the period when the United States Army was known as the Legion of the United States, military justice was harsh and severe. At the same time, it was uneven, arbitrary and inconsistent.[13]

Between 1812 and 1833, Congress revoked its permission for courts-martial to impose stripes and lashes. But because of strong pressure from military officers who believed this type of punishment was necessary to enforce military discipline, Congress relented and restored whipping. In one case, following the congressional action, a convicted deserter received fifty lashes, had his head shaved, and was branded before being drummed out of the Army.[14]

In 1861, Union generals complained that the Bull Run debacle was a result of a lack of adequate discipline among the civilian soldiers, and that the lack existed because civilian authorities in Washington were diluting military law.[15]

Appeals from courts-martial sentences could, by statute and tradition, go from a regiment to the White House. In the generals' view, this appeal process weakened their authority and destroyed the effect of swift capital punishment following serious offenses.[16]

By the end of 1861, the military commanders got their way. The Law of 24 December 1861 gave divisional commanders the final determination in appeals for death sentences.[17] But civilian officials were not comfortable with the provisions.

Eight months later, the procedure was modified. Under the 17 July 1862 amendment, the president was to review every death sentence imposed by courts-martial.[18] "With us," Abraham Lincoln wrote to Count Agenor Etienne de Gasparin on 4 August 1862, "every soldier is a man of character and must be treated with more consideration than is customary in Europe."[19]

Within the same amendment a new Judge Advocate General's Office was established, with a civilian — Joseph Holt — in charge. Holt's role was to make the administration of military and martial law more uniform, humane and effective — and not to create political crises.[20] Field commanders, however, were still unsatisfied. They complained that Holt was too gullible; Lincoln, too lenient. This was the reason, they claimed, for the deterioration of Union Army discipline — and the repeated losses at the hands of the Confederates. A lack of understanding of military regulations on the part of the greatly uneducated mass of soldiers might have been more to the heart of the problem.

The unrest created by Army commanders brought about yet another new law, which Lincoln signed on 3 March 1863. Under its provisions, corps commanders would be the *usual* final appeal level for death sentences by courts-martial. The president could interfere in exceptional cases — and did.[21]

The conflict over who had control over military offenses goes back to the earliest days of this country, when the founding fathers feared a standing army and the possibility of the military's assuming control over the civilian government. This fear helped create the disparity in justice systems.

To a civilian it might seem ironic that, during a period of enlightened thinking and the creation of a democratic form of government, this nation allowed its military to be governed by archaic and undemocratic rules. Perhaps the reason is simple. The military has never been considered equal to the civilian population, despite the American notion of the "citizen-soldier." A soldier is unlike his civilian counterpart. He can't quit his job and go home because he's dissatisfied with working conditions. He can't organize his colleagues into a collective bargaining unit. "Practically," Richard D. Knudten writes, "the serviceman exists within a welfare state committed to order and to discipline in order to accomplish a defense function. And yet, this state is the most undemocratic of all institutions."[22]

The rationale for separate systems of justice is valid; the implementation, however, leaves much to be desired. The army must have the power to discipline its own for offenses, since military discipline is the responsibility of military commanders. At the same time, the army asserts its responsibility to prosecute offenses which would be crimes if committed by civilians. Military crimes are not, in most cases, analogous to civilian crimes, proponents of the dual system contend; therefore they cannot be prosecuted in the same manner. In peace and war, additional rules of conduct are needed for the training and operation of a disciplined army.

Military discipline cannot be maintained by any civilian body, based on the punishment/conviction rate and the crowded civilian court dockets. In time of war, a viable civilian judicial court system may not exist.[23]

"The primary object of the system of military justice must always be to maintain discipline within the organization and to ensure prompt compliance with its dictates," Colonel Samuel H. Hays stated at a March 1970 conference on "Human Rights of the Man in Uniform." "With the other systems," Hays stated, "it must be focused more on providing organizational effectiveness than on punishing or protecting individual action."

Hays felt that the military system was "subject to great stress, pressure and responsibility and enforce rules and regulations that have no counterpart in civil life." The punishments for military crimes, he continued, "must be viewed more from its effects on the organization as a whole than its effects on the individual. Hence military justice must act as deterrent to undesirable standards and command control."

Efforts to change the dual systems of justice have been unsuccessful because civilian criminal justice and military justice have been created with different purposes in mind. "While the civilian code seeks to prevent antisocial acts," Knudten writes, "the military code enforces the military demand that the soldier perform disagreeable and often dangerous responsibilities rarely asked of civilians."[24]

Proponents of the status quo contend that military trials are more efficient than civilian ones because of necessity. The lack of legal formalism allows officers and troops to return to the field promptly. The military, however, since the 1775 articles, have prosecuted, tried and convicted military personnel for both military and civilian offenses during war — and peace.

Efforts to change the system have always met with strong opposition. Testifying before Congress in 1879, General William T. Sherman stated:

> It will be a grave error if by negligence we permit the military law to become emasculated by allowing lawyers to inject into it the principles derived from their practice in the civil courts, which belong to a totally different system of jurisprudence. The object of the civil law is to secure to every human being in a community all the liberty, security, and happiness possible, consistent

with the safety of all. The object of military law is to
govern armies composed of strong men, so as to be
capable of exercising the largest measure of force at the
will of the nation. These objects are as wide apart as the
poles, and each requires its own separate system of laws,
statutes and common. Any army is a collection of armed men obliged to obey one man. Every enactment, every
change of rules which impairs the principle weakens the
army, impairs its values, and defeats the very object of
its existence. All the traditions of civil lawyers are an-
tagonistic to the vital principle, and military men must
meet them on the threshold of discussion, else armies will
become demoralized by even grafting on their code their
deductions from civil practice.[25]

The arguments for and against separate systems of justice have remained the same for the past two hundred years. Though changes have been made,
notably the creation of the Uniform Code of Military Justice, signed into law
by President Harry S Truman on 5 May 1950, which took effect 31 May 1951,
military justice remains dissimilar to civilian forms of justice.

Since Truman's efforts, the only other changes occurred during the Viet-
nam era, in the Military Justice Act of 1968, which adopted further civilian
courts practices. It did not, however, change the structure of courts-martial procedures.[26]

For the 267 men the government lists as executed during the Civil War
years, the words of Richard M. Nixon, at the 1969 Air Force Academy commencement, might seem ironic:  "I believe that every man in uniform is a citizen
first and a serviceman second, and that we must resist any attempt to isolate
or separate the defenders from the defended."

# ENDNOTES TO CHAPTER ONE

1. Joseph Warren Bishop, *Justice Under Fire, A Study of Military Law* [New York, 1974], p. 10.

2. James G. Randall, *Constitutional Problems Under Lincoln* [Urbana, Illinois, 1964], p. 521.

3. Harold M. Hyman, *A More Perfect Union: The Impact of the Civil War and Reconstruction on the Constitution* [New York, 1973], p. 149.

4. Robinson O. Everett, *Military Justice in the Armed Forces of the United States* [Harrisburg, Pennsylvania, 1956], p. 22.

5. Bishop, *op. cit.,* p. 26. Other revisions took place after the Civil War, viz., 1874, 1916, 1920, 1950, and 1968.

6. Everett, *op. cit.,* p. 22

7. Clifton B. Bryant, *Military Law and Boards of Office* [Washington, 1963], pp. 21-22.

8. Leon Friedman, ed., *The Law of War: A Documentary History* [2 vols., New York, 1972], pp. 26-27.

9. From Theodor Mommsen, *History of Rome,* Book II, Ch. 8 [Dickinson trans., 1889], as quoted in Bishop, *op. cit.,* p. 3.

10. Bishop, *op. cit.,* pp. 3-4.

11. *Ibid.,* pp. 4-5.

12. *Ibid.*

13. Friedman, *op. cit.,* p. 27.

14. Stanley Silton Graham, "Life of the Enlisted Soldier on the Western Frontier" [M.A. thesis, 1972], pp. 201-202.

15. Hyman, *op. cit.,* p. 188.

16. *Ibid.*

17. *U. S. Statutes at Large,* XII, 330.

18. *Ibid.,* XII, 598.

19. *Collected Works of Abraham Lincoln,* ed. Roy P. Basler, *et. al.* [New Brunswick, New Jersey, 1953], V, p. 355.

20. Hyman, *op. cit.,* pp. 190-91.

21. *Ibid,.* p. 191.

22. Richard D. Knudten, *Crime in a Complex Society: An Introduction to Criminology* [Homewood, Illinois, 1970], p. 487.

23. Bryant, *op. cit.,* pp. 6-7, and Bishop, *op. cit.,* pp. 21-25.

24. Knudten, *op. cit.,* p. 479.

25. Everett, *op. cit.,* p. 23.

26. *Ibid.,* pp. 28-29.

# CHAPTER TWO

## THE MANUAL OF COURTS-MARTIAL

Captain Stephen Vincent Benét, author of *A Treatise on Military Law and the Practice of Courts-Martial,* is better remembered in American society as the ancestor of the author of *John Brown's Body.* His work on the practice of courts-martial stood as the cornerstone of critical thinking on military justice into the twentieth century.

"Military law," Benét wrote,

> is that portion of the law of the land, designed for the government of a particular class of persons, and administered by special tribunals. It is superinduced to the ordinary law for the purpose of regulating the citizen in his character as a soldier; and although military offences are not cognizable under the common law jurisdiction of the United States, yet the articles of war clearly recognize the superiority of the civil over military authority.[1]

He might have added "in theory," because in actual practice the two are at odds.

Building on the establishment of a separate judicial system to deal with military personnel and offenses against good military order is the unique institution called the court-martial.

"A court-martial is a lawful tribunal," Benét wrote,

> existing by the same authority that any other court exists by, and the law military is a branch of law as valid as any other, and it differs from the general law of the

land in authority only in this, that it applies to officers and soldiers of the army, but not to other members of the body politic, and that it is limited to breaches of military conduct. [*Grant. vs. Gould* ii: H. Blacks, 64, 98, 100].

During the Civil War period, the military was called upon to exert judicial control in several areas under martial law. Civilians suspected of spying or treason were arrested by military authorities. In many areas, the line between military and civilian jurisdiction was vague to the point of non-existence.

To establish a hierarchy of importance, courts-martial were arranged in command categories:

*General.* A general court-martial could be convened by "any general staff officer commanding an arm, or colonel commanding a separate department [Article 65], and in time of war by a commander of a division or separate brigade [Act approved 24 December 1861]." In a case where the accuser was the person authorized to convene the panel, the next higher authority — including the president of the United States — was authorized to act as convenor. The president, however, never took advantage of this provision.

*Regimental.* The panel of this tribunal could be appointed by any officer commanding a regiment of corps.

*Garrison.* This type was open to all officers commanding a garrison, fort, barracks, or "other places where the troops consist of different corps [Article 66]."

In practice, however, special courts-martial were more often convened. In several recorded instances, drumhead courts-martial took place.

*Drumhead courts-martial*[2] are the most intriguing, because they are conducted at the whim of a commander, or as the result of emergencies or special situations. Usually they are swift trials conducted in the field with little attention paid to legal formalities. Very little paperwork was generated to substantiate these trials, although a detailed account of a drumhead trial exists in the service records file of at least one man, Private William Ormsley.[3]

*Composition of Courts-martial.* The composition of courts-martial was restricted to a panel "exclusively of 'commissioned officers' " [Articles 64 and 66]. This provision excluded chaplains, surgeons, assistant surgeons, paymasters and others "not clothed with rank." The reasoning behind it was explained by Attorney General J. McP. Berrien in 1829: "If we look to the origin of courts-martial in England [from whence we borrow them], it would be difficult to believe that a tribunal which has succeeded there to the ancient court of chivalry, could be composed of other than military men." Berrien contended that "the nature of the subjects which are generally submitted to the decision of these tribunals, the knowledge of military discipline and usage, and frequently of tactics [which are indispensable to those who preside there], it would seem that non-combatants, whose duties do not lead them to acquire this species of information and who have no rank, either real or assimilated, could not be deemed competent to sit in courts-martial."

Though not excluded by the code, enlisted men did not sit in judgement of other enlisted men. In practice, enlisted men were denied trial by their peers, and were usually cowed in the presence of authority figures.

*Triable Persons.* Persons who could be brought before a court-martial included officers [Article 1], enlisted men [Article 10], anyone "receiving pay or hire" from the army [Article 96], "militia or others mustered and in the pay of . . . the United States [Article 97], sutlers and retainers [Article 60], and spies [Article 57].

Key items to remember are the stipulations "receiving pay or hire" and "in the pay of" the government. To try a man for a military offense legally, the tribunal had to be certain that the person had received payment as a soldier. In several cases under consideration, this provision was overlooked; yet men were tried, convicted and executed.

Because of the fine line between military and civil justice brought about by martial law, another form of military tribunal existed: the military commission. While courts-martial had special and limited jurisdiction under the Articles of War, they did not have jurisdiction over persons not covered by the Articles. "But the laws of the United States, as well as the military usages of other countries," Major-General Henry Wager Halleck wrote to Major-General William S. Rosecrans on 20 March 1863, "recognize courts of general military jurisdiction, over civilians as well as soldiers, under the common law of war."[4] These tribunals were called military commissions. Several civilians, including Congressman Clement L. Vallandigham of Ohio, were tried by military commissions during the war.

*Punishments.* The punishments delivered by a court-martial panel were regulated, as Benét indicated, by

> the restraining provision of the eighth article of the amendments to the constitution . . . Punishments were *cruel* when they are indicative in their character, going, both in kind and degree, beyond the intention and necessity of their infliction for the vindication of the law; they are *unusual,* in kind only, when unknown to the statutes of the land, or unsanctioned by the customs of the courts.

The critical point in the rendering of punishment was the perception of the punisher. What is cruel to a civilian might not, in fact, be cruel to a combat-hardened military commander.

*Crimes Calling For Execution.* The sentence of death by either hanging or musketry could be rendered only for selected offenses, including mutiny [Article 7], aiding in mutiny [Article 23], sleeping on post [Article 46], misbehavior before the enemy [Article 52], giving away a watchword [Article 53], giving aid and comfort to the enemy [Article 56], and corresponding with the enemy [Article 57]. Before an execution could be carried out at the beginning of the Civil

War, the proceedings had to be transmitted to the Secretary of War for consideration of the sentence by the president [Article 65]. This provision was modified by the law of 3 March 1863 and other statutes cited above.

*Other Crimes.* For non-capital crimes, the 99th Article stressed that "though not mentioned in the foregoing articles of war, [they] are to be taken cognizance of by a general or regimental court-martial, according to the nature and degree of the offence, and be punished at their discretion." This provision allowed commanders to demand capital punishment for convictions in cases of theft, pillage and plunder.

It is further stipulated in Article 67 that neither garrison nor regimental courts-martial had the power to try capital cases. Further, such courts were restricted in the degree of punishment they could render. This article was ignored in the cases of several men executed during the war.

*Treatment of Officers.* In regard to officers, none of whom were executed during the Civil War, the punishments of courts-martial tended to be minor. In the most drastic cases, officers were cashiered and their shame was publicized in their local newspapers. In 1862, the War Department announced that it had stricken from the rolls one hundred officers, absent without leave. "This is the first installment," one newspaper reported, "of the thousands now absent, skulking,"[5] Even officers who had committed murder were mildly chastised — and promoted in rank as will be seen in a later chapter.

In England, prior to 1815, court-martialed officers were removed from command. The inconvenience of depleting the commissioned ranks forced the British to drop this practice. In the Union Army, however, there were always sufficient numbers of men seeking political favors in the form of commissions so that cashiering remained.

*Confinement.* According to Article 79, accused men — regardless of rank — were to remain in confinement no "more than eight days, or until such time as a court-martial can be assembled." Though during the later periods of the war, standing courts-martial panels existed, this deadline provision was ignored, possibly because of the heavy case loads.

*Court-Martial Panel.* The court-martial panel was composed of several members. In general courts-martial, the number of commissioned officers could range from five to thirteen; "but they shall not consist of less than thirteen where that number can be convened without manifest injury to the service" [Article 64]. Garrison and regimental courts-martial could be convened with a minimum of three officers [Article 66].

The key members were the president and the judge advocate general. The president or presiding judge was instructed to keep order and conduct business. The judge-advocate, on the other hand, had more complicated duties.

Appointed by the officer ordering the court [Article 69], the judge advocate had as his primary responsibility to prosecute the case in the name of the United States. In addition, under the same article, he was to consider himself counsel to the accused, after the prisoner had entered his plea. In this Solomon-like role, the judge advocate did not have to supply the prisoner with a list of prosecution witnesses who were not on the original list. If the prisoner was unhappy with this situation, he might apply for the assistance of outside counsel, as provided in the Sixth Amendment. Assistance in a court-martial case was, however, restricted

> to giving advice, framing questions which are handed by the accused to the judge advocate on separate slips of paper, or offering, in writing through the same channels, any legal objections that may be rendered necessary by the course of the proceedings.

Counsel could not address the court; "his presence is only tolerated as a friend of the prisoner."

Courts-martial panels could object to a specific attorney and could revoke their permission for him to attend the proceedings once he was in attendance.

The record of the courts-martial proceedings was recorded by the judge advocate in general courts-martial; in others, by the junior member or recorder. The court-martial itself had the right to prevent any record from being made "which might have the baneful tendency to pervert the public mind in regard to the trial and its results, and moreover, have improper influence on the witnesses whose testimony is yet to be delivered."

Such a provision provides an insight into why the majority of court-martial proceedings were brief, in most cases, no more than ten pages of testimony. Apparent censorship was such that only the barest details of testimony remain — innocuous comments about how long a witness knew the defendant; what was his character as a soldier; a listing of the officers on the panel; charges and specifications; and the decision. It is only on reading appeal documents that one can find how sparse is the court-martial information remaining.

*Questioning.* In military courts-martial during the Civil War, there was no such thing as peremptory challenge. The accused could not challenge until the court was sworn in. By then it was too late.

Challenges were allowed for "bias, prejudice, or malice," the principal challenge being "he [a court member] has been a former juror in the same case." The *proper time,* Benét indicates, "for challenging a member is immediately after the order convening the court has been read, and before the court is sworn." The decision to expel a member, however, rested with the panel — including the challenged member. In the case of Private William H. Howe, he objected to several members of the group who sat in judgement — including the presiding officer, who sat in judgement of him in a prior court-martial. His objection, of course, was overruled.

*Double Jeopardy.* The principle of double jeopardy was also addressed in the Articles of War. According to the 87th Article, no officer or man could be tried a second time for the same offense. A second trial could be ordered, nonetheless, "and held for the benefit of the prisoner and upon his motion." In the case of Private Howe, the only executed soldier to have two trials, the second court-martial was convened upon the orders of the army and not "upon his own motion." At his first trial, Howe was convicted and sentenced to execution. The results were thrown out because of certain irregularities. The second decision, the same as the first, was not questioned for irregularities. The military's position on this was simple: since the first court-martial was dismissed by the army, it did not, in fact, exist.[6]

*Confessions.* Contrary to the practices in civil courts, confessions were admissible in courts-martial

> even when undue influence has been exerted, if it has been
> made under such circumstances as to create a reasonable
> presumption that the threat or promise had no influence,
> or had ceased to have any influence upon the mind of
> the party. . . . but there must be very strong evidence of
> an explict warning not to rely on any expected favor, and
> that the prisoner thoroughly understood such a warning,
> before his subsequent confession can be given in evidence.

If a confession were obtained by *"artifice or deception,* but without the use of promises or threats, it is admissable." Leading questions were also allowed — in both theory and practice — in Civil War military courts.

*Court Decisions.* Following the presentation of witnesses and evidence, the panel retired to decide on the case. The decision to convict had to be made by a two-thirds majority. Following that, the minority was required to vote for the sentence as if they had voted in the majority.

*Revisions.* If the decision reached was challenged by the prisoner, a revision could be made, but within a limited scope. During this process, no witnesses could be called and no additional information or evidence brought forth. The court "confines itself exclusively to a reconsideration of the record for the purpose of correcting or modifying any conclusions thereon . . . ." On revision, "any illegality as to the constitution of the court, or any defect in its composition, cannot be amended . . . ."

*Court of Last Appeal.* The place of last resort to which a condemned prisoner could turn was the office of the President of the United States. The president did pardon or commute the sentences of some of the men who pleaded with him — sometimes for capricious reasons. There were formalized procedures for final review as outlined previously. However, many convicted men, knowing Lincoln's reputation for compassion, used the presidential route to gain pardon, though this was not a guarantee of commutation of sentence.

With provisions such as those outlined above, it would seem that the rights of the individual soldier were restricted, that the avenues available to an unsophisticated soldier without family or political connections were quite limited. Under these circumstances, one might expect that the number of sentences for execution would be much higher than the 267 acknowledged men.

## ENDNOTES TO CHAPTER TWO

1. Captain Stephen Vincent Benét, *A Treatise on Military Law and the Practice of Courts-martial* [New York, 1862, Revised Edition, 1864]. The primary source for this chapter is Benét. Rather than confuse the reader with endless lists of *Ibid.* and *Op cit.,* the author will cite only those other sources in this chapter.

2. The name "drumhead" is derived from the informality of the trial. Since most units traveled with a drummer to summon the troops, and not a desk, the drum itself became the judge's bench.

3. National Archives. *RG 94. Records of the Adjutant General's Office, 1780s-1917.* Compiled Military Service Records. William Ormsley file.

4. Harold M. Hyman, *A More Perfect Union: The Impact of the Civil War and Reconstruction on the Constitution* [New York, 1973], p. 152.

5. *Philadelphia Inquirer,* 20 November 1862.

6. In Howe's case, the first court-martial transcript was "lost," until the diligent Dale Floyd located it among other — nonrelevant — files at the National Archives.

# CHAPTER THREE

## THE IMPLEMENTATION OF JUSTICE

Benét and other legal scholars had developed a framework for the practice of courts-martial and delivery of military justice. It was now the responsibility of the administration in Washington and the commanders in the field to react to infractions of military discipline and violations of the Articles of War.

One of the major problems facing Union commanders, besides their Confederate adversaries, was desertion. It seemed that a day did not go by without one or more soldiers slipping through the picket lines and making their way home or to enemy lines. Some, as illustrated in letters to family and friends, had seen enough war to last them a lifetime; others seized the opportunity to take advantage of the government's generous bounty and substitute systems and deserted one day to enlist the next.

Regardless of the reasons for desertion, Union officers found that this offense, more than any other, dominated their concepts of command and discipline. Though the Articles of War indicate desertion to be one of the most heinous crimes a soldier can commit, there is no clear definition of desertion. The interpretation of what constituted desertion was left, in many cases, to the commanding officer.

When Private William C. Dowdy [Company E, 1st U. S. Volunteers] decided to change the location of his sleeping quarters aboard the steamer *Effie Deans,* sailing along the Missouri River, Captain Alford F. Fay, his company commander, preferred charges against the man for violating the 7th and 21st Articles of War, because Dowdy "did absent himself from his Company without leave from his Comd'g Officer on the night of the 5th of September, 1864 and did remain absent until apprehended by his Comd'g officer on morning of the 6th of Sept. 1864. All this on board Str. Effie Deans . . . . "[1] Dowdy, who had never left the ship, was tried, convicted and shot for desertion.

Following the promotion of a new brigadier general, a disappointed aspirant for that position, Charles R. Jennison, made "an intemperate speech . . . during which he practically advised the men to desert."[2] Private Alexander Driscoll, Company H, 7th Kansas Cavalry, took the advice and left his unit.[3] He was charged, convicted and executed for desertion.

Private Charles Williams, Company D, 4th Maryland Infantry, on the other hand, "deserted from his company when it was drawn up in line of battle, expecting to meet the enemy" on 20 September 1862, near Hagerstown, Maryland.[4] Private Williams was an exception, not the rule, in Civil War desertions. In an analysis of the data derived from the study of Union executions, it was determined that only four men deserted from battle:   Privates William F. Hill, Company K, 20th Massachusetts Infantry, William H. Devoe, Company B, 57th New York Infantry, Adam Smalz, Company E, 66th New York Infantry, and Williams.

The majority of men deserting their units — and who later were executed — did so during periods of post, garrison or guard duty. The location from which the largest number [15.48%] of men deserted was the siege before Petersburg. A small number departed the army while on leave, assigned to work, or as a patient, in a hospital.

If published records of the desertion rate are correct — and that the flow of deserters reached tidal proportions during several periods of the war — it appears it was not a crime against which most military commanders desired strong enforcement. Several commanders, and their subordinates, put themselves on record in letters and petitions to Lincoln recommending commutation and clemency in specific cases of desertion. In reading through numerous regimental accounts, it becomes quite evident that the execution of deserters was performed to set examples for the rest of the troops — and for imprisoned deserters and bounty jumpers — rather than as punishment for a crime committed.

Another problem that faced Union commanders in dealing with this crime, besides determining what constituted desertion, was how to proceed in dealing with it.

Since Private William H. Johnston [Company D, 1st New York Cavalry] was the first Union soldier to be executed for desertion, the army had to take great care in its procedures for the court-martial and conviction. His crime occurred following the battle of Bull Run. In a letter to Brigadier General William B. Franklin, the assistant adjutant general wrote: "Inasmuch as this is a very flagrant case the utmost exactness is necessary and the offence must be described in the *very words* of the article of war, or the record will not support a capital sentence."[5]

Franklin followed the adjutant general's direction. Johnston was tried and convicted quickly. He was executed 13 December 1861 by musketry.[6] The approach recommended by the adjutant general's office was followed in all subsequent courts-martial for desertion.

Because Johnston's case was the first, it would be expected that the army would have taken a great deal of time trying him. This was not the case. Johnston's desertion took place while his unit was assigned to the defenses of

Washington, sometime after 7 September 1861. The letter to Franklin is dated 9 December, and the order [General Order 52, Army of the Potomac calling for his execution was promulgated 11 December — a span of only two days. Johnston was executed 13 December.[7] Justice in his case was swift.

On the whole, men who were convicted — and executed — for desertion received quick justice, even though a look at the average time spans from crime to order certifying the court's decision to execution does not, at first, indicate this. Chart 2 presents the *average* time lapses.

CHART 2:  TIME LAPSES IN DESERTION CASES [159 Cases]

| YEAR | CRIME TO ORDER | ORDER TO EXECUTION |
|---|---|---|
| 1861 | 487.00 days | 13.00 days |
| 1862 | 441.41 days | 29.58 days |
| 1863 | 151.10 days | 19.74 days |
| 1864 | 89.30 days | 5.77 days |
| 1865 | 23.10 days | 9.40 days |
| Average | 190.85 days | 14.54 days |

In analyzing the data, however, one can see that the median time between crime and order is actually thirty-eight days; between order and execution, six days. In reality, therefore, the speed with which military authorities handled execution cases was indeed swift. In some cases, particularly those of Privates Michael Landy, Company A, 10th Connecticut Infantry, and Charles King, Company L, 3rd New Jersey Cavalry, the lapse between crime and death was one day; Privates Henry Holt, Company F, 2nd New Hampshire Infantry, two days; and Thomas Dix, Company G, 1st Connecticut Heavy Artillery, and John Eagen, Company A, 2nd Connecticut Infantry, four days.

Others had their lifespan increased because of the difficulties in apprehension and appeal procedures, notably Privates John McMann, Company B, 11th Infantry, Regulars, 869 days from crime to death; George W. Prince, Company B, 22nd Ohio Infantry, 850 days; John W. Hardup, Company A, 43rd Ohio Infantry, 806 days; and William H. Howe, Company A, 116th Pennsylvania Infantry, 608 days. Howe, it must be noted, had his life prolonged 323 days because of lengthy appeal procedures instigated by his counsel and former officer, Edmund Randall.[8]

The popular notion that substitutes and bounty jumpers were the primary individuals to be executed does not stand up to the close scrutiny of the data on executed soldiers. Of all the men executed for desertion, the analysis shows that 53.55 percent of all men executed for desertion were enlisted including a number of men with previous service [It is possible that some of these enlistees may have been, in fact, bounty jumpers.]; 27.1 percent, substitutes; 1.94 percent, drafted; and the remaining 17.42 percent, of unknown status.

The problem of bounty-jumping, in connection with the substitution program, was real; however the setting of examples in this category were limited. The single, most critical execution involving alleged bounty-jumpers took place 29 August 1863, when five foreigners, substitutes in the 118th Pennsylvania, some of whom did not even speak English, were executed by musketry in a field near Rappahannock Station, Virginia.

Because desertion, bounty-jumping and re-enlistment plagued the Army of the Potomac, "the death penalty became necessary as the surest method to prevent their recurrence," the historian of the 118th wrote. Military authorities ". . . had instructed courts-martial . . . to impose the severest penalty known to law."[9]

The execution of the five was carried on with "unusual publicity, officially and otherwise . . . ,"[10] including a large rendering of the scene by an artist for *Frank Leslie's Illustrated Newspaper.*[11]

The 118th was reluctant to accept the five as bona fide members of the unit. "They had been thrown into an organization where they were entirely strangers . . . ," their historian indicated, "and as they come there as prisoners only for the stern administration of military justice, they could look for little sympathy."[12]

Though the proceedings of these men's court-martial and the evidence supporting the contention they were bounty-jumpers cannot be located, the evidence was strong enough for President Lincoln to communicate to Major General George Gordon Meade that the five "were very flagrant cases, and that you deem their punishment as being indispensible to the service."[13]

Probably the first actual bounty-jumper to be executed was Private Charles Williams, Company D, 4th Maryland Infantry, who deserted 20 September 1862 when his unit was preparing for battle near Hagerstown, Maryland. Using the alias of Charles Smith, he was arrested in a party of substitutes, returning only "when he was paid as he admitted $300 . . . ."[14] Williams was shot to death at the Rapidan River, Virginia, 25 September 1863.

In addition to the loss of strength that the exit of bounty-jumpers caused the army, the Rev. Mr. John R. Adams wrote, "there were those in the ranks of every regiment, men who had no interest in the cause. . . . They not only shirked duty, but their acts and conversations were demoralizing good men."[15]

The execution of Private John Starbird, Company K, 19th Massachusetts Infantry, ended all that, in Adams' estimation: "Men who had straggled and kept out of battle now were in the ranks, and the result to our corps alone was as good as if we had been reinforced by a full regiment."[16] Starbird, a frequent bounty-jumper, was executed at Spotsylvania, Virginia, 21 May 1864.

Not all the men who were convicted of desertion were, in fact, executed. When Privates Henry Schumaker, Company C, 6th Connecticut Infantry, and Henry Stark, Company E, same regiment, were executed, their partner-in-crime was freed — because of a typographical error.

Schumaker, Stark and Gustav Hoofan of Company B had a habit of escaping custody. They were substitutes who deserted, were arrested, and escaped at least three times before the authorities were able to keep them confined. "They were very bold, ingenious men," the historian of the 6th Connecticut wrote, "and their skill and perseverence might have won them honor if rightly applied."[17]

When the trio was finally forced before the firing squad, "an error was discovered in the writing [of one man's name], the name Hoofan had been written Hoffman by the Judge Advocate . . . . [Hoofan] was saved from death and ordered to return to his regiment." The officer, however, was reprimanded for "his inexcusable carelessness and fatal error."[18] The records do not shed any light on Hoofan's future. He is not, however, listed among those executed. The correctly-named soldiers were executed at Hilton Head, South Carolina, 17 April 1864.[19]

The most outstanding case of desertion was that of bounty-jumper Samuel W. Downing, alias John W. Ball, Company H, 4th Maryland Infantry. By his own admission, Downing obtained $7,550 between 16 August 1863 and 31 June 1864 by repeated false enlistments. His confession reads like a tour of the federal states. He enlisted and deserted from most major recruiting centers in the North — sometimes more than once. He developed a network of contacts who, for a sum between $5 and $100, helped him enlist and escape. He implicated several by name, including his partner in crime, a substitute broker in the Bowery, New York City, who shared half of Downing's gain. The sharing only went so far. Downing was shot 16 September 1864 — alone.[20]

For the most part, these were the type of examples used by unit historians and the print media of the day to draw attention to the desertion situation. In the majority of desertion cases, the circumstances themselves were dull repetitions of each other. Some men, like Howe, had suffered debilitating disease and went home, others merely tired and slipped away.

The last execution for desertion was that of Private Alexander McBroone, Company B, 1st Arkansas Infantry. He was shot to death 21 April 1865 at Fort Smith. The McBroone execution, five months after the end of the war, indicates that executions themselves did not stem the flow of deserters. In fact, it is possible that Union soldiers considered the odds in being returned from desertion to face a possible death, and decided there was a greater probability that they would never be caught.

The next most frequent offense for which Union soldiers were executed was murder. In an environment where men are trained to kill or be killed, it does not seem incomprehensible that soldiers would settle grievances and arguments with weapons.

Sixty-three individuals died at the hands of Union soldiers — in 49.21 percent of the cases the victim was unknown [or the archival] records do not indicate the status of the individual]. Civilian victims represent 19.05 percent as do enlisted personnel; officers, 12.7 percent.

Though the records do not indicate a larger number of murders, it is possible that other individuals were killed and the culprits never prosecuted, such as in the case of the shooting death of Sergeant Joyce, 2nd Kentucky Infantry.

Though it might seem likely that the lapsed time between the perpetration of a murder and the application of justice would be less than that for desertion, it is not the case. An analysis of the times between incident and order and death demonstrates that it took longer to bring a murderer than a deserter to justice. Chart 3 (below) shows this.

CHART 3: TIME LAPSES IN MURDER CASES [64 Cases]

| YEAR | CRIME TO ORDER | ORDER TO EXECUTION |
| --- | --- | --- |
| 1861 | 29.00 days | 3.25 days |
| 1862 | 130.33 days | 14.00 days |
| 1863 | 192.60 days | 29.00 days |
| 1864 | 84.70 days | 18.36 days |
| 1865 | 47.80 days | 24.00 days |
| 1866 | 51.00 days | 17.00 days |
| Average | 95.48 days | 20.15 days |

The median from crime to order is 56.5 days, almost double that of desertion. The median from order to execution is 13 days, again more than double that for desertion.

In the case of the murder of a civilian, the average time between crime and conviction was 72.75 days, with a median of 45.5 days; from order to execution, 26.36 days, with a median of 12 days.

Military officials were more diligent in their handling of civilian murders than military ones. In the case of murdered officers, the time between crime and order was 56.33 days, with a median of 60.5 days; 9.89 days from order to execution, with a median of 7 days. With the murder of enlisted personnel, it took 77 days from crime to order, with a median of 58 days; 19.78 days from order to execution, with a median of 10.5 days.

The first Union soldier to be executed by order of the military was Private John W. Cole, Company G, 1st Kansas Infantry. Cole, a native Pennsylvanian but a resident of Leavenworth, Kansas, enlisted 29 May 1861.[21] Two months later, he argued with a member of his company. "They agreed to go out and settle the difficulty by a fight." As the two left, Cole "stabbed him in the back, killing him instantly."[22] He was tried quickly by a military commission and convicted. "The poor fellow," a newspaper reported following his execution 14 July 1861, "fell instantly, pierced with seven bullets, one of which passed through his neck, and was sufficient to produce instant death. Such," the writer concluded, "are the tendencies and the severe discipline of war."[23]

Private Robert Kerr, Company A, 1st California Cavalry, an Irish immigrant, was executed by musketry at Franklin, Texas, 20 March 1864, for the murder of 1st Lieutenant Samuel H. Allyne near San Elizio, Texas.[24] Kerr had a drinking problem of long standing, which propelled him into an earlier confrontation with a Lieutenant Harvey. For that incident, he spent several months imprisoned at Fort Yuma. He was freed from that confinement on the pleas of his company officers who felt sorry for him.[25]

Shortly after his release from Fort Yuma, Kerr deserted. He was returned to duty after his capture, without punishment. Following his return he resumed his argumentative behavior. This time an officer died.

First Lieutenant David W. Levergood died 16 April 1865, two days after Corporal Frank Hudson deserted.

When apprehended, Hudson was charged with both desertion and murder, though no proof exists in his file or the transcript of his court-martial that he had caused the lieutenant's death. To his death, Hudson pleaded innocence. In a plea to Major General Irwin McDowell, he stated: "I never was an enemy of Lieut. Levergood's he had enemies in the Company and they or some of them took advantage of my desertion to accuse me of the crime of killing him."[26]

McDowell responded he did not modify his orders. He did indicate, however, that he reviewed the case with "Judge Hoffman of the U. S. District Court and Judge Field of the United States Supreme Court."[27] Hudson was hanged at Camp Union, Sacramento, California, 16 June 1865.

Private Robert Rodgers, Company B, 77th Ohio Infantry was executed 16 December 1866 at Brownsville, Texas, more than a year after the war ended. Rodgers, after his 1863 discharge, reenlisted in the Ohio regiment. He saw combat, and, during 1865, was held as a prisoner-of-war for almost four months. Following his parole and while on leave, Rodgers was arrested by civil authorities for stabbing a citizen in Marietta, Ohio. Once turned over to military control, Rodgers' case becomes intriguing. In the first place, the lawyer he requested to advise him was unable to meet with him, because of bureaucratic red tape and harrassment.[28]

The lawyer requested admittance to the military prison to counsel his client, but was refused because his pass was out-of-date: the commanding officer had been relieved and another took his place. He then countered that the person countersigning the pass was still in charge. When asked to see the slip of paper, the lawyer obliged. ". . . On my subsequent demand for the return of this paper, *as my property*" the lawyer complained, "Capt. Ayers at first denied having received the paper at all, and afterward declared it was *mislaid*!"[29]

Rodgers, apparently felt he didn't need an attorney and took matters into his own hands. On the day before he was to be shot [27 April 1866], the convicted murderer was reported missing from the jail.

Captain J. H. Evans reported "that the prisoner Rodgers made his escape from the Military Prison last night . . . ."

According to Evans, Rodgers had "filed or sawed off his irons, climbed over the partition of the room . . .," and ran through a "yard of the prison where two sentinels were on duty, and made his escape over a brick wall about ten feet high." The three sentinels on duty at the time were arrested.[30]

A month later, an unsigned letter requested that a new date be set for the execution of Private Rodgers. The red-faced anonymous author recounted the actual events of the night of 26 April: Rodgers had escaped, but not from the prison. He had hidden himself under the floor of the building and had spent that time digging a tunnel.[31]

Robert Rodgers' execution took place two days later.

In the case of Private Fortune Wright [Company A, 96th Infantry, USCT], it is quite possible that his execution should not have taken place, and that he was a victim of unfortunate circumstances.

Wright was walking down a New Orleans street in December 1863, when he was "accosted by a colored woman, dissipated and immoral . . . acting her willingness to prostitute her body." She asked Wright for money. When he refused, she became abrasive, attracting the attention of two white men. Not witnessing the earlier parts of the argument, they assumed the soldier was abusing the woman. One of the men, Dr. Octavius Undecimen Tresgerant, attacked the soldier with his cane, calling him "a damn black Son of a bitch." The doctor's companion urged the physician on, yelling, "Kill him. Kill the damned black Yankee Son of a bitch." In what appears to have been self-defense, Wright drew a knife and lashed out at Tresgerant, who subsequently died.[32]

Wright received quick court-martial and conviction. His unit commander, Lieutenant Colonel O. Fariola, tried to get the sentence removed or reduced. In a letter to the assistant adjutant general, Department of Louisiana, he wrote that "Dr. Tresgerant himself, on his death-bed, requested that the man who stabbed him be unmolested: These last words may go to show that in Dr. Tresgerant the community lost a noble Heart, could they not show too, that he felt himself somewhat responsible for the fatal occurrence?"[33]

In addition, a number of Dr. Tresgerant's friends petitioned Major General Edward Richard Sprigg Canby for executive clemency, noting that it was "an act of self-defence on the part of the prisoner, while resisting two assailants; and that, if not self-defence, his crime at most is that of manslaughter."[34]

Wright received a three-week stay of execution, but not a new trial. A review of a court-martial, as previously noted, does not permit the introduction of new witnesses or evidence. If military justice would have had such a provision, Private Wright's fate might have been different. Fortune Wright was hanged at New Orleans, 23 February 1866.

In reviewing the Adjutant General's Office report, a number of men, listed as murderers, were found to have been convicted and executed for different offenses. Private John Willis, Company D, 52nd Infantry, USCT, deserted Camp Hibbin, Mississippi, 21 August 1863. He was executed for that offense 26 May 1865.[35]

Otto Pierce, a Private in Company L, 5th U. S. Colored Artillery [Heavy], was another "murderer." Pierce was officially charged with "absence without leave" — he was missing from camp from noon to 4 p.m. one day — and "disobedience of orders" — he had failed to get permission to be away from camp.[36] He was hanged at Vicksburg, Mississippi, 26 May 1865.

The case of Private James Quinn, Company A, 11th Heavy Artillery, USCT, is a baffling one. Quinn confessed at his court-martial that he was guilty of the charges brought against him, specifically absenting himself from duty and sleeping out of his quarters in violation of the 42nd Article of War.[37] In a letter from Cornelius W. Harris, 20th Infantry, USCT, however, it is noted that the regiment witnessed the execution of Quinn, who "shot one of the sergeants with a pistol, and killed him on the spot . . . ."[38] Quinn's casualty sheet does not list murder. Whichever the case, Quinn was executed by musketry at Camp Parapet, Louisiana, 25 November 1864.

Perhaps the most fortunate "murderers," as listed in the Adjutant General's report, are Privates David Geer, Company D, 28th Illinois Infantry, and Homobono Carrabojal, Company D, 2nd New Mexico Volunteers.

Geer, tried by a special court-martial, was sentenced to death. According to Adjutant General's records, his sentence was commuted to dishonorable discharge from the service without pay, allowance, or bounty.[39] According to the 1885 report, Geer was shot to death 4 March 1865 at Vicksburg, Mississippi. His final fate remains a mystery.

Carrabojal, probably H. Molina Carabajal,[40] was reported in some government files as being executed at Denver City, Colorado, in either October or November 1863. He was described in other official documents as an "assassin, suicide, mental [his] execution suspended until he was better."[42] He was ordered to an asylum in Washington, D.C., and discharged from the service February 1866.[43] His whereabouts after that are unknown.

In reading the literature, specifically the works of Ella Lonn [*Desertion During the Civil War*] and George Convers Murdock [*Patriotism Limited, 1862-1865, The Civil War Draft and the Bounty System*], one gets the distinct impression that a large number of men whose job it was to retrieve deserters died in the course of their duties. A study of archival records dealing with military executions indicate that only two men were actually executed for the murder of bounty-hunters: Privates Reuben Stout, Company K, 60th Indiana Infantry, and William H. Howe, Company A, 116th Pennsylvania Infantry. It is possible — and probable — that many murderers of bounty-hunters were never apprehended.

Stout deserted his unit shortly after enlisting, and returned to Indianapolis, Indiana. A little more than a year later, when Solomon Huffman, an apparent bounty-hunter, tried to arrest him, Stout shot and killed the man. He was arrested and tried by general court-martial; convicted and sentenced to death by musketry. He was executed 23 October 1863 at Indianapolis.[44]

Howe's case was similar, but with more shocking implications. William H. Howe had distinguished himself at the battle of Fredericksburg; in fact, he retrieved the regimental colors from the field. Sick and unable to gain medical attention, the young soldier returned to his home in Perkiomenville, Pennsylvania. More than a year later, the bounty-hunters came to arrest him in the dark of night. In a gunfight, precipitated by the hunters, one of them, Abraham Bertolet, was killed. Evidence brought forth at Howe's second court-martial indicated that the weapon used by him could not have been the one used to kill the bounty-hunter.

Howe was apprehended a few weeks later and returned to Philadelphia for trial. Convicted and sentenced to execution, Howe was given a surprise reprieve by the military. The findings of his trial were overturned for "informality," and he was retried — with several members of the original panel sitting in judgement. He was again convicted. Despite numerous appeals to the president, including a detailed analysis of the legal shortcomings of the trial, Howe was hanged at Fort Mifflin, Philadelphia, 26 August 1864.

Howe's case demonstrates a number of the inequities of the military justice system of the period: He was twice tried for the same offense; a confession was drawn from him under the most adverse conditions; a defense witness at the first trial became a prosecution witness at the second — shortly after receiving a promotion — and the execution was conducted almost in burlesque fashion. The man who cut the body down, after the execution, was eating a loaf of bread while performing his duty! Howe's execution did perform one service; it permitted the government to incarcerate a number of antiwar activists from Columbia County, Pennsylvania, at Fort Mifflin to watch Howe's last hours — and thereby neutralize their opinions.[45]

The last name on the Adjutant General's report presents an even stranger situation. William Loge, nicknamed French Bill, is not listed by state or unit; he apparently held no rank. There are no records of his enlistment, offense or trial in the National Archives. All that is known about him can be found in correspondence from and to Brigadier-General John D. Stevenson. Stevenson wrote Major-General Philip H. Sheridan that one of his men had captured French Bill, "a notorious murderer and bushwacker . . . He is a deserter from the Sixty-first New York Infantry."[46] Sheridan telegraphed back tersely: ". . . take him out and hang him. This will be your authority." French Bill was executed 2 December 1864 " in accordance with orders."

A careful search of archival records did not turn up a William Loge, nor is he mentioned in the files of the 61st New York Infantry, or the 28th New York [a note on file mentions that unit]. Who French Bill was — and what he did — remains a mystery.

In many respects, desertion is a silent protest against the military system. Mutiny, on the other hand, is a more vocal demand for a change of command or a change in the system itself. But, similar to desertion, mutiny required an interpretation by a commander.

An inspection of actual casualty sheets for executed soldiers reveals only eighteen cases of soldiers executed for mutiny; 72.22 percent of these acts of mutiny were attributed to members of the United States Colored Troops [USCT]. Does this indicate that black soldiers were less disciplined, and more likely to disrupt military order by violent protest? Or does it indicate that white commanders looked on any unusual action by black soldiers as blatant violations of the Articles of War? Some white Commanders, despite Lincoln's emancipation position, harbored resentment toward the former slaves and were less tolerant of them. Black soldiers, on the other hand, were unaccustomed to their new freedom and were more disruptive than their white counterparts.

According to Article 7,

> Any officer or soldier who shall begin, excite, cause, or join in, any mutiny or sedition, in any troop or company in the service of the United States, or in any party, post, detachment, or guard, shall suffer death, or such punishment as by a court-martial shall be inflicted.

In other words, any man under arms who seriously endangers the discipline of a military unit can be charged with mutiny.

Sergeant William Walker, Company E, 21st Infantry, USCT, a twenty-three-year-old Georgian, was the first black soldier to be executed for mutiny [29 February 1864].

Prior to joining the army, Walker served as river pilot and considered himself partially responsible, for the sinking of a Confederate steamer, near Fort McAllister.[47]

Walker was charged with mutiny because he helped organize other black soldiers in protest against the inequitable wages they were receiving. In June 1863, the War Department decided to pay black soldiers $3 less per month than their white counterparts, and to deduct an additional $3 for clothing. This scale reduced the monthly pay for blacks to $7 as opposed to $13 for whites. The order deeply affected many of the black men who felt they had been cheated by the system. Opposition to the discriminatory pay structure centered in the South Carolina Sea Islands where the black regiments, for the most part, were stationed.

At first the protests took the form of normal enlisted griping. Then, an attempt to resolve the problem exacerbated the issue and turned mild protest into organized action. On 25 August 1862, Secretary of War Edwin M. Stanton ordered General Rufus Saxton to enlist 5,000 black soldiers, stipulating they "receive the same pay and rations as are allowed by law to volunteers in the service."[48] The order did not rectify the difference in pay for any other black soldiers, only those recruited by Saxton.

The protest reached fever pitch during the summer and fall of 1863. In mid-November, Walker led one company of blacks to the tent of the regimental commander, Lieutenant Colonel Augustus G. Bennet, where they stacked their arms. They informed Bennet that they would not serve until the pay matter was resolved. Not responsible for the policy and possibly in favor of equitable wages, Bennet was placed in a difficult situation. He warned the company that what they were doing was mutiny and punishable by death.[49] This statement neither calmed the group, nor their white officers.

In the course of the confrontation, Walker argued with 1st Lieutenant George N. Wood and threatened to kill him. Walker then refused to obey Captain Edgar Abeel, who tried to calm him down. Abeel finally ordered Walker to his tent under arrest. Walker threatened "to go to the Provost first," then obstructed the arrest of the company drummer, and released another black soldier from confinement.

Though faced with a volatile situation, Bennet was sympathetic to the plight of the black soldiers, because he did not press the issue by placing Walker in armed arrest. Walker violated Bennet's confidence and left his tent, without the commanding officer's permission, to go to another tent to play cards. He was charged with "breach of arrest."[50]

Bennet had no choice but to let the system run its course. Walker was court-martialed, found guilty and sentenced to death. He was shot the next day, 19 February 1864, in front of the entire brigade at Jacksonville, Florida.[51]

Several months later, another pay protestor, Wallace Baker, Company I, 55th Massachusetts Infantry, Colored, followed Walker. His case was intensified by his intense desire to be treated as an equal to all white soldiers. "You damned white officer," he shouted at 2nd Lieutenant T. F. Ellsworth of his command, "do you think you can strike me, and I not strike you back again? I will do it, I'm damned if I don't."[52]

After a general court-martial found him guilty of mutiny and disobedience of orders, Private Wallace Baker was executed by musketry 18 June 1864 at Folly Island, South Carolina.

The mutinous conduct of the black soldiers can best be described as a result of a failure of federal authorities to live up to their word. Black enlisted men, despite rank, were paid $7 a month. A black first sergeant received the same pay as a white private. As a result, the pay protests were not limited to one specific area. Private Samuel Mapp, Company D, 10th Infantry, USCT, was executed 20 April 1865 at City Point, Virginia, for his participation in another pay protest.[53] Sergeant Giles Simms, Company F, 49th Infantry, USCT, and Private Washington Tontine, Company F, 40th Infantry, USCT, mutinied in the Army of the Tennessee. They were executed together near Vicksburg, Mississippi, 25 September 1864.[54]

The end of the war did not end the execution for black soldiers who had mutinied. First Sergeant William Kease and Sergeant Doctor Moore were shot to death at Ringgold Barracks, Texas, 11 August 1865.[55] The final executions for mutiny were the largest conducted during the entire Civil War period. On 1 December 1865, six privates of the 3rd Infantry, USCT — James Allen, Jacob Plowder, both of Company E, David Craig, Nathaniel Joseph, both of Company K, Joseph Grien, and Thomas Howard, both of Company I — were executed by musketry at Fernandina, Florida.[56]

In an ironic footnote, Craig's life might have been spared. Lincoln telegraphed Major General J. G. Foster "to suspend sentence & transmit record here."[57] Craig was not a mutineer, it was alleged; he was only following orders. He had been ordered "to take the guns from some of the mutineers, and in so doing he was arrested."[58] Unfortunately for Craig, the president's telegram was received two weeks too late.

The desire for an equal pay structure was not limited to the black soldiers. Many high-ranking officers sustained the protest in some units, and limited prosecution of larger number of troops.[59]

In June 1864, Congress finally acted and authorized equal pay retroactive to 1 January 1864 — with the provision that all black soldiers, free on 19 April 1861 when the war began, were entitled to the pay that was allowed at the time of their enlistment.[60] Though this was not what the former slaves wanted the law to say, it did allow some white commanders to administer what was known as the "Quaker Oath." Black soldiers were required to swear that at the start of the war "no man had the right to demand unrequited labor of [him]."[61]

Congress finally acknowledged Stanton's pledge in an 1865 enrollment act and recognized, as legitimate, the equal pay provision for all U. S. Colored Troops from the day of their enlistment.

The inequities of pay and status acted as a stimulant to the black troops. It created a common issue for them. It generated leadership in the ranks, men who were willing to die for equal footing with whites. After all, wasn't that one of the reasons for which the war was fought? The Black Mutinies also pointed out another inequity: that of the lack of education brought about by the institution of slavery. Former slaves were ignorant of due process and the fact that individual commanders had no policy position in determining pay structures. Mutiny against a company commander was mutiny against the wrong individual. The newly-freed blacks were unaware of this.

Not all mutineers, however, were black. The first Union soldier to be executed for mutiny was a white soldier: Corporal Charles Smith, Company K, 1st California Infantry.

In November 1862, Corporal Smith was part of a guard detail at Mesilla, District of Arizona, when a prisoner escaped. Colonel Joseph Rodman West suspected that the sergeant of the guard and several of his men helped the man escape. As a result, he placed the sergeant and three guards in irons until they could prove their innocence.

The following day, members of Company K refused duty until the sergeant was released. Corporal Smith acted as spokesman for the group. West, however, did not wish to have his decision questioned, so he had Smith shot. "He died," West reported,

> within an hour . . . No one can regret more than myself the painful necessity of taking the life of one of our own soldiers:  this course had to be pursued or all authority to command ceased . . . ."[62]

The prisoner who had caused the confinement of four men and the death of another was recaptured the same day, and proved to West's satisfaction that members of the guard had not offered him any assistance.

Brigadier General Isaac H. Carleton, commanding the Department of New Mexico, ordered a military commission to investigate the matter. When West responded to Carleton, he respectfully asked that the commission be instructed "to inquire into the accidental shooting of [another enlisted man] on the same day and occasion."[63]

If West had not been premature in his display of authority, and had called for a court-martial, as provided by the Articles of War, enough time would have been gained and Smith might have lived.

Mutinies were handled with great dispatch by military commanders, as Chart 4 (below) indicates.

### CHART 4:  TIME LAPSES IN MUTINY CASES [18 cases]

| YEAR | CRIME TO ORDER | ORDER TO EXECUTION |
|---|---|---|
| 1861 | — | — |
| 1862 | 1.00 days | 0     days |
| 1863 | 61.25 days | 3     days |
| 1864 | 50     days | 27.2  days |
| 1865 | unknown | 48.33 days |
| Averages | 49.50 days | 17.83 days |

The median time span from crime to order, however, is 49 days; from order to execution, 18 days. Though slower than justice in the case of desertion or murder, the resolution of mutiny cases was swift by any standard.

The only military crime directed solely at civilians that was punishable by execution was rape. Rape has followed armies since the dawn of recorded history. It is a symptom of the conquerer complex. Commanding officers who must maintain control over any civilian population must curtail their men, or lose the respect and assistance of the citizenry. Incidents of rape, or alleged rape, according to existing records, were prosecuted with force and speed. In fact, once convicted, a soldier could expect to be executed within seventy-two hours! Chart 5 (below) illustrates this point.

### CHART 5: TIME LAPSES IN RAPE CASES [22 Cases]

| YEAR | CRIME TO ORDER | ORDER TO EXECUTION |
|---|---|---|
| 1861 | — | — |
| 1862 | 5.00 days | 2.00 days |
| 1863 | 198.50 days | 9.75 days |
| 1864 | 20.00 days | 7.00 days |
| 1865 | unknown | 53.00 days |
| Averages | 106.13 days | 10.82 days |
| Median | 104.00 days | 3.00 days |

There were only twenty-two executions for rape during the Civil War; 50 percent of them involved members of the United States Colored Troops. The most glaring rape case, however, was one involving a white soldier, Private James Preble, Company K, 12th New York Cavalry. In several hours' time on 16 March 1865, Preble attempted to rape two women, and actually raped a third.[64] Once apprehended, the soldier was tried, convicted, and executed within two weeks. He was shot to death at Goldsboro, North Carolina, 31 March 1865.

Private John Bell, Company I, 2nd Kansas Cavalry, the first man to be legally executed in the state of Kansas, was sentenced at drumhead for the rape of an Iola, Kansas, woman 4 July 1862.[65] The army's main intention in his execution was a swift and strict enforcement of military justice. The residents of Iola, however, misunderstood this intention, and looked upon Bell's execution as a event for "the amusement of the citizens . . . ."[66]

The execution took place at sunrise, when military officials thought the citizens would be in bed. "Several men," a local newspaper reported, "laid all night in the wet grass to see a soldier hang . . . ."[67]

Thomas R. Dawson, Company I, 20th Massachusetts Infantry, had seen prior service in the British army and wore medals to prove it.[68] One night, while on picket, Dawson left his post and got drunk. While in that condition, he allegedly assaulted an elderly woman.[69] Dawson admitted that he and two others had wandered from camp and found some liquor. He also admitted that the alcohol made him "so stupid he knew not what followed . . . ."[70]

His story was believed by the Catholic chaplain who visited him, and his company officers. Despite pleas from the chaplain and the officers to Lincoln and General George Gordon Meade for clemency, Dawson was hanged, near Stephensburg, Virginia, 25 April 1864.

Dawson's case brings out the pressures that the military exerted on the president, and the president's reluctance to provide mercy unless a commander did so first. Was the decision on Dawson's death Lincoln's way of giving Meade what he and other high-ranking officers wanted — strong discipline? Or was it the president's way of excusing himself from intervention in a rape case? Lincoln had provided clemency for all types of military offenders, except rapists.

Three men, according to the Adjutant General's report, were executed for rape and theft. All three were members of Company H, 2nd New Jersey Cavalry, and were executed at Memphis, Tennessee, 10 June 1864.

Though Privates John Callaghan, Thomas Johnson, and John Snover were listed as rapists, there is no record that they, in fact, committed anything other than desertion. Callaghan was a probable bounty-jumper; Johnson and Snover were reduced from corporal shortly before they deserted.[71]

Privates Daniel Geary and Ransom S. Gordon, both of Company E, 72nd New York Infantry, were tried for the rape of a camp follower. They were hanged with great ceremony by Provost Marshal General Marsena R. Patrick 15 July 1864.[72] Gordon might not have been a soldier at the time of the offense; he had been mustered out one week before the attack took place.[73]

Sergeant Charles Sperry, Company E, 13th New York Cavalry, was listed on the Adjutant General's report as being executed for rape. Though charged with the rape of a 15-year-old — and quitting his post without urgent necessity or leave; with drunkenness on duty; with assault and battery, with intent to commit rape — and was found guilty on all counts — except rape.[74] He was shot to death 3 March 1865, in Washington, D.C.

Private Lloyd Spencer and two of his friends, John W. Cook and John M. Smith all members of Company B, 55th Massachusetts Infantry, Colored, were executed near Jacksonville, Florida, 18 February 1864, for rape.[75] Though the testimony of the victim indicated there were four rapists, only Spencer and Cook were tried and convicted. Smith, though executed with the other two, was actually a deserter and had neither been tried nor convicted of rape.[76]

Errors in the Adjutant General's report also may have distorted the case of Private John Carroll, Company D, 20th Wisconsin Infantry. Carroll actually was tried and convicted for desertion.[77] Another source, however, indicates he was executed "for crimes committed in Brownsville, Texas."[78]

Private Lawson Kemp, Company A, 55th Infantry, USCT, is listed as being executed for rape 19 November 1863. But, his company muster roll lists him as "died of disease" the same day he was allegedly executed. Kemp was tried by drumhead, and no transcript was made.

Throughout the research on the rape cases, it was apparent that no Union soldier was accused of or executed for the rape of a black woman. In several of the cases, substantial material in the files indicated that the accused were convicted on circumstantial evidence. It became apparent that black soldiers were accused, convicted and executed for rape rapidly, more rapidly than white soldiers. In the cases of black soldiers, testimony was quite limited and, in most cases, based on hearsay, not fact.

In the cases of rape and murder, commanders did not have to make major judgements as to whether a crime was or was not committed. That was not the case with spying, acting as a spy or treason. In these cases, there is a fine line . . . a line which commanders oftentimes could not distinguish.

Though listed on the Adjutant General's report as being executed for desertion, John Rowley, Company D, 7th Connecticut Infantry, was actually accused, convicted and executed for murder and treason. The charge of treason, however, was perceived not actual. Rowley shot a member of his unit, while they were engaged in battle. Therefore, the accusing officer considered Rowley's action as treason: he gave "aid and comfort to the said enemies at war with the United States, by shooting [his comrade] . . . ."[79]

Rowley confessed to murder, but not to treason.

Privates Charles King and Henry Regley, both of Company L, 3rd New Jersey Cavalry, were both convicted of spying. In reality, the two deserted the Union Army near Winchester, Virginia. As they attempted to leave their own lines, they encountered a man they presumed to be a Confederate. In exchange for rebel uniforms, they provided him with military information. At that point, he told them he was a Union staff officer. The two were arrested and, without benefit of trial, were shot to death by order of Major-General Philip H. Sheridan 6 January 1865.[80]

Private Thomas Abraham, Company G, 139th New York Infantry, was executed 7 March 1864 for "acting as a spy." He was convicted of "allowing a prisoner . . . to escape from the Guard House, and thus get within the enemy lines."[81]

There is no proof that Abraham actually assisted the man in his escape. The court-martial specifies that Abraham accumulated information on troop movements and passed them along to the prisoner.[82] He was not found guilty of acting as a spy, but for giving intellgence to the enemy in violation of the 57th Article of War, and persuading another soldier to desert the service, in violation of the 23rd Article. It is interesting that Abraham would have been found guilty of persuading the man to desert, since the man was in confinement on a murder conviction. His execution had been stayed by the president.

The offenses of treason and spying did not appear in the records until the last years of war. Because of the gravity of the charges, they were handled with great dispatch. [See Chart 6, page 33]

Another area of criminality for which the capital sentence was issued was that of theft, including stealing and highway robbery. Only one soldier was executed for theft. That man, however, Frank L. Newton, had been discharged from the 13th Connecticut Infantry *before* the crime took place.

CHART 6:  TIME LAPSES IN TREASON/SPY CASES [3 Cases]

| YEAR | CRIME TO ORDER | ORDER TO EXECUTION |
|------|----------------|--------------------|
| 1864 | 25 days | 7 days |
| 1865 | 2 days | 0 days |
| Average | 13.50 days | 3.50 days |
| Median | 13.50 days | 3.50 days |

Newton and his associates never received a formal trial or court-martial. In fact, they were condemned on the word of an accomplice who was given a prison sentence . . . not hanging like the rest.

Private John T. Barnett, Company A, 11th Pennsylvania Cavalry, a reported deserter from the 63rd Georgia, joined Private Hiram Evans, of the same unit, to rob four entrepreneurs "who made a living by following raids, and, taking advantage of the frightened farmer, bought up negroes at low rates and shipped them back to the South." While Barnett and Evans were being brought back to camp, Evans escaped.[83] Tried and convicted of highway robbery, with assault and intent to commit murder [the two had fired in the air after the fleeing slave merchants],[84] Barnett was shot to death at Portsmouth, Virginia, 18 September 1863. No action was taken, however, in regard to the slave traders.

Convictions and executions in theft cases took somewhat longer for conviction and execution, based on the length of time required in apprehension. When a suspect had been apprehended, justice was swift. [See Chart 7]

CHART 7:  TIME LAPSES IN THEFT CASES [5 Cases]

| YEAR | CRIME TO ORDER | ORDER TO EXECUTION |
|------|----------------|--------------------|
| 1861 | 1 day | 1 day |
| 1862 | 783 days | 8 days |
| 1863 | 17 days | 25 days |
| Average | 204.50 days | 14.80 days |
| Median | 17 days | 5 days |

There were no executions in this category during the last years of the war, which is quite interesting considering the complaints that were lodged against General William T. Sherman and his troops during the March to the Sea.

In addition to the men who were executed for stated crimes, whether the information was accurate or not, there was also Private Michael Connel, Company E, 24th Ohio Infantry. He was executed on 5 March 1862, at Camp Jackson, Tennessee. There are no records of the charges lodged against him, no transcripts of trials or general orders, not even the method used to terminate his life. Connel's death and the reasons that brought it about will forever remain a mystery.

But these men's stories only touch at the inconsistencies and incongruities of military justice during the Civil War.

# ENDNOTES TO CHAPTER THREE

1. National Archives. *RG 94. Records of the Adjutant General's Office, 1700s-1917.* Compiled Military Service Records; hereinafter cited as *RG 94.* William C. Dowdy file.

2. S. M. Fox, *The Seventh Kansas Cavalry: Its Service in the Civil War* [Topeka, 1908], p. 19.

3. *The Conservative,* 27 March 1862.

4. *RG 94.* George Gordon Meade to Abraham Lincoln. Charles Williams file.

5. *RG 94.* J. Williams, Assistant Adjutant General, Headquarters, Army of the Potomac, to Brigadier-General W. B. Franklin, 7 December 1861. William H. Johnston file.

6. General Order 52, Army of the Potomac, 11 December 1861

7. *RG 94.* William H. Johnston file.

8. Robert I. Alotta, *Stop the Evil: A Civil War History of Desertion and Murder* [San Rafael, Calif., 1978]; specifically Chapter 10, "Out of the Depths."

9. Henry T. Peck, *Historical Sketch of the 118th Regiment Pennsylvania Voluneers, "Corn Exchange Regt."* [no publisher, 8 September 1884], pp. 294-305.

10. *Ibid.*

11. General DuChanal, "How Soldiers Were Tried," *Civil War Times Illustrated,* VII [February 1969] 10:10-15.

12. Peck, *op. cit.,* pp. 294-305.

13. *The War of the Rebellion: A Compilation of the Official Records of the Union and Confederate Armies* [4 series, 70 vols. in 128 vols., Washington, 1880-1901], I, 29, part 2, pp. 102-103; hereinafter cited as *OR.*

14. *RG 94.* George Gordon Meade to Abraham Lincoln. Charles Williams file.

15. John R. Adams, *Memorials and Letters of Rev. John R. Adams, D. D.* [Cambridge, 1890], p. 94.

16. *Ibid.*

17. Charles K. Caldwell, *The Old Sixth Regiment: Its War Record, 1861-5* [New Haven, 1875], pp. 82-86.

18. *Ibid.*

19. General Order 7, Headquarters, Hilton Head, 16 April 1864.

20. *RG 94.* Samuel W. Downing file.

21. *RG 94.* David W. Cole file.

22. *Lawrence Republican*, 25 July 1861.

23. *Ibid*

24. *RG 94.* Robert Kerr file.

25. *RG 94.* Major D. Ferguson to Captain Benjamin C. Butler, 8 August 1862. Robert Kerr file.

26. *RG 94.* Frank Hudson to Major-General Irwin McDowell, 13 June 1865. Frank Hudson file.

27. *RG 94.* Major-General Irwin McDowell to Brigadier-General George Wright, 15 June 1865. Frank Hudson file.

28. *RG 94.* Frank E. MacManus to Major-General George Washington Getty, 28 February 1866. Robert Rodgers file.

29. *Ibid.*

30. *RG 94.* Captain J. H. Evans to Lieutenant-Colonel D. D. Wheeler, 27 April 1866. Robert Rodgers file.

31. *RG 94.* Headquarters, District of the Rio Grande, to Brevet Colonel C. H. Whittelsey, 24 May 1866. Robert Rodgers file.

32. *RG 94.* Statement of Prisoner. Fortune Wright file.

33. *RG 94.* Lieutenant-Colonel O. Fariola to Major Wickham Hoffman, 4 June 1866. Fortune Wright file.

34. *RG 94.* Petition to Major-General Edward Richard Sprigg Canby, undated. Fortune Wright file.

35. *RG 94.* John Willis file.

36. *RG 94.* Charges and Specifications, 17 November 1864. Otto Prince file.

37. *RG 94.* James Quinn file.

38. Lydia Minturn Post, ed., *Soldiers' Letters, from Camp, Battle-Field and Prison* [New York, 1865], pp. 233-34.

39. Special Order 476, Adjutant General's Office, 4 September 1865.

40. Company Muster Roll.

41. *RG 94.* Homobona Carrabojal file.

42. *Ibid.*

43. *Ibid.*

44. General Order 279, Adjutant General's Office, 8 August 1863.

45. A detailed account of the courts-martial and execution of Private William H. Howe can be found in Alotta, *Stop the Evil. op. cit.*

46. *OR* I, 43, part 2, p. 721. Brigadier-General John D. Stevenson to Major-General Philip H. Sheridan, 1 December 1864.

47. *RG 94.* William Walker file.

48. *OR* I, 14, p. 377.

49. Ira Berlin, *et al.,* "Writing Freedom's History," *Prologue,* 14 [Fall 1982] 3:134. A more detailed account of the Black Mutinies can be found in *Freedom: A Documentary History of Emancipation 1861-1867,* Ira Berlin, ed. [Cambridge, 1982], particularly Chapter 7: "Fighting on Two Fronts: The Struggle for Equal Pay."

50. General Order 29, Headquarters, Department of the South, 28 February 1864.

51. *RG 94.* William Walker file.

52. General Order 90, Department of the South, 19 June 1864.

53. General Court-Martial Order 55, Department of Virginia, 9 April 1865.

54. General Order 20, Army of the Tennessee, 4 August 1864.

55. General Court-Martial Order 4, Military Division of the Southwest, 14 July 1865.

56. General Court-Martial Order 39, Department of Florida, 13 November 1865.

57. *RG 94.* David Craig file.

58. *RG 94*. H. C. Marehead to Congressman E. Cowan, 10 December 1865. David Craig file.

59. Berlin, *op. cit.,* p. 134.

60. *OR,* III, 4, p. 448.

61. Berlin, *op. cit.,* p. 135.

62. *RG 94*. Colonel Joseph Rodman West to Captain Benjamin C. Cutler, 27 November 1862. Charles Smith file.

63. *Ibid.*

64. General Order 20, Department of North Carolina, Army of the Ohio, 26 March 1865.

65. Kansas Adjutant General's Office, *Official Military History of Kansas Regiments During the War for the Suppression of the Great Rebellion* [Leavenworth, 1870], p. 21.

66. *The Manhattan Express,* 27 July 1862.

67. *Ibid.*

68. Captain Gregory B. Adams, *Reminiscences of the Nineteenth Massachusetts Regiment* [Boston, 1899], pp. 84-86. Very Rev. William Corby, *Memoris of Chaplain Life* [Notre Dame, 1874], pp. 220-28.

69. Frederic S. Klein, "On Trial," *Civil War Times Illustrated,* VII [January 1969] 9:46

70. Corby, *op. cit.,* pp. 220-28.

71. Adams, *op. cit.,* pp. 84-86.

72. Corby, *op. cit.,* 220-28.

73. *RG 94*. Files of John Callaghan, Thomas Johnson and John Snover.

74. David S. Sparks, ed., *Inside Lincoln's Army: The Diary of Marsena Rudolph Patrick, Provost Marshal General, Army of the Potomac* [New York, 1964], pp. 388-89, 419.

75. *RG 94*. Ransom S. Gordon file.

76. General Order 31, Department of Washington, 27 February 1865.

77. Massachusetts Adjutant General's Office.

78. *RG 94*. John N. Smith file.

79. *RG 94*. John Carroll file.

80. W. J. Lemke, *Chaplain Edward Gee Miller of the 20th Wisconsin: His War 1862-1865* [Fayetteville, 1960], p. 26.

81. General Order 97, Headquarters, Department of Virginia and North Carolina, 23 August 1864.

82. *RG 94*. Charles King file.

83. *RG 94*. Thomas Abraham file.

84. *RG 94*. Brigadier-General I. J. Wistar to Major-General Benjamin F. Butler, 8 February 1864. Thomas Abraham file.

85. General Order 26, Department of Virginia and North Carolina, 29 February 1864.

86. *RG 94*. John T. Barnett file.

87. *Ibid.*

# CHAPTER FOUR

## THE RITUAL OF EXECUTION

The ultimate punishment for a Union soldier who had been tried and convicted of a major crime against military or civilian authority was death — execution by musketry or by hanging.

From the time man discovered a lead ball could be propelled at a target by black powder, execution by musketry was considered a soldier's death. Though the end result of a bullet or a rope was the same, the military felt more comfortable with the bullet, perhaps because the bullet is an integal part of the military profession — weapons always are present in a military unit, or because a well-aimed bullet will produce instant death. Another reason for this choice might be that a convicted man can stand before a firing squad and demonstrate the ultimate fear: facing rifles pointed directly at him — with no chance for escape. Hanging, on the other hand, does not fit into the military mode. As a result, it is usually restricted to the punishment of ignoble — if there is any such thing as noble — crimes.

In the early days of the Civil War, death by hanging was restricted to those men who had committed crimes against civilians, such as rape, pillage, and robbery, while musketry was limited to deserters, mutineers and murders. As the war intensified and the need for more and more executions increased, the choice of one method of execution over the other ceased to be of any importance.

The availability of planking and carpenters and the proximity of an experienced hangman allowed some commanders to use the rope and scaffold. But armies on the move did not have such luxuries, even though there are some accounts of hanging a convicted soldier from the nearest tree. The ever-present musket or rifle in every military command made it more convenient to execute by the bullet. According to the Adjutant General's 1885 report, only eighty men were hanged; 186, shot. One man was executed by some undisclosed means, though it is probable that he was shot.

The physical act of execution prevents the doomed individual from repeating his offense. Execution will not, however, prevent others from duplicating his crime unless potential criminals can see what will happen to them if they commit crime — and are caught. To learn the proper lesson of correct military behavior and adherence to military order, potential offenders must experience — vicariously — the pain, anguish and suffering associated with the death of another. This can only be accomplished by public execution. And, to be truly effective, the public execution must be attended with suspense and drama, filling the minds and souls of all witnesses with fear and images of their own mortality.

"With regard to the mode of carrying the sentence into execution," Benét wrote,

> . . . it should be rendered . . . as extensively useful as possible, by the publicity which attends its execution. Capital punishment, for instance, should be carried into effect in the presence of all troops, or of such proportions of the command as the convenience of the service may dictate.[1]

Military executions conducted by the Union Army during the Civil War, whether by musket or rope, were carefully orchestrated events, outlined, before Benét, in Alexander Macomb's *The Manual of Courts-Martial.*[2] The procedures and directions left little to the imagination, and very few details were left to the discretion of the commanding or executing officer.

The execution of Privates Henry Schumaker and Henry Stark at Hilton Head, South Carolina, 17 April 1864, was typical.

Following a brief period of prayer with the clergymen of their choice, Schumaker and Stark were taken from their cells and escorted, under heavy guard, to a waiting army wagon which contained a pair of roughly-made coffins. The men wore plain "citizen's clothing"; they were not allowed to wear the uniforms they had dishonored.

Once in the wagon, they were seated astride the pine boxes and led into a military parade. The provost marshal, mounted on a horse, led the entourage. He was followed by his mounted assistant, a drum corps in two ranks, the firing squad, the wagonload of prisoners, and an ambulance, carrying the clergy, a surgeon, and a civilian witness or two.

As Charles K. Caldwell[3] remembered it, "The funeral escort of a corporal and eight men, marched to funeral music, with arms reversed." The somber music was integral to the mood that was to be created. Men in combat, those constantly facing death at the hands of the enemy, live each day in fear that this day will be the last. The dirges and funeral tones accentuated those feelings and produced shudders in even the strongest individuals.

"Slowly," Caldwell continued, "the procession proceeded to the appointed place; the square was formed on three sides, and the victims were driven around once that all might see them and avoid their fate . . . ."

The "square" was the "hollow square," a military conrivance that grouped the soldiers in ranks so that all witnesses had a clear view of the execution — and each other. No man could stand in the ranks and look up without seeing the eyes of a comrade. This was designed to accentuate the emotions in the individual. The men to be executed were placed at the open end, with the firing squad facing them.

The convicted men, faced with imminent death, were frightened, and this mortal fear in many cases paralyzed their limbs. In this disordered state, they were paraded before their former comrades-in-arms — rigid at attention. The contrast was not lost on most witnesses. The apparent vulnerability of humanity was expressed graphically in action, not in words. The sight of a fellow soldier, unable to stand erect with tears and saliva mingling on his face, being half-carried, half-dragged to his death, was designed to achieve maximum impact on all witnesses and underscore the complete and total power of military command over each and every member of the army.

After each spectator had the opportunity to see the condemned, the convicted men were helped out of the wagons. Members of the guard detail lifted the coffins from the carts and placed them on the ground, next to newly-dug graves. The doomed men were then made to sit upon the coffins while the provost marshal intoned the charges, specifications and sentence.

The reading of the orders, complete with all details of the crime[s] committed, was a necessary component of the execution ritual. It underscored the fact that someone had blatantly violated the strict rules and regulations of military order. When the provost marshal reached the sentence statement, no question would remain in any listener's mind, military authorities thought, that he too could — and would — be punished for any transgression.

"After a short prayer by the priest," Caldwell wrote,

> they were blindfolded and their hands tied behind them and made to kneel upon their coffins, facing the center of the square. The firing party came up and halted at six paces distant, when, at a signal from Capt. Babcock [the provost], they fired and the victims fell upon their coffins. Schumaker was pierced with nine bullets and Stark with six.

The executed men were left where they fell, until the officers had the opportunity to march the entire command in review past the lifeless forms. Usually the march was accompanied by a sprightly tune — an apparent attempt to celebrate life in the face of death.

After everyone had seen the results of transgression against military order, a burial detail laid the bodies in the coffins — face down. This procedure apparently was derived from strong Christian tradition. . .those who were thought to be saintly where laid to rest facing the heavens; those who were not, facing hell. Once sealed, the pine boxes were placed in the holes and covered with dirt. Careful attention was paid to leveling off the ground, so that passersby would never know a grave existed in the site. Neither mound nor marker, however, was needed to remind the soldiers who witnessed the execution that a man, a former soldier, had died there.

The ritual attached to the executions of Privates Schumaker and Stark was typical of most musketry executions. The shooting of both men was clean and humane. This was not always the case.

Privates Thomas Dix, John Hall, Henry McCurdy, John Smith, and James Thompson were executed by musket fire near Laurel Hill, Virginia, on 21 December 1864. After the first volley echoed across the field, one eyewitness

> looked toward the graves, but to our astonishment each man yet remained standing, showing conclusively that the detail had fired high. The second or reserve detail was at once marched into position . . . and at the same signal the smoke puffed from their carbines, and their fire proved more accurate, but not entirely effective. The prisoners all fell. Three were dead, while two were trying hard to rise again, and one of them even got upon his knees when a bullet from the revolver of the provost marshal sent him down. Again he attempted to rise, getting upon his elbow and raising his body nearly to a sitting posture, when a second bullet in the head from the marshal's revolver suddenly extinguished what little life was left and a third shot put out the life of the second prisoner.[4]

The execution of two deserters, Privates Edward Elliott and George Layton, at the Rapidan River on 18 September 1863, "was a very bungling affair," Charles Davis Page wrote,

> . . . not more than one cartridge out of five did any service. After repeated firing the men were pronounced dead and the division was marched by companies past the graves and the bleeding forms of the victims. New recruits of the regiment were after that marched by the graves as a silent example.[5]

Disastrous executions such as these were sometimes viewed by the troops as sickening displays of callous authority. In some situations, the existence of such motivations was not only possible but probable.[6] Some officers, those who did not command the respect of their subordinates, did, either on their own or at the direction of higher authority, make circuses out of the executions.

In most cases, however, the shoddy craftsmanship of an execution was the result of poorly-loaded cartridges, inadequately-trained marksmen, and the army's own attempt to reduce the guilt of firing squad members. The common soldier found it distasteful to take the life of a comrade, regardless of the crime. To minimize the personal guilt that might have plagued the mind of an executioner, arrangements were made so that no member of a firing squad would know that the fatal shot came from his rifle. "Five men from each company," an 1861 news account read, "were then detailed to execute the sentence. The guns were loaded without the intervention of the men, two only out of each five having ball cartridges."[7] When Private John Cole's time arrived, "some thirty of the guard were detailed for the execution . . . Most of the guns," the *Lawrence Republican* reported, "were loaded with blank cartridges, and no one knew the nature of the cartridge he fired."[8] "Eleven men in each section [of two] had rifles loaded with ball cartridges and one with a blank" at Frank McElhenny's execution at Deep Bottom, Virginia, on 8 August 1864. "No one knew who had the latter," Captain John N. Partridge wrote, "so that each had the right to suppose that he held it."[9]

This involved procedure, however, was only for effect. The recoil of a weapon fired with a blank charge — even when double-charged [there are no records that this technique was employed] — does not produce the same impact as one with a lead ball. A practiced rifleman, and the men selected usually had some experience, must have felt the difference. No one let on, and not one account, including recollections of members of the shooting squads, mentioned this fact. Apparently, the guilt-minimizing effort was effective — and no one let on they knew.

Execution by hanging followed much the same ceremonial ritual as that by musketry. But, because of the mechanical necessity of a gallows, hangings lacked much of the inherent pageantry of death by bullet.

Hangings usually took place in or near a garrison, where labor was readily obtainable for the erection of the required scaffold. In one instance, that of the execution of Private William Howe, at Fort Mifflin, Philadelphia, 26 August 1863, the entire apparatus was borrowed from nearby Moyamensing Prison and reconstructed at the fort.[10]

What hangings lacked in military drama was made up for in the lengthy period of tension-producing construction. A hanging place could not be built overnight. If a fort or garrison had the dubious honor of possessing a permanent gallows, it stood as a daily reminder that military crimes were punishable by death. On the other hand, because of its permanence, some installations were used by other commands for executions of men not from the garrison command. This sometimes minimized the effect on the rank and file stationed at that particular post.

If an installation did not have a permanent gallows, and one had to be built, the actual construction work served as another reminder of impending doom. Some references, especially accounts of Howe's execution, draw attention to the proximity of the prisoner to the work. "Thus," a newpaper account charged,

> the few remaining hours of the prisoner . . . must have been disturbed by the sight of the preparations for his death. He could see all that passed and could hear the thoughtless remarks of those who came to examine the structure.[11]

In the implementation of an execution by hanging, the parade was eliminated for obvious reasons: the victim, standing high above the crowd, could be seen by everyone present. At the same time, a band was not required since there was no procession through the ranks. In hangings, the band was replaced by one or more drummers who beat out a staccato sound before the trap was pulled.

Because of the principal focus, the victim and the rope, all attention was drawn upwards, in an almost-religious gesture. At a shooting, a man's attention could be drawn toward other things, the firing squad, the provost marshal or the faces of other soldiers.

When a hanging was complete, the body would remain suspended for a period of time, before the men were dispersed, so all could derive maximum benefit from the spectacle. Standing at attention, soldiers were mesmerized by the gentle motion of the taut rope, with the dead weight of a fellow-soldier at its end. Following the public display, the body would be cut down, embalmed at government expense, then shipped to the victim's family for final disposition. The main reason for this procedure was that the majority of forts and posts had limited burial space for men who died in garrison hospitals. The intrusion of the blood of cowards and criminals, it was felt, would desecrate the sacred soil reserved for the honored dead. The black soldiers who were hanged outside Petersburg, however, were interred near the execution site. It is probable, since the men were former slaves, the government did not have next of kin to whom the bodies could be sent.

Because the bodies of many of the hanged victims were returned home, their remains can be found in private burial plots — and military cemeteries, where they were buried with "the usual military honors."[12] One must wonder if the army — or the federal government — relented or apologized for the executions in this way.

The basic reason for the executions, as it has been explained, was to present an object lesson to all witnesses. In this regard, military authorities achieved their goal. Chaplain H. C. Trumbull's comment that "none who witnessed [the execution] could ever forget it"[13] is common in most eyewitness accounts.

And the memory would stay with the men until the day they died. Following the execution of Private Henry Miller at Jacksonville, Florida, 16 April 1864, a member of the 3rd New Hampshire remarked that the unit "had no more desertions for many months."[14] The effect of the execution of Private John D. Starbird was more positive, as Captain Gregory B. Adams recalled. The impact was "as good as if [the corps] had been reinforced by a full regiment."[15] But not all the comments were so positive. "I presume," Captain Adams remarked following another execution,

> that the impressions desired were produced upon the minds of the men, but the remarks were that it was too hard to hang men when they were so hard to get, and if they had let him alone a few weeks Johnnie Reb would have saved them the trouble.[16]

Some units, such as the Pennsylvania Reserve Corps, were resentful of being forced to witness the execution of a fellow soldier. "The Bucktails," as Edwin A. Glover remembered, "did not consider that they needed this object lesson. Possibly to show their resentment, that night more than one succeeded in finding some cheap whiskey and getting gloriously drunk."[17]

Executions took place infrequently during the first two years of war and then intensified, until they occurred with such great frequency that it seemed a day did not go by without an execution taking place somewhere within the Union Army. Chart 1 (below) summarizes the executions by year.

The executions of Union soldiers impressed everyone who witnessed them. But the mental image of the execution was all that endured, not the reason for the shooting or the hanging. Men continued to desert the army; men continued to rape, rob and murder, as the data indicates. The only ones who were stopped were the ones executed.

The following chapters will provide the reader with year-by-year accounts of how military justice was administered and delivered during the Civil War.

CHART 1: UNION EXECUTIONS BY YEAR [287 Cases]

| YEAR | NUMBER | PERCENTAGE |
|------|--------|------------|
| 1861 | 9 | 3.14 |
| 1862 | 15 | 5.23 |
| 1863 | 65 | 22.65 |
| 1864 | 96 | 33.45 |
| 1865 | 78 | 27.18 |
| 1866 | 4 | 1.39 |

A full day-by-day listing is included in the succeeding chapters. However, 10.11 percent took place during December 1864; 6.38 percent, March 1865; 5.99 percent, May 1865; 5.62 percent, September 1863; 5.24 percent, in both April 1864 and January 1865.

# ENDNOTES TO CHAPTER FOUR

1. Captain Stephen Vincent Benét, *A Treatise on Military Law and the Practice of Courts-Martial* [New York, 1862, Revised Edition, 1864], p. 166.

2. Alexander Macomb, *The Manual of Courts-Martial* [New York, 1841]

3. Charles K. Campbell, *The Old Sixth, Its War Record, 1861-5* [New Haven, 1875], pp. 82-86.

4. James I. Robertson, "Military Executions," *Civil War Times Illustrated* V [May 1966] 2:34-39.

5. Charles Davis Paige, *History of the Fourteenth Regiment, Connecticut Vol. Infantry* [Meriden, 1906], p. 15.

6. Examples of the callous display of authority are illustrated in the chapters dealing with the individual soldiers and their cases.

7. *Daily Conservative,* 26 November 1861.

8. *Lawrence Republican,* 25 July 1861.

9. Alfred S. Roe, *The Twenty-fourth Regiment, Massachusetts Volunteers 1861-1866, "The New England Guard Regiment"* [Worchester, 1907], pp. 424-32.

10. *Daily Evening Bulletin* [Philadelphia], 26 August 1864.

11. *Sunday Dispatch* [Philadelphia], 28 August 1864.

12. Several examples of executed soldiers being interred in military cemeteries, complete with military honors, have been found in individual soldiers' files at the National Archives. They are duly noted in the chapters on individual cases.

13. Roe, *op. cit.,* pp. 424-32.

14. Colonel Elbridge J. Copp, *Reminiscenses of the War of the Rebellion 1861-1865* [Nasua, 1911], pp. 216-17.

15. Captain Gregory B. Adams, *Reminiscences of the Nineteenth Massachusetts Regiment* [Boston, 1899], p. 94.

16. *Ibid.,* pp.84-86.

17. Edwin A. Glover, *Bucktailed Wildcats: A Regiment of Civil War Volunteers* [New York, 1960], p. 219.

# CHAPTER FIVE

## 1861:
### *". . . the severe disciplines of war."*

*14 July 1861*

The first Union soldier to be executed for a military crime during the Civil War was JOHN W. COLE, a 21-year-old teamster and a native Pennsylvanian.[1]

The *Lawrence Republican* [Lawrence, Kansas] reported on 25 July 1861 that

> Two soldiers of Capt. Stockton's company, first regiment of Kansas volunteers, got into a quarrel in their tent. They agreed to go out and settle the difficulty by a fight. As one of the beligerents was leaving the tent the other stabbed him in the back, killing him instantly.

"The assassin," Private Cole, was tried by military commission, convicted, and sentenced to be shot. Thirty men were assigned to the shooting squad 14 July 1861, near Springfield, Missouri. It is no wonder that Cole fell instantly; his body was "pierced through with seven bullets . . . ."

"Such," the reporter concluded, "are the tendencies and the severe disciplines of war."

*2 August 1861*

In 1861, the Union Army was still operating under court-martial policies used in the Mexican War, as the service file of Private WILLIAM F. MURRAY, Company F, 2nd New Hampshire Infantry, indicates.

Murray, a three-year-enlistee, was accused of shooting "with musket" Mary Butler 26 July, in Alexandria, Virginia. Miss Butler did not survive.

A military commission, similar to the one used to try Private Cole, was called for 8 a.m. the same day as the murder, which may indicate the crime was committed earlier than the specified date. By 1 August, the panel, presided over by Colonel Henry Whiting, 2nd Virginia Volunteers, found Murray guilty and called for him to be hanged.

James B. Fry,[2] assistant adjutant general, wanted to ensure the successful completion of military justice. In a letter to Colonel Henry E. Davies, commanding in Alexandria, Fry wrote:

> We will take the most effective measures to render the rescue or escape of this man impossible and to carry out the sentence promptly. Make some officer or officers responsible (with ample guards) for the security of the man tonight and until he is executed. Let there be no hesitation for failure in carrying out his sentence.

There was no hesitation or failure. Murray was hanged between 4 and 5 p.m., 2 August 1861 at Fort Ellsworth, Alexandria.

### 28 August 1861

Sergeant [no first name given] JOYCE, a member of the 2nd Kentucky Infantry, was shot to death by Lieutenant Ira Gibbs on 28 August 1861 — for failing to order his men on a work detail.[3]

### 2 October 1861

ROBERT DICKMAN [Dickerman], 27, a bachelor farmer from England, enlisted in the 18th Illinois Infantry at Anna, Illinois, 28 May 1861.

Dickman was accused of the 2 October murder of a William Evans in Mound City, Illinois. By regimental court-martial — with no records, no date, no orders — the man was hanged the same day at Mound City.

### 24 November 1861

Army life in Leavenworth, Kansas, was neither peaceful nor tranquil, if *The Daily Conservative* was accurate in its reporting!

On Friday, 21 November 1861, a number of men went into town. As the night progressed, a number got drunk and were arrested — "though not without resistance," a reporter wrote. JOSEPH RAYMOND [Joseph Ramon], 23, a private in Company C, 7th Kansas Cavalry,

> with two others, an American and an Irishman went to a German boarding house and saloon . . . They violently demanded admittance, firing into the house, and breaking the windows. They obtained an entrance, though informed by the barkeeper they did not sell liquor to anyone.

The trio drew revolvers, and took what liquor they could find, "placed pistolas at the hearts of" the owner's two daughters and ordered them upstairs. The owner was able to protect her daughters' virtue by drinking "some wine" with the men. They confiscated "a small amount of silver and a silver watch," then left, "going to a private dwelling and insulting the lady in the same manner."

Both women identified Raymond as "the Mexican, who was marked in a peculiar manner, by reason of one finger of his right hand being shot off. His hand was also bloody from the glass of the windows."

Colonel Charles R. Jennison called a "regimental court of inquiry . . . and a very full investigation [was] made." The investigation was so thorough that only Raymond was tried, convicted and sentenced to death for stealing. Jennison took full responsibility for the execution order.

"Nothing had ever given [Jennison] more pain," the newspaper concluded,

> than the necessity of ordering the death of this man, who, when sober, had always shown himself to be a good soldier; but the case was extreme, and the necessity of an example so great that he could not show any clemency. If such things were allowed to go unpunished, the lives of no man was safe, the honor of no woman was secure, and all property in danger. Besides the lives and honor of the regiment were at stake in such a matter. It was painful, but still it was a duty.

On Sunday, 24 November 1861, the regimental chaplain, the Rev. Mr. Ayres made "a most impressive prayer" with Raymond. The convicted man "stood unflinching and did not want to have his eyes bandaged." He fell after one volley; his body "pierced with a dozen bullets."

Joseph Raymond, the "honest and faithful" soldier died with "pay due him from enlistment." At the same time, his file indicated "he owed the government $35.86 for extra clothing at the time of his death."

### 13 December 1861

While Company D, 1st New York Cavalry defended Washington, one of its members, Private WILLIAM H. JOHNSTON, deserted. Though desertion was not uncommon, Johnston's case was singled out for very special treatment.

William Johnston was the first Union soldier executed for desertion. Because of this, his trial and execution became the model for those that followed throughout the Civil War.

In a letter, dated 7 December 1861, Assistant Adjutant General J. Williams outlined to Brigadier-General William B. Franklin, the standard technique to be employed by court-martial panels — in this case, and hundreds that followed:

. . . Inasmuch as this is a very flagrant case the utmost exactness is necessary and the offence must be described in the *very words* of the article of war, or the record will not support a capital sentence. No one can be punished for desertion from the service of the United States (Art. 20th of war) unless *he has received pay in the service of the United States* or has *been duly enlisted* in it. It is necessary that the deserter should be described as having done the one or the other of these acts. The *proof* of having been duly enlisted or of having received pay, in the service of the U. S. is another matter. His own admission, or conduct inexplicable upon any other hypothesis that that of regular enlistment, *may* in the absence of regular evidence, be resorted to: but it is supposed that at any rate there will be difficulty in knowing that he has *received pay* in that service. This can be proved by anyone who saw him receive such pay as well as the Paymaster, though if that officer be acceptible, resort had better be made to him among others. Without some proof a Capital Sentence will in all probability fail of execution.

Realizing that Franklin had not been involved in cases like this previously, Williams went into great detail . . .

I have taken the liberty of framing a charge & specification against Johnston. I have so drawn it as to admit of proof either that he was duly enlisted or that he received pay. The court will, if he be not proved to have been duly enlisted, negative so much of the specification. If he be not proved to have received pay they will negative that averment: but of the failure to prove that he has received pay I can scarcely conceive. If the reporting officer adopts the form I send the charge can be tried without preliminary return to this office.

The form that Williams suggested was used, with the expected results. Johnston was executed 13 December 1861, and the ritual itself was memorialized in *Frank Leslie's Illustrated Magazine.* The publicity did nothing to stem the flow of deserters, and Williams' format was used throughout the war.

### 20 December 1861
RICHARD GATEWOOD, 21, a steamboat cook, joined the 1st Kentucky Infantry for a very simple reason: he and a large number of other river-

men were out of work because of the suspension of steamboat traffic in Southern waters. The rivermen were rough and tough, and didn't adhere to strict military discipline. They provided a fair amount of business to the military courts.

Private Gatewood left his unit — without authority — 3 August 1861. While he was gone, trouble started at Camp Tompkins, the regimental headquarters. On 28 August, Lieutenant Ira B. Gibbs shot and killed a Sergeant Joyce, for refusing to order his men on a work detail, mutinying and advising his men to resist. General Jacob B. Cox was within earshot, and put Gibbs under arrest. He assured the uneasy soldiers that the matter would be thoroughly investigated, and justice delivered.

Gatewood was arrested in late September. While in confinement, the soldier threatened Major Bart Lieper, 1st Kentucky, and, on 8 October, attempted to escape — assaulting a guard.

A general court-martial was convened to hear the cases of Gatewood, Gibbs, and others, with General Cox as the presiding officer, and Major Rutherford B. Hayes, 23rd Ohio, as judge advocate.

Lieutenant Gibbs was acquitted — and promptly promoted to captain; Gatewood, however, was convicted on all accounts and sentenced to death.

Major Hayes, later to serve as the 19th President of the United States, was unnerved by the court's decision. In his diary for 29 October, he wrote:

> I have tried twenty cases before a court-martial held in Colonel Tompkins' house this past week. One [Gatewood] convicted for desertion and other aggravated offenses, punished with sentence of death. I trust the General will mitigate this.

Hayes was not alone in his desire to see a mitigation of sentence. Silas Gatewood, a relative, wrote Brigadier-General William S. Rosecrans from Madison, Indiana, ". . . has the sentence been executed? If not will you ask its suspension until I can reach your camp. There are mighty reasons that can be presented for your respite please answer!! . . . the whole family await answer in Madison."

Silas Gatewood's communique was three days late. On 20 December 1861, Richard Gatewood was carried in an ambulance to the shooting site. General Cox took command of the execution, as he had the court. In his *Military Reminiscences,* Cox notes that Gatewood "fell dead at the volley which sounded like a single discharge."

Sensing that his action to punish Gatewood — but not Gibbs — was unpopular, Cox spared his command the customary finale: the parade past the corpse. Instead, the units were formed into columns and marched directly back to their camps.

"The moral effect of the execution was very great," Cox wrote, "for our men were so intelligent that they fully appreciated the judicial character of the act, and the imposing solemnity of the parade and execution made impression all the more profound."

### 23 December 1861

A month after William F. Murray murdered Mary Butler in Alexandria, Virginia, Private JOHN LANAHAN [Lannagan], Company I, 46th Pennsylvania Infantry, murdered his commanding officer, a Major Lewis.

A general court-martial was convened, and Lanahan was convicted. He was hanged 23 December 1861.

### Undated

A private in the 8th Illinois was hanged for murder sometime in 1861, following a drumhead court-martial. "All partners," an English observer noted, "felt that they had performed a virtuous act."[4] A search of the 8th's records failed to turn up any mention of the incident — or the man.

# ENDNOTES TO CHAPTER FIVE

1. The majority of information on the executed soldiers has been obtained from two key sources: National Archives. *RG 94, Records of the Adjutant General's Office, 1780s-1917.* Muster Rolls of Volunteer Organizations, Civil War, and *RG 94, Records of the Adjutant General's Office, 1780s-1917,* Compiled Military Service Records. Unless otherwise cited in text or note, the material is drawn from these sources. The names enclosed in braces [ ] indicate other spellings and aliases used by the men.

2. After serving as assistant adjutant general in Washington, Fry was named Colonel and Provost Marshal General 17 March 1863.

3. Press release issued by Education Foundation, Inc., Charlestown, West Virginia, 28 January 1962.

4. Quoted in Victor Hicken, *The American Fighting Man* [New York, 1969], p. 199.

# CHAPTER SIX

## 1862:
## *". . . deeply to be regretted."*

**6 January 1862**

MICHAEL LANAHAN, a private in Company A, 2nd Infantry, Regulars, was part of the City Guard at Washington when he was accused of murder. His file does not indicate whom he murdered.

Lanahan, however, was convicted by general court-martial, and hanged 6 January 1862.

A haunting suspicion that the last man executed in 1861 [John Lanahan] and the first man in 1862 were related did not result in any concrete evidence. John Lanahan joined his unit in Scranton, Pennsylvania; records do not indicate the place of origin for Michael Lanahan.

**5 February 1862**

SAMUEL H. CALHOUN, 26, was executed 5 February 1862 at Bardstown, Kentucky. He was accused of murder, though no record of a general court-martial exists.

A letter in his file, however, indicates he confessed to the crime after the adjournment of the court.

**5 March 1862**

MICHAEL CONNEL, an Irish laborer, was executed for an unknown offense at Camp Andrew Jackson, Tennessee, 5 March 1862.

Connel's service record indicates he was a 3-month volunteer in Company E, 24th Ohio Infantry from 29 April to 29 May 1861.

On the date of the completion of his service, Connel joined up for a 3-year enlistment. At the time of his offense, the 24th Ohio was part of the advance on Nashville.

Could Connel have been a deserter? His company muster roll does not state whether he was absent or present in May/August or September/October, but does show that he "Was priv. in 3 months service from Apr. 29 to May 29/61 for which back pay is due." The entries for January/February 1862 repeat that back pay is due him. But in the muster out roll, it is stated that he was "last paid to" 31 August 1861.

The March/April 62 entry is simple: "Was executed at Camp Andrew Jackson, Tenn., Mar. 5, 1862, by sentence of General Court Martial." There is no record that Connel was ever tried.

### 7 March 1862

> In the case of Private WILLIAM KUHNES, Company "I" 2nd Regiment Maryland Volunteers the proceedings are confirmed. The Major General Commanding perceives no palliation of the offence committed. It was not merely the highest military crime of which short of deserting to the enemy the accused could have been guilty, but it was cold blooded assassination for which a false pretext was with perverse ingenuity elaborated before hand.[1]

Kuhnes was convicted by general court-martial of the shooting death of 2nd Lieutenant David Whitson, of his company, at Camp Carroll, Baltimore, 10 December 1861.

Lieutenant-Colonel Thomas Clark, 6th Michigan Volunteers, presided over the panel that called for Kuhnes' death by hanging. The sentence was carried out at Fort McHenry, 7 March 1862.

### 18 March 1862

Company H, 7th Kansas Cavalry, according to Simeon M. Fox in *The Seventh Kansas Cavalry: Its Service in the Civil War,* had a fine contingent of fighting men, but lacked proper discipline "at first."

This lack of discipline, Fox noted, took several forms. When Captain Marshall Cleveland resigned from the unit, many of his men deserted — only to join Cleveland's newly-organized unit. When Colonel James G. Blunt was made a brigadier general. Fox continued, Charles R. Jennison, who was an aspirant for promotion himself, "was highly wroth, and made an intemperate speech while in camp at Lawrence, during which he practically advised the men to desert."

Following his speech, a number of men, mostly from Company H, took his advice. That company, according to Fox, was largely made up of former members of Cleveland's "jayhawkers," who had operated on the Missouri border. It had a reputation as a "black horse company."

ALEXANDER DRISCOLL, 27, an Irish shoemaker and a resident of Leavenworth, joined the unit 10 October 1861. According to *The Daily Conservative* [Leavenworth], Driscoll fit right into Company H . . .

deserting from the British at Sebastapol, repeating the crime at Lexington under Price, he had since becoming one of our number robbed a Union man in Missouri, stabbed a fellow soldier in his company here, from the effects of which his life is even now [27 March 1862] jeopardized, Driscoll determined to reach the highest round on the ladder of infamy, stole a horse and saddle, after relieving himself of his shackles and leaping a bluff of rocks, escaped the guards and fled again towards the camp of secesh. — But man proposes and God disposes. Spraining his ankle and becoming swollen and painful, he was obliged to halt at a farmhouse some thirty miles from camp, being unable to ride farther. Here he was taken by a scout . . . and compelled to return.

Driscoll, according to the 1885 Adjutant General's Office report, was tried by general court-martial; however, no record of one exists. *The Conservation* explains this lack:

The convening of a court martial, the trial, the conviction and the sentence were the work of but a few hours, and on Saturday last, on dress parade, in the presence of the whole regiment, his body was pierced by five balls, and the soul of poor Driscoll was ushered in the presence of Him who deals justly and loves mercy.

Based on the newspaper account, Driscoll was executed at Humboldt, Kansas, 22 March 1862; he is listed in his company rolls as having died 18 March.

## 6 April 1862

JOHN TANSEY, a recruit in Company K, 3rd Cavalry, Regulars, committed murder somewhere in the Department of New Mexico, and was executed 6 April 1862.

Research, however, conducted at the National Archives, did not uncover records for John Tansey. Records can be located for John R. Tansey, a recruit in the 3rd Cavalry, who joined 6 March 1863, and deserted a little over a month later. No evidence exists to indicate that Tansey was ever apprehended or convicted.

## 8 April 1862

DARIUS [Durius] A. PHILBROOKS, 28, 1st Sergeant in the 1st Regiment Colorado Infantry [The Adjutant General's report mistakingly placed Philbrooks in Company K, 1st Colorado Cavalry, a unit that didn't come into existence until 1 November 1862 — eight months after the man's execution.].

Tried by general court-martial for violating the 9th Article of War — striking a superior officer in the performance of the officer's duties, Philbrooks was shot to death at Fort Union, 8 April 1862.

### 13 June 1862

JOHN McMAHON, 24, an Irish laborer who joined the 99th New York Infantry 10 December 1861, shot and killed a fellow soldier, Michael Dolan, while the unit was stationed at Fort Monroe, Virginia.

Tried by general court-martial, McMahon was convicted, and confined at Fort Wool, Rip Raps, Virginia, before he was executed. McMahon was hanged at Fort Wool on 13 June 1862.

### 16 June 1862

General Benjamin F. Butler, while he commanded the occupation of New Orleans, May-October 1862, prided himself on the general good conduct of his troops, and the resulting esteem of the general citizenry.

Around the first of June, a band of burglars, representing themselves as Union officers empowered to search for arms and contraband papers, preyed on the city. "With forged orders and in disguised uniforms," Homer Baxter Sprague remembered in his *History of the 13 Regiment of Connecticut Volunteers During the Great Rebellion,* "they forced their way at dead of night into dwellings of peaceable citizens, searched trunks, drawers, wardrobes, seized whatever money or plate they could lay hands on, and made off with the booty."

The burglars operated with quiet efficiency leaving few if any clues as to their identity. "It became," as Butler recalled, "a very annoying scandal and disgrace." Butler could not allow this to continue.

On the morning of 12 June, he announced to his officers' mess that "This system of night thieveries must be put an end to, and I am going to attend to nothing else, routine duty excepted, until it is done."

Later that morning, "a respectable looking Spanish gentleman" visited Butler. His home had been entered the night before by an officer and four men. This small detachment, the citizen stated, "searched everything in the house . . . ." When they left, they took with them "all of the jewelry in the house and somewhere in the neighborhood of $10,000 in money . . . ." The lieutenant did, however, leave a receipt with the owner, signing himself: "J. William Henry, first Lieutenant of the Eighteenth Massachusetts Volunteers," and testifying that he had searched the premises "No. 93 Toulouse Street, and find to the best of my judgement that all the people who live there are loyal. Please examine no more."

Butler looked at the receipt and realized immediately that it was a forgery: there was no 18th Massachusetts regiment under his command. Was there any way the civilian could identify the men, Butler asked? The only thing the man could remember was that the detachment drove away in a cab.

"In the name of heaven," Butler yelled, "did you get the number of the cab?" He had, it was No. 50!

The general dispatched his provost guard lieutenant to catch the cab and driver. The driver was brought in and, after some prompting, recalled the destination of the party from 93 Toulouse, it was a popular coffee house.

**Benjamin Franklin Butler, while he commanded New Orleans, single-handedly stopped crime in that city...or so he wrote. Butler is depicted in a very general-like pose by Thomas Nast.**

*Massachusetts Commandery, Military Order of the Loyal Legion*
*and the US Army Military History Institute.*

"Lieutenant," Butler ordered, "take a party of the provost guard and go to this coffee-house, and bring to me every live thing in it including the cat, and don't let one speak to the other until after they have seen me."

Three-quarters of an hour later, the officer returned with the prisoners. When they marched before the general, Butler recognized a face. It was that of a man who had come before him when Butler served as a judge in Boston. The man had been tried and convicted of burglary, but had been pardoned on the provision he enlist in the army. He had subsequently been discharged because of a rupture.

When Butler threatened to hang the man "to save all further trouble," the man told the story that there was a party of seven that had formed a secret society. For the past two weeks they had ransacked eighteen different houses. He also gave Butler the names, including three who had not been picked up at the coffee house.

All seven were brought before Butler, including a second familiar face: that of the mate of Butler's own steam yacht. Three confessed the same night: Theodore Lieb, of New Orleans; George William Craig, former first officer of the *City of New York;* and FRANK NEWTON, 22, formerly a private in the 13th Regiment Connecticut Volunteers. Newton had been discharged due to a "disability" 20 May 1862. William M. Clary, formerly the second officer of the steam transport *Saxon,* and Stanislaus Roy, of New Orleans, also confessed. Most of the property was recovered . . . except for three or four hundred dollars.

Four of the five were tried by Butler personally, and sentenced to execution by hanging — a sentence that was carried out at 10 a.m., at the parish prison on 16 June. Theodore Lieb, "a boy," Butler wrote, "at the intercession of his mother and upon evidence that he had not been a bad boy before his connection with the gang, and being only a sort of page for them, I sentenced to prison for a short term." The informer was given a sentence of five years at hard labor to be served at Ship Island.

"From that hour," Butler prided himself, "no burglary was ever committed in New Orleans; at least none were complained of."

### 11 July 1862

JOHN BELL, 24, a private in Company I, 2nd Kansas Cavalry, is a footnote in Kansas history. He was the first man to be legally executed in the state.

By sentence of a drumhead court-martial, approved by Colonel W. F. Cloud, Bell was sentenced to death by hanging for the 4 July 1862 rape of a woman near Iola, Kansas.

*The Manhattan Express,* 22 July 1862, published an account of Bell's death...

> It was intended to hang him at sunset on the 9th inst.,
> but the citizens heard of it, and men, women and children
> flocked in and around camp, as though there was to be
> some great show.

It appeared there was little entertainment in those days in Kansas. Realizing this problem, Colonel Cloud

> wisely decided that though John Bell should die, to pay the penalty of his crime he should not die for the amusement of the citizens, so there was no parade or execution that day. The next day the citizens hovered around camp all day like so many fools. Last night commanders of companies were ordered to have their companies ready for parade at sunrise. This morning our companies were formed and marched to the place prepared for the execution . . .

Even with the change in agenda, Cloud was outfoxed by the townsfolks. "As soon as we arrived there," the account continued, "several citizens could be seen poking their heads out of the grass. Our duty has been performed, the criminal has been executed — and the citizens of Iola have made *fools* of themselves. Several men laid all night in the wet grass to see a soldier hung . . . ."

Bell might have been the first legal hanging in Kansas history, but he was not the only man to be hanged by military authority. In Louise Barry's "Legal Hangings in Kansas," she notes that two others took place: those of John Shirley [6 May 1863] at Fort Leavenworth, and CLAUDEUS C. FRIZELL [27 May 1863] at Fort Scott. Shirley was a civilian, but Frizell was a militiaman from Vernon County, Missouri.

The *Daily Conservative* [17 May 1863] also indicates that JOHN W. SUMMERS, Company E, Second Kansas Cavalry, was executed for desertion by a military firing squad at Fort Scott on 13 May 1863. Quite possibly there had been other military executions of military personnel at army posts in Kansas and elsewhere — without the facts published by the military or the public press.

### 21 September 1862

Little is known about LEWIS STIVERS, a private in Company B, 7th Kentucky Infantry.

What few records exist indicate he was executed 21 September 1862 for murder by some unspecified delivery of military justice.

### 26 November 1862

Members of Company K, 1st California Cavalry, were assigned as guards for a deserter. On the morning of 25 November 1862, the man escaped, and Colonel Joseph Rodman West suspected that the sergeant of the guard and several sentinels helped him to escape.

With swiftness, West ordered the sergeant and three privates, all of Company K, placed in irons. "Members of the guard," West wrote to Captain Benjamin C. Cutler, "have heretofore done such things here, and it is difficult to decide whom to trust."

Head Qrs. Dist. of Arizona
Mesilla, November 27, 1862.

Captain

I have to report, for the information of
the Genl. Comg, the following Serious occurrence
at this post. Corporal Clifton of Co. B 2 Cavalry
Cal Vols., a prisoner in irons awaiting Sentence for
desertion, escaped from the guard house on the evening
of the 25th Inst. under such circumstances as to induce
the belief that the Sergeant of the guard and Sentinels
on post, connived at his escape. I ordered the Sergeant
and three Sentinels (all of K Company 1st Infl. C. V.) to
be placed in irons until some account could be given
for such dereliction of duty. Members of the guard
have heretofore done such things here, and it is difficult
to decide whom to trust.

Yesterday morning all the privates of K
Co. refused duty, a Corporal Smith acting as spokesman. The long roll was beat, Comp'y K appearing
by orders, without arms: Corporal Smith was
called to the front and asked by myself:
"Will you do your duty Sir?" His reply was
"I will do as my Company does". On my repeating the question he answered "Not until
Sergeant Miller is released". Corporal Smith

was then shot by my orders: he died within
an hour.

Comp'y A 5th Inf and D of my regiment
were on duty: the latter executed my orders to
shoot the mutineer, but missed him entirely
the first volley, and fired the second so wild
as to wound a soldier of A Co. 5th who was acting
as Capt Smith's Servant and Standing at the
door of his quarters. The Captain supposes
that the man, being hard of hearing, did not
hear the long roll beat: he is seriously wounded
and may not recover. It was the evident intention
of the men of D Co: to avoid shooting the prisoner
by firing wild, and to this circumstance is to
be attributed the wounding of Capt Smith's man.

The men of Company K were then
separately called to the front, and all answered
that they would resume duty. The escaped
prisoner was recaptured the Same day, and
as by his examination it is proved that the
members of the guard were no way cognizant
of his escape, the latter have been released.

No one can regret more than myself
the painful necessity of taking the life of
one of our own Soldiers: this course had to
be pursued or all authority to command

*ceased.* The command has become somewhat demoralized by desertion, and remaining in a town where whisky, gambling and women are plentiful. The course that I have taken, was, in my judgement, unavoidable, and I trust that the Genl Comg may see nothing in it to disapprove of.

I am Captain
very respy Yr Ob Srt.

J. R. West
Col. 1st Infy
Calvols
Comg.

To Capt. Ben. C. Cutler
Asst Adjt Genl
Santa Fe.

Col. [later brigadier general] J. R. West was quite unhappy — or at least that's what he wrote to Assistant Adjutant General Capt. Benjamin Cutler, at Sante Fe — at taking the life of one of his own men. West acted precipitously; Corp. Charles Smith [Co. K, 1st California Infantry] had been right: members of the guard had not conspired to assist a "prisoner in irons" from escaping West's camp.                                                        *National Archives*

The next morning, all the privates of Company K refused duty, with CORPORAL CHARLES SMITH acting as spokesman. "The long roll was beat," West continued, "Company K appearing, by orders, without arms."

West called Smith to the front: "Will you do your duty sir?"

Smith replied: "I will do as my company does."

West repeated the question, only to hear Smith answer: "Not until Sergeant Miller is released."

West wheeled about, and ordered Smith to be shot on the spot. The order was carried out within the hour.

Companies A and D were assigned the execution duty. Members of Company D missed Smith entirely with the first volley, indicating either their lack of marksmanship or their distaste with West's decision. The second was so wild "as to wound a soldier of A Co. 5th who was acting as Capt. Smith's Servant and standing at the foor of his quarters. The Captain supposes that the man, being hard of hearing, did not hear the long roll beats: he is seriously wounded and may not recover. It was the evident intention," West declared, "of the men to avoid shooting the prisoner by firing wild, and to this circumstance is to be attributed the wounding of Capt. Smith's man."

Later that day, members of West's command recaptured the escaped prisoner. After questioning him, West realized the sergeant and the guard had not assisted the prisoner in his escape. They were released from custody. "No one can regret more than myself," West wrote, "the painful necessity of taking the life of one of my own soldiers: the course had to be pursued or all authority to command ceased."

Brigadier General Isaac H. Carleton, commanding the Department of New Mexico, suggested on 3 December that West [by now a brigadier general] request a court of Inquiry. West complied the next week, but no further action was taken.

"The whole affair," as West wrote to Carleton, "is deeply to be regretted."

### 1 December 1862

WILLIAM W. LUNT, 22, a member of Company I, 9th Maine Infantry, was charged with and convicted of desertion and highway robbery.

Lunt's offense may have been viewed as more than plain desertion at the time of his court-martial. In a report written by Lieutenant-Colonel H. Bisbee, Jr., 9th Maine, 27 April 1862, from Fernandina, Florida, the man was suspected of providing information to the enemy, information which resulted in the death or capture of a whole company of Union soldiers.[2]

On the day Lunt deserted, a party of men who held a Mr. Heath in custody were positioned at a railroad bridge separating Amelia Island from the mainland. Three days later, when the group was ordered to return, the scouts found one dead man — a new officer, Lieutenant Wiffin — and evidence that the rest had been killed or captured. Colonel Elbridge J. Copp, in his *Reminiscences of the War of the Rebellion 1861-1865,* suggested that several deserters, Lunt was the only one to be apprehended, had given information to the enemy as to the location of the outpost.

Six men escaped the raid, including one drummer who stated that the unit was surprised in their sleep.

The assertion that Lunt had passed along information to the enemy does not seem likely. His second alleged offense, highway robbery, disputes it. Lunt stood accused of taking $268 from a Miss Ellen Manning aboard a train running from Fernandina to Baldwin, Florida — 8 April — the day after his desertion. If he had confided information to the Confederates, he would not have been able to rendezvous with them and be allowed to go off immediately. That was not the usual procedure. It must have been someone else.

It is not known whether these allegations were taken into account by the general court-martial, presided over by Colonel Alfred H. Terry, 7th Connecticut Volunteers. Lunt, however, was found guilty, and shot to death at Hilton Head, South Carolina, 1 December 1862.

### 5 December 1862

On 17 September 1862, 1st Lieutenant Fernando Linzy, Company K, 103rd New York Infantry, was bayoneted, at the foot of 6th Street, in Washington, D.C. The key suspect was JOHN KESSLER, 36, a German farmer and enlistee in the unit, allegedly "inflicting a wound" which caused the officer's death. Linzy was "in the performance of his duty" at the time of the attack.

Kessler apparently had brushes with military authorities prior to this incident. According to his service record, he was a prisoner at Washington, D.C. 15 May. The murder apparently took place while Kessler's unit was engaged in the Maryland campaign.

Court-martialed, with Colonel W. R. Murphy, 10th New Jersey Volunteers, presiding; and convicted, Kessler was hanged in Washington. His case had been reviewed by Lincoln, and the sentence approved. Though the Adjutant General's report is silent as to the date of his death, Kessler was executed 5 December 1862.

## ENDNOTES TO CHAPTER SIX

1. Union Soldiers, Maryland Roll #82, Microcopy No. 384, 2nd Inf, J-Lam.

2. *OR,* I, 6, p. 132.

# CHAPTER SEVEN

## 1863:
### "... the painful necessity ...."

*2 March 1863*

On 5 September 1862, privates WILLIAM DORMADY, 19, and CHARLES CLARK [Clarke], both members of Company H, 1st Pennsylvania Light Artillery, quit their posts "to plunder and pillage the citizens of York County, Va." Together with other members of their unit, they encountered a civilian, Hezekiah Stokes of Yorktown County, and "with clubs, pistols and knives," the band of soldiers did "beat, shoot and stab" the man. "While divers malicious persons were assaulting" Stokes, "and doing him great personal violence," Dormady and Clark were "present aiding, abetting, and assaulting the same."[1] No one else was charged in the crime.

Dormady and Clark were court-martialed by a military commission at Yorktown, Virginia, and convicted of murder and quitting their post to plunder and pillage. A unique aspect of this case is that the men were also accused of assault with intent to kill. Of that charge, the panel found them not guilty. The two men, however, pleaded not guilty to all charges except their unauthorized leave from camp.

The findings of the panel were forwarded to Washington, and the sentence, to be "executed under the orders of Major-General John A. Dix, commanding the Department of Virginia," was approved by Lincoln. Both men were hanged at Fort Yorktown 2 March 1863.

*27 March 1863*

ROBERT GAY, 27, a private in Company D, 6th Indiana Cavalry [71st], entered the service of the Union 18 August 1862 and immediately was noted on his unit's muster roll as being sick and absent with leave [18 August-31 October]

While Gay was listed as sick for duty, the same record lists him as being captured by Confederate forces at Richmond, Kentucky, 30 August. He signed a parole oath sometime in September.

At that point, he became listed as a deserter. He was returned to his company under arrest in October, and was confined until November, when a general court-martial was convened. Gay was tried and convicted of desertion. He was shot to death 27 March 1863.

A haunting question hovers over the case of Robert Gay: Was the parole oath as binding on Union soldiers as it was expected of Confederates? It appears that was not the case.

### 26 April 1863

The Union forces had tried everything to eliminate straggling and pillage by the troops. By the spring of 1863, all efforts had been exhausted. "It has become necessary, to prevent demoralization, that the fate of this wretched man should be measured out to all who follow his example." read Special Order 106, Department of the Gulf, 2 May 1863.

The "wretched man" was HENRY HAMILL, 39, a private in Company D, 131st New York Infantry. "The safety of this army is more important than the life of any man in it," Major General N. P. Banks' order read, "from the humblest private to the commanding general."

Hamill quit "his colors to plunder and pillage, while the brigade was on detached service in an exposed position and in the presence of the enemy. . . ."[2] In a draft letter found in Hamill's file, a further description of the crime can be found: Hamill "has confessed his crime — He entered the house of a citizen, he terrified women and children, he stole clothing (and shot guns —) . . . " The commanding general regreted "the necessity for this act. . . " Earlier in the same letter, the commanding general of the Department of the Gulf is quoted as saying that "soldiers guilty of plunder and pillage 'fight a fool's fight and deserve a dog's death'. . . ."

Hamill was shot to death in front of the command at sundown 26 April 1863.

### 15 May 1863

JULIUS MILIKA [Mileka. In his correspondence, he signed Julien Milaka], 30, a native of Prussia, enlisted in the 10th Michigan Infantry in February of 1862.

On or about 12 September, he deserted his unit at Nashville, Tennessee. He was returned from desertion at Nashville 8 February 1863. Following a general court-martial, Milika was shot to death at noon on 15 May 1863 on the commons west of Granny White Pike, Nashville.

Milika is buried in Plot 4553, City Cemetery, though some sources have him buried in the National Cemetary in the same city.[3]

**12 June 1863**

The quality of military mercy can be strained just so far, as the Union leadership found out in the case of JOHN P. WOODS [Wood].

Woods, 19, an Ohio farmer, enlisted in the 19th Indiana Infantry 29 July 1861. It was not until 20 August 1862, at Rappahanock Station, Virginia, that he deserted. Recovered and reinstated, Woods then deserted 17 November and 13 December, at Fredericksburg. He was apprehended 1 January 1863.

Each time he was captured, he was returned to duty without penalty. But he had stretched the point to its maximum. He learned that fact when he deserted — for the final time — 28 April.

After his arrest, he was tried by general court-martial, found guilty, and sentenced to execution. He was shot to death at Falmouth, Virginia, 12 June 1863.

His execution elicited response from his comrades, such as Sergeant Sullivan Green, 24th Michigan, who wrote:

> As the Marshal stepped toward him, the prisoner took off his hat, placed it on the ground, and as he turned to his coffin, he stood face to face with his executioners, and beyond them the long line of his comrades, who gave him a last sad, pitying look. However just and necessary the penalty, there is nothing in such a moment that can scarcely be felt but once. . . A comrade had died at the hands of his fellow soldiers, by the same death he feared to meet in the ranks of patriotism. He had cravely deserted them in an hour of danger and had now paid the penalty. The Division marched by the corpse, the column moved forward to the dusty road on its march, and we leave each to his own reflections.[4]

**14 June 1863**

On 10 September 1862, WILLIAM MINIX [also Minx], 25, a member of Company A, 9th Kentucky Infantry, took leave of his unit at Bowling Green, Kentucky, while they were on the march to Louisville.

Following the announcement of his death sentence, Minix wrote to Colonel Thomas J. Cram 14 June 1863:

> . . . as you are doubtless aware I am sentenced to be shot on Tuesday next — others have also been sentenced the same as my selfe who have done much worse then my selfe and yet have been reprieve and I feel shure if you would intrest your selfe on my behalfe my life might be saved and I will promase no swear if I escape that awful degrading death I will hence forth be a true and loyal and a law abiding soldier may God help me for I cannot — help my selfe

His plea went unanswered and, on 16 June 1863, William Minix stood before a firing squad at Murfreesboro, Tennessee, in front of General Horatio P. Van Cleve's division . . . and met his death.

## 16 June 1863

WILLIAM LYNCH, 26, a private in Company G, 2nd Massachusetts Cavalry, stood accused of mutinous behavior 9 April 1863 in Boston.

In the charges and specifications sheet for his court-martial, it was indicated that Lynch "did begin, excite, cause and join in a mutiny and sedition in a squad of men [in his company] . . . by saying to the men: 'Kill the Sergeant!' meaning 1st Sergeant H. G. Burlingham . . . and further, that no man should be ironed in the camp, and that no man could or should iron him; further that he would kill Sergeant Burlingham . . ., and Corporal Balcom, Co. A . . . and he did further say over the dead body of PENDERGAST (late of Co. G . . .), 'I will avenge that man's blood,' or words to that effect . . . ."

In addition to mutiny, he was charged with violating the 8th Article of War, in that he "did not use his utmost endeavor, nor any endeavors at all, to suppress the same," and violating the 9th Article of War since he struck "his superior officer . . ., whilst in the execution of his office." Lynch was also accused of drawing a sabre on Burlingham. That charge was not sustained.

It would appear from the court-martial testimony that Private Pendergast, though not listed as an executed soldier, was the victim of summary punishment. The reaction from Lynch and others in his unit, though not thought out carefully, was natural under the circumstances. As in many other examples of military discipline during the period, only one man was set aside as an example.

The court-martial panel, presided over by Major James W. McDonald, 11th Massachusetts Volunteers, found Lynch guilty, and convicted him. He was shot to death at Fort Independence, Boston Harbor, 16 June 1863.

## 19 June 1863

"While at Leesburg," Samuel Toombs wrote in his *Reminiscences of the War,* "we were kept busily employed with the rest of the Brigade, building a line of earthworks for defence against the army. On the 19th June, we witnessed one of the most affecting sights of the war."

WILLIAM GROVER [also Gruver], WILLIAM McKEE, 19, both of Company A, 46th Pennsylvania Infantry, and CHRISTOPHER KRUBERT, 36, a married German shoemaker and a member of Company B, 13th New Jersey Infantry, had been found guilty by court-martial of desertion; Krubert, 18 January from Wolf Run Shoals, Virginia; the other two, on or about 4 June from Stafford Court House.

"The sky was cloudless," Toombs wrote:

> the sun shone resplendent on Leesburg and the camps surround[ing] it. When the information first reached the troops, a hushed stillness pervaded the whole of the First

Division, and as the drums of the different Regiments beat the first "Assembly" call, the men marched to their positions with sobered looks.

Thirty-six men were detailed to the shooting party; eight for each man, with twelve in reserve.

The death sentence was read, and Chaplain Beck of the 13th read a short prayer; then the rifles fired "and three lifeless bodies fell backward upon their coffins. The troops were marched past the graves," Toombs related, "and they shudderingly looked upon the ghastly sight. Krubert's body was pierced by seven balls in the vicinity of the heart. No burial service was read. The bodies were placed in the coffins prepared for them, and at once consigned to mother earth."

### 23 June 1863

DAVID BLAZER [Blaser], 22, an Ohio farmer, was a member of the 4th Indiana Light Artillery for little more than a month [he was mustered into service 18 February 1863 at Nashville, Tennessee] before he deserted near Liberty, Tennessee, 24 April 1863

Five days later he was captured at Alexandria, Tennessee, "wearing ordinary dress of rebel soldier and said he belonged to Morgan's Cavalry."

Blazer was tried by general court-martial, presided over by Lieutenant-Colonel E. S. Walts, 2nd Kentucky Cavalry, 6 May and convicted. He was shot to death 23 June near Murfreesboro.

Like Private Blazer, JOHN SCHOCKMAN [also Shockman], 20, spent little time with the 1st Kentucky Infantry. He was mustered into the unit 5 June 1861, and deserted from Camp Ganley 1 December.

According to his records, he enlisted in the Ohio Volunteer Cavalry, but was discovered as a deserter from the Kentucky unit.

He was tried for desertion 23 May 1863, and executed by musketry a month later.

### 15 July 1863

WILLIAM H. LAIRD, a 27-year-old married man from Berwick, Maine, enlisted in the 17th Maine Infantry 18 August 1862. He deserted 11 October at Fort Rickets, Maryland, while his unit was near Sharpsburg.

Though his case was cut-and-dried, one letter in his service file indicates a heretofore unknown problem facing military authorities charged with the duty of executing condemned soldiers.

Major George S. Andrews wrote to the Assistant Adjutant General, Department of the East, 9 July 1863, indicating that he understood executions were to be "as private as possible." With his letter, acknowledging the arrival of Laird, he enclosed two newspaper clippings "to illustrate how news circulates here. The evening paper from which sent is published Portland at 5 o'clock P.M. while the prisoner did not arrive at the post until 4 o'clk P.M. yesterday."

Head Quarters Fort Preble Me
July 9. 1863

Major,

        I have the honor to report the arrival this P.M. of private William H. Laird of Company "G" 17th Regt. Me. Vols. now under sentence of death and to be executed on the 15th inst.

        As the Maj. Genl commanding desires the proceedings to be as private as possible, I wish to place before him the situation of this post and other evidence tending to show the impossibility of anything being kept private here.

        The security of the Rebel prisoners now here requires one half my force for guard each day. The Engineers at work on the Fort have 150 men employed. The post now has as many entrances to the parade as there are individuals desiring to enter and nothing but a chain of Sentinals encircling the whole grounds can keep them out and my whole garrison is not large enough for such a purpose

        I enclose slips from two newspapers to illustrate how news circulates here. The evening paper from which I sent is published in Portland at 5 o'clk P.M. while the prisoner Hutchinson did not arrive at the post until after 4 o'clk P.M. yesterday

        Should the Maj. Genl Commanding in view of these facts decide to send the prisoners to Fort Independence or some

other isolated or enclosed post, I respectfully request a
guard may be detailed from such post and send here
for the prisoners as I have neither Officers or men suf
- ficient to admit of my furnishing such a guard as
would be required. without jeopardizing the safe Keeping
of the prisoners of war

                                                          I am Sir, very
                                                          resp'y Yr obt sevt
                                                          Geo L Andrews
To                                                        Maj. 17th Infy
Maj. C. T. Christensen                                    Comdg Post
Ast Adj't Genl
Dept of the East
New York City

**Maj. George Andrews was not too intent of the task of executing Pvt. William
H. Laird [Co. G, 17th Maine Infantry]. His men, he contended, were over-
worked as it was in guarding prisoners of war. His request was refused.**

*National Archives*

Andrews was concerned over his primary charge of guarding "Rebel prisoners now here" which required

> half my force for guard each day. The Engineers at work
> on the Fort have 150 men employed. The post now has
> as many entrances to the parade as there are individuals
> desiring to enter and nothing but a chain of Sentinals en-
> circling the whole grounds can keep them out and my
> whole garrison is not large enough for that purpose.

He suggested that condemned prisoners be sent to "an isolated or enclos-ed post."

The tone of the major's letter stresses his concern over the security of prisoners of war rather than the onerous task of executing Union soldiers.

### 17 July 1863

PETER KLEINKOFF, a German shoemaker, was executed by musketry for desertion, assault with intent to commit robbery, and assault with intent to commit murder 17 July 1863 at Benicia Barracks, California.

By his own court-martial testimony, Kleinkoff admitted to having deserted . . . but with mitigating circumstances.

He had, as he wrote

> beenn a prissoner in the State Prisson of this State and
> gott my Liberty after having suffert for the term 6 Six
> Years and at the time I escap did not posses the means
> of leaving the country when I fount that some of the camp
> at Benicia would soon goh away frome heer so I went
> and enlisted thinking that the company would be leaving
> in a few Days whitch was the gennerall talk at that time
> in and about the Garrison.

Thinking he had found the ideal hiding place, the soldier resumed his life as a free man. He remained, he admitted, "undisrurbt and was in hopes of remaining so," until in town he met one man, then another from the prison; both knew of his past.

"It was not but a few Days," the soldier continued, "when som of the men of my respected Comp fount out that I hath formerly been an inmate at the States Prissen." Several men of his company confronted him with the fact "and I was feart to look any man in the face after that. I fot it as long as I was able to bear it." Finally, Kleinkoff could bear it no longer; he deserted.

The reason he gave for desertion is touching: "I was about to tell [his company commander] and ask his advis but on accountt of me being or hav-ing excapt from the most horrible Pla that a Man can be in and dit not wish to dissgrace the Comp."

On the night of 12 February 1863, Kleinkoff left Benicia Barracks, and went to town. There he assaulted a Private John Williams [Company E, 4th Infantry, California Volunteers] "with intent to commit robbery." According to the general order that sentenced him,[5] he inflicted "great bodily injury and dangerous wounds upon the head and body of [Williams]."

Kleinkoff was apprehended at Sacramento and confined at Benicia Barracks 22 May. A brief mention in his service record suggests that he once served in the 3rd Artillery, USA, under the name of Charles Smith. That allegation was never substantiated.

Kleinkoff pleaded guilty to desertion, but not to the two charges of assault. He admitted he "comited a Crime for which Gott alon can pardon me that is of forfitting the sollards Oblication and Oth that That sathen in regard to serv the united States . . . ."

At his court-martial, there was little or no discussion. He was found guilty of all three charges, and shot to death 17 July 1863 at Benicia Barracks.

### 1 August 1863

"August 1. — [Gordon's Division] Broke camp at Warrenton Junction and moved to Greenwich, 12 miles. Same day" Private BRADFORD BUTLER, 26, a farmer in the 157th New York Infantry," was shot in the presence of the division for desertion."[6]

Butler, an enlisted man, had joined the Union Army 19 September 1862, at Hamilton, New York. On or about 27 April 1863, He deserted his unit from Acocek Creek, Virginia, while the unit was part of the Chancellorsville campaign.

### 12 August 1863

HIRAM REYNOLDS, 33, a Tennessee widower with two children, was a gambler by trade. A veteran of the Mexican War, and honorably discharged from Union service twice, Reynolds was convicted of murder 25 May 1863 by a general court-martial, presided over by Lieutenant-Colonel Judson Wade Bishop, 2nd Minnesota Infantry.

As a teenager, Reynolds had fought in the Mexican War, under Colonel James Lane, 3rd Indiana Infantry. He was in the 27th Indiana Infantry at the start of the Rebellion. He transferred to the Navy, serving under Admiral Andrew H. Foote. Reynolds was discharged from the Navy because of a disability. When he was able to serve again, he re-enlisted. This time in the 82nd Indiana Infantry.

He stood accused of murdering Private Washington Mosier 19 May 1863 in the regimental camp near Triune, Tennessee. At his court-martial, evidence was brought forth that Mosier had fired the first shot in what appears to have been a duel.

Regardless of the circumstances, Reynolds was hanged at Nashville, 14 August 1863.

The Rev. John R. Adams, Chaplain of the 5th Maine, knew more about the anguish attached to executions than many officers and enlisted men.

In his *Memorials and Letters,* he recalls how, on 3 May 1863, THOMAS JEWETT, 33, an English laborer, deserted his regiment at Salem Heights, near Fredericksburg, "in the face of the enemy."

Jewett was captured; tried by general court-martial, convicted and sentenced to death by musketry. The sentence was carried out 14 August, at New Baltimore.

The day after, the Rev. Mr. Adams wrote:

> . . . it was my painful duty to be with him. He never said a word about reprieve, or a commutation of sentence; all his thoughts have been centered in one earnest desire for the good of his soul. Yesterday morning he was very calm and hopeful; when the provost marshal was called, and he was delivered over for execution, he gave his hand to the guard in the regiment, and to personal friends, with a smile, and then, being ironed, he walked to the wagon prepared for him. On the coffin he took his seat with a little hymn-book in his hand, and was occupied in reading till he reached the place of execution. He had to ride two miles and a half. I rode on my horse next to the wagon (surrounded by a strong guard), till within a half-mile of the place of execution. We entered the wagon and sat with the prisoner on his coffin. The whole division was present, drawn up in two lines. We rode past, the bands playing a dirge as we passed. At this time the prisoner was wonderfully calm; once he looked round brightly, with a smile, and said, "I see it now, it is all bright." We arrived at the fatal spot, — an open space, — the vacant side of a square, the troops occupying the other sides; the coffin was placed in position, the culprit led to it, and seated; I sat with him. His hands were then pinioned behind him, and those who were to fire took their position. The provost called upon me to pray; this done, his eyes were bandaged, and I retired. I took the Testament and hymn-book from his hand, and walked several rods. The word was then given: "Make Ready! Take aim! *Fire!*" and his soul was in eternity in an instant. The division surgeon examined the body, and pronounced it dead. The bugle sounded, and the troops marched by the body as it lay in its blood. I remained and placed the Testament in his coffin, hoping that He who had promised to comfort the penitent and the dying, would be the Resurrection and Life to his soul in the great day when all in their graves shall come forth.

It was a sad and solemn scene. Oh, how trying to me!
The culprit was an Englishman, and had deserted from
the English army; he had no parents living, nor brothers
nor sisters. He gave me his money to purchase tracts for
the regiment.

### 14 August 1863

FRANCIS SCOTT, a private in Company F, 1st Louisiana Infantry, was
executed 14 August 1863 for the murder of his commanding officer, Major D.
Bullem.

Since the murder of one's commanding officer could not be treated light-
ly, his execution by musketry was conducted in the grand manner with massed
troops.

### 25 August 1863

HENRY McLEAN, 18, a farmer from Sparta, Illinois, joined Company
C, 2nd Illinois Light Artillery, at Paducah, Kentucky, 10 July 1862.

McLean deserted his unit the day after Christmas the same year, while
the unit was at Corinth.

He was apprehended, tried by general court-martial, convicted and
sentenced to be shot to death by General Order 105, Department of the
Cumberland, dated 9 May 1863.

The sentence was carried out 25 August 1863, at Fort Donelson,
Tennessee.

### 28 August 1863

During the Civil War, civilians were encouraged to provide information
to the military authorities on the whereabouts of deserters, disloyal persons and
the like. It was another of Lincoln's distorted views of the Constitution. The
informers were free to lie or "get even" with enemies. There was no mechanism
in place to test their veracity. In June of 1863, Hiram Bingham, an enrolling
officer from North Brookfield, Massachusetts, sent a letter to the authorities
about WILLIAM F. HILL.

Hill, the letter alleged, was an inmate of the local poor house, along with
Moses, his father. "Sometime last winter Wm came back to us in a destitute
& filthy condition having the appearance of a *Deserter*." Bingham wrote to
find out if his impression was right, and received a reply that a young man by
the name of William F. Hill "*did* enlist & got his bounty of $100 . . . . Wm
(to me) denies ever being in the Service or securing the bounty — says he went
to camp & visited on the Caps. Some months but was never sworn in or mustered
from the camp with the Regiment which he says was the 33d.

"I think I have grave reason to believe," Bingham confided, "that he
was in the Battle of Antietam thus he deserted at or about this time threw away
his arms & equipment & . . . clothing with some confidante & found his way back

to us." Hill was described as "a Stout heavy but Shiftless fellow — has ever since his return complained of one Knee but gives no satisfactory answer how he was injured."

Records indicate Hill enlisted at Camp Massasoit, Readville, Massachusetts, 6 August 1862. It is possible he was a deserter at Antietam, but the list of units that participated in that campaign does not include the 20th Massachusetts Infantry, the unit in which Hill enlisted. He was, however, court-martialed, and executed along with Private JOHN SMITH, 35, a Philadelphia mechanic in the 1st Company, Massachusetts Sharpshooters, attached to the 15th Massachusetts Infantry.

Smith, a three-year man, deserted his unit before the Mud March from a camp near Falmouth, Virginia 11 January 1863. He was apprehended 15 August at Morrisville, Virginia.

Both men were shot to death 28 August 1863, at Morrisville.

### 29 August 1863

By the end of August 1863, Union military authorities needed some example that would help stop the neverending string of deserters leaving the Army of the Potomac.

Such an example was made of JOHN FOLANCY [Folaney; aka Geacinto Lerchzie], 24, EMIL LAI [also Emile; aka E. Duffie or Duffe], 30, GEORGE KUHNE [aka G. Week], 22, JOHN RIONESE [Rainese; aka George Rionese], 23, and CHARLES WALTER [aka C. Zene], 29. Together, these men would make up one of the largest executions in the Civil War.

These five unassigned recruits, called bounty-jumpers by Henry N. Blake in his *Three Years in the Army of the Potomac*, caused great consternation among the officers of the 118th Pennsylvania Infantry, "who could not be held responsible for a lax state of discipline if the villians were pardoned by the President, and by the substitutes who made preparations to leave if the execution was postponed."

They were all foreign-born, and "unacquainted with the English language, except one. Two were Roman Catholics, another a Hebrew, and the others, if of any faith," Henry T. Peck, in his *Historical Sketch of the 118th Regiment Pennsylvania Volunteers, "Corn Exchange Regt.*," recalled, "were Protestants." The men had never joined the 118th and, as a result, were unknown to its members. "Charged with a crime, conviction for which was likely to be followed by capital punishment." Peck continued,

> they were sent to the regiment only as a forum where judi-
> cial cognizance could be taken of their offence . . . They
> had . . . been thrown into an organization where they
> were entirely strangers and which had with them neither
> friendship, memories nor associations, and as they had
> come there as prisoners only for the stern administration
> of military justice, they could look for little sympathy.

Military authorities, especially in the Army of the Potomac, had been plagued with repeated desertion, bounty-jumping and reenlistment. "The authorities," Peck asserted,

> having determined, if possible, to eradicate the shameful practice of bounty-jumping, had instructed courts-martial in all well-established cases, upon conviction, to impose the severest penalty known to law. This failing to entirely remove the evil, and "to be shot to death by musketry" being deemed too honorable a death for such abandoned characters, the mode of execution was subsequently changed to the rope and gallows.

Folancy, Kuhne, Lai, Rionese, and Walter were arrested when they tried to recross the Potomac after escaping from Captain Henry O'Neill's unit. It is quite possible that, based on the lack of knowledge of the English language, the men had never realized they had joined the Union Army. Notwithstanding that supposition, the men were tried by general court-martial, presided over by Colonel Joseph Hayes, 18th Massachusetts Volunteers, and convicted. "The numbers arraigned, the frequency of the crime, the expected severity of the sentence," Peck recalled, "attracted the attention of the whole Army of the Potomac. Besides, it was almost the first, if not the first, of this class of cases, and was given unusual publicity, officially and otherwise."

When the time came for their execution neared, the five men petitioned Major-General George Gordon Meade for clemency. In a letter from Beverly Ford, Virginia, dated 25 August 1863, the prisoners wrote:

> We . . . implore your mercy in our behalf for the extension of our sentence, so that we may have time to make preparations to meet our God; for we, at the present time, are unprepared to die. Our time is very short. Two of us are Roman Catholics; we have no priest, and two are Protestants, one is a Jew and has no rabbi to assist us in preparing to meet our God. And we ask mercy in behalf of our wives and children, and we also desire you to change our sentence to hard labor instead of death, as we think we have been wrongfully sentenced; as we, being foreigners, were led astray by other soldiers, who promised us there would be no harm done.

Meade did not reduce the sentence, but did make efforts to locate the proper clergymen to console the prisoners. Compassion did exist in the Army of the Potomac.

The Rev. Constantine L. Egan, O.P., a Roman Catholic priest was summoned by the War Department, and asked to minister to two of the prisoners. The Very Rev. William Corby, C.S.C. related Egan's experiences in *Memoirs of Chaplain Life: Three Years Chaplain in the Famous "Irish Brigade," Army of the Potomac.*

The day after the request was made, Egan traveled to the headquarters of the 118th and was given access to the prisoners.

> I went to the tent where the prisoners were confined,
> heard their confessions that evening . . . Next morning
> a tent was erected, where I said Mass for the condemned
> men, and administered to them Holy Communion.

It was not until shortly before noon of the day of execution that Dr. Zould, a Jewish rabbi, could be obtained. He had little time to spend with Kuhne, a barber.

Kuhne's civilian occupation did provoke some troubles for him while in confinement. Lieutenant Samuel N. Lewis, one of the officers assigned to guard the men, searched the prisoners. "He found a pocket-book from the Hebrew," Peck related, "who pleaded earnestly for its return. Lewis, yielding to his entreaties, was about returning it without examination when Major Herring, who had supervised the operation, promptly directed him not to do so until he had carefully examined its contents. Concealed in its folds was a lancet." Lancets were used by barbers in some of their non-tonsorial work. Herring and Lewis believed it could have been used as a weapon in a possible suicide attempt; it was confiscated.

After all opportunities to have the sentence changed or clemency obtained, the five resolved themselves to their fate.

Theodore Gerrish, an eyewitness and the author of *Army Life: A Private's Reminiscences in the Civil War*, recalled

> The impressive silence was not broken by a single sound.
> Each line of soldiers looked more like a section of a vast
> machine than a line composed of living men. The silence
> was suddenly and sadly broken by the sounds of ap-
> proaching music — not the quick, inspiring strains with
> which we were so familiar, but a measured, slow and
> solemn dirge, whose weird, sorrowful notes were poured
> forth like the moanings of lost spirits. Not a soldier spoke,
> but every eye was turned in the direction from which came
> the sad and mournful cadences, and we saw the
> procession.

Edwin A. Glover was also there. In his *Bucktailed Wildcats: A Regiment of Civil War Volunteers*, he explains how the entire Fifth Corps was drawn up on a hillside "from which every last man had a clear view of the plain below." Since the execution was expected to act as a deterrent to future desertions, every device to heighten the drama was employed: five wagons, each bearing a coffin, were wheeled before the troops; each man was seated on his coffin; a military band played the "Death March"; black blindfolds were placed over the men's eyes; the chaplains were given a final moment of private prayer with the men; then the firing squad of sixty — twelve for each condemned man — assumed their position.

A touch of gallows humor did emerge at this execution. Father Egan and Rabbi Zould had a slight dispute. As Henry Blake reported: ". . . the rabbi and the priest . . . had a dispute about precedence, and urged their respective claims upon theological tenets; but the commander of the provost-guard viewed the subject in a military light, and decided the novel question by allowing the rabbi to walk first, because his faith was the oldest and outranked the other."

As orders were read, and prayers said, Brigadier-General Charles Griffin grew annoyed with the delays, Henry Peck remembered; Only fifteen minutes were left of the time allotted for the execution. "Shoot these men," he shouted to Captain Orne, "or after ten minutes it will be murder."

An officer stepped forward and in a thin voice shouted: "Ready, aim, *fire*"!

Four bleeding bodies fell across their coffins; one man remained standing. Pistol in hand, Orne moved to the man still standing, prepared to fire a bullet through his brain if he were still living. But, Surgeon Thomas pronounced the man dead.

The troops were then marched by the bodies to the tune of "The Girl I Left Behind Me." Father Egan remained and read the funeral service over the dead.

### 30 August 1863

By order of Colonel H. Robinson, 1st Louisiana Cavalry, WILLIAM DAVIS, 23, Company G, 2nd Rhode Island Cavalry, and RICHARD SMITH, 26, Company G, same unit, were shot to death for mutiny.

The execution and the crime apparently took place at Camp Hubbard, Thibodeaux, Louisiana 29-30 September 1863. There is neither record of the execution nor orders to execute.

### 4 September 1863

Five men were executed in the Department of the Ohio 4 September 1863, all members of the 27th Kentucky Infantry: JAMES M. ANDERSON, FRAZIER CARMEN [or Carmen Frazier], CHRISTOPHER and JOHN W. COFFEY [or Coffee], and JAMES A. POINTER.

All five, accused of desertion, had joined the Kentucky unit 12 October 1861. At various times in 1862, they left their unit without authority; Anderson, a cook at the hospital in Corinth, Mississippi, deserted the hospital in the summer, and was arrested a year later; Carmen, at an unknown date; the Coffey brothers, around 1 October; and Pointer, 3 September.

Tried by general court-martial, they were convicted and sentenced to be shot to death. They were executed together at Mumfordsville, Kentucky, 3 September 1863.

Pointer had a brother, James H., who was a member of the same regiment. He deserted along with his brother; was retrieved, tried and convicted. He did not join his brother in front of the firing squad. James "died of disease" 24 February 1863.

### 17 September 1863

JACOB AIERDAIN [Aierdeim], 29, a member of Company G, 119th New York Infantry and a Bavarian farmer, was shot to death by order of a general court-martial 17 September 1863 for desertion. Though records are not specific on the date of his desertion, it is known that he was in arrest July/August, suggesting that his desertion might have taken place while his unit was in the Gettysburg campaign.

### 18 September 1863

EDWARD ELLIOTT, 22, a Massachusetts bookkeeper, and GEORGE LAYTON [Laton, aka Charles Eastman], 20, a Maine farmer and miller, entered the 14th Connecticut Infantry within a month of each other in New Haven, Connecticut; Elliott, a substitute for Isaac P. Butsford, 11 August 1863, and Layton, an enlistee, 18 July 1863.

Within the week after Elliott joined the unit, the two apparently became acquainted and they deserted together, 18 August 1863 near Elk Run, Virginia. They were apprehended 28 August "in citizen's dress." Elliott claimed to be a deserter from "the Rebel Army." It would seem, based on the records, that Layton fell into bad company when he was befriended by Elliott. In his *History of the Fourteenth Regiment, Connecticut Vol. Infantry*, Charles Davis Page questioned the character of a large number of the regiment's recruits, and the many desertions — including the acts of Elliott and Layton.

Because of the desertion problem and the quality of manpower, Elliott and Layton were used as examples.

The execution of these two men was "a very bungling affair . . . not more than one cartridge out of the five did any service," Page recalled. "After repeated firing the men were pronounced dead and the division was marched by companies past the graves and the bleeding forms of the victims." As a reminder, Page noted, "New recruits of the regiment were after that marched by the graves as a silent example."

"On the road four Jews [Samuel Hoffhermer, Farmsville, Virginia, Benjamin Adler, Louis Hamburger, and Samuel Mann][7] were met who made a living by following raids," the historian for the 11th Pennsylvania Cavalry recounted, "and, taking advantage of the frightened farmers, bought up negroes at low rates and shipped them to the South. They were examined and allowed to pass. But after the column had passed," two members of the unit: JOHN T. BARNETT, 20, called "a deserter of the Sixty-third Georgia," and Hiram Evans, of Company A, "went back and robbed them of $15,900, State bank bills and jewelry."

While the unit was resting at Brandywine, "one of the Jews came and reported their loss." Company A had been sent to guard Nelson's Bridge, so a detachment of troops with the Jewish entrepreneur was sent there. "The Jew recognized both of the assailants . . ." They were arrested, and $6,970, two watches, a diamond pin, etc., was recovered.

"On the way back Evans cut the rope that tied him to his horse and escaped, and was never heard of afterwards," Barnett, however, was tried by general court-martial, presided over by Major Samuel Wetherill, 11th Pennsylvania Cavalry.

Barnett was convicted of highway robbery, assault with intent to commit murder, and desertion. Though he pleaded guilty only to being absent from his unit and stopping the carriage, he was found guilty on all counts. Barnett apparently escaped from jail, because his service record indicates he was recaptured 6 September.

After his case was reviewed and approved by Lincoln, John Thomas Barnett was shot to death on a field "now used by the Ambulance camp, Portsmouth," Virginia, 18 September 1863. No action, however, was taken in regard to the Jewish merchants and their slave trade.

Not far from where Barnett was executed, another — much larger — execution took place. Four deserters: ALBERT JONES, 22, Company K, 3rd Maryland Infantry, a Baltimore boatman; WILLIAM SMITH, 35, Company E, 78th New York Infantry, a Boston farmer; CORNELIUS TREECE [Truce, Trus], 23, Company K, 78th New York Infantry, an Indiana mason; and GEORGE VAN [Vane], 22, Company D, 12th New York Infantry, a farmer, were shot to death "on low ground, camp near Culpepper, VA, between 2nd and 3rd Brig. 18 Sep 63 . . . ."

All four had deserted between May and June, and had been recovered. Their case was apparently cut and dried. However, there was a problem or two which existed. In Van's file, a letter from Brigadier-General Charles Griffin to the assistant adjutant general, Lieutenant-Colonel Fred J. Locke, dated 15 September, indicates some concern: "I would respectfully call the attention of the Maj. Genl Comdg 5th Corps to the fact that [Van] does not belong to the 1st Div: but to the Provost Guard of 5th Corps & the execution ought not to be imposed upon another command."

Locke's response was swift — and direct: "The corr is unnecessary. The order of the Genl Comd the Army directs that the execution shall take place & it is certainly within the provice of the Corps Comdr to say by whom it shall be done . . . ."

Van requested — and was denied — executive clemency. The Adjutant General's Office responded to his request in terse terms: ". . . to inform you that the case is not considered a proper one for the exercise of executive clemency." Jones also requested a pardon. This too was denied in a letter to Lincoln from Meade: "This being his second desertion [he had deserted 29 June at Frederick, Maryland] and it having occurred after your proclamation and solemn warning to the Army. I do not consider him a fit subject for executive clemency."

### 25 September 1863

CHARLES WILLIAMS [aka Charles Smith], 26, Company D, 4th Maryland Infantry, was a two-time deserter. He deserted the first time at Hagerstown, Maryland, 20 September 1862. By 18 November, he was confined at Fort McHenry. Apparently he was not court-martialed for the offense, because his service records state he deserted again 9 April 1863. He was returned to divisional headquarters 5 August.

Little more than a month later, Williams was tried by a general court-martial, presided over by Colonel E. B. Fowler, 14th New York. He was charged not only with desertion, but also with inciting to mutiny. The second charge was not substantiated, but he was found guilty of desertion, and sentenced to death.

Williams asked for executive clemency, but the transmittal letter, dated 21 September, from General Meade could not recommend it. Meade outlined Williams' offenses, including how he was picked up in a

> party of substitutes for the 90th Pa . . . And as he not only failed to avail himself of your Proclamation and returned to his duty, but only came back when he was paid as he admitted $300 — with the same offense a second time . . . .

Brigadier-General S. Williams, however, disagreed with Meade on 23 September, and recommended something else . . .

> for the reason that in my judgement clemency would be well timed. From representation made to me as to the character of the man's mind and disposition, I am satisfied that he committed the offense without due appreciation of the heniousness of the offence.

Meade's view, however, prevailed.

Together with JOHN TIMLIN [Temlaw], 19, Company D, 145th New York Infantry, an Irish newsman, Williams was shot to death near Brandy Station 25 September 1863. Timlin was a deserter tried by court-martial, presided over by Colonel James L. Selfridge, 46th Pennsylvania Volunteers.

### 2 October 1863

According to the final report of the Adjutant General's Office, ADAM SCHMALZ [Smalz], 18, Company E, 66th New York Infantry, and WILLIAM SMITZ, Company F, 90th Pennsylvania Infantry, were executed by musketry 2 October 1863, at a camp near Culpepper, Virginia.

Schmalz, a German laborer, enlisted at New York City 23 October 1861. He was accused of deserting on or about 1 July 1863 at Gettysburg. Smitz [the National Archives has no record of his existence under various spellings of the name] was also accused of desertion, and it is possible that he too departed the army at Gettysburg.

Schmalz was apprehended at Hanover, Pennsylvania, 27 July, by the provost marshal. He received a general court-martial 1 September by a panel, presided over by Lieutenant-Colonel A. B. Chapman. Both men were ordered to be executed by General Order 92, Army of the Potomac, 27 September. That order was carried out 2 October.

### 9 October 1863

JOSEPH CONNELLY [Conley, Conelly], 19, died as a private in Company H, 4th New Jersey Infantry. That much can be determined. How he got to the execution field is quite another story.

According to his company returns, Connelly was charged with desertion 21 June 1862, at Mechanicsville, Virginia. But, the return also indicates he was "absent sick" since that date in a Philadelphia hospital. It is also stated that he deserted from the hospital 29 August, but returned under arrest 3 March 1863, and sentenced by general court-martial to forfeit all pay due him "due to the publication of sentence" 14 April 1863. On the march to Gettysburg 2 July, he again deserted. He was returned under arrest 7 September. His final court-martial, presided over by Colonel William H. Penrose, 15th New Jersey Volunteers, found him guilty and sentenced him to death by musketry.

The War Records Office, New Jersey Department of Defense, offers a different story. In their records, Connelly was mustered into the 4th Regiment 24 August 1861, but deserted 7 August. He was then mustered into the 12th New Jersey 4 September — and promoted to corporal 20 August — almost two weeks after his alleged desertion. He was reduced to a private 8 November. Transferred to Company H, 4th Regiment 3 March 1863, he deserted 2 July, and was arrested 5 September.

Which file is correct? Both agree, nonetheless, that the man was executed 9 October 1863

**16 October 1863**

HENRY C. BEARDSLEY, 24, Company G, 5th Michigan Infantry, was mustered into the Union Army 28 September 1861, at Detroit. By January 1862, he was the company clerk; July, a pioneer. In September, he was dropped from the unit's rolls at Alexandria, Virginia — yet his service record lists him as missing since 22 August 1862.[8]

JAMES HALEY, 23, a Chester, Pennsylvania, farmer, was mustered into Company B, 116th Pennsylvania Infantry, at Philadelphia, 11 July 1862. Haley apparently took sick prior to the battle of Fredericksburg, because his service records locates him in the regimental hospital at Falmouth, Virginia, July/August and November/December 1862. If he were in the hospital at the times indicated, he probably was not with the 116th at the battle that reduced the regiment to slightly more than company strength. Haley is listed as deserting near Frederick City, Maryland, while the unit was in pursuit of Lee, following the battle of Gettysburg.

He and Beardsley were tried by general court-martial; Beardsley by a group, headed by Colonel Bryon R. Pierce, 3rd Michigan Volunteers. Both were convicted and sentenced to execution. Though the Adjutant General's Office lists Beardsley's death date as 8 October, both men were shot to death eight days later at Fairfax.

**23 October 1863**

REUBEN STOUT, 28, a farmer from Pewn, Pennsylvania, was mustered into the 60th Indiana Infantry 25 February 1862 at Indianapolis. On 1 April, he deserted and returned to Indiana.

On or about 14 March 1863, he shot and killed a civilian, Solomon Huffman, in Madison Township, Carroll County, Indiana. Huffman was a bounty hunter who was trying to arrest Stout. Stout was finally arrested ten days later; tried by general court-martial, presided over by Colonel John S. Williams, 63rd Indiana Volunteers, in Indianapolis 14 May; and sentenced to be executed 26 July.

Because of efforts on his part to get his sentence commuted, Stout received a reprieve of three months — but to no avail. He was executed by musketry 23 October 1863

**30 October 1863**

Justice was not meted out evenly in the 15th Massachusetts Infantry.

Andrew Ford, in *The Story of the Fifteenth Regiment Massachusetts Volunteer Infantry in the Civil War 1861-1864*, recounts that one member of his unit was found guilty of desertion and sentenced

> To forfeit all pay and allowance now due him; to have one half of his head shaved; to be dishonorably discharged; to be drummed out of the service of the United States in the presence of his brigade and then to be confined to hard labor for eighteen months on public works.

Months later, another deserter was sentenced to hard labor at Dry Tortugas, Florida, for the rest of the war.

Only one deserter from the 15th was executed: JOHN ROBERTS, of Company H. Roberts, 21, a native of St. John, New Brunswick — though Ford recalls he was born in Hedford, County Galway, Ireland — and a blacksmith, was a substitute for Benjamin B. Russell of Boston. He deserted near Bank's Ford, Virginia, on or about 3 September 1863, but returned under arrest three weeks later. Tried by general court-martial, Lieutenant-Colonel Ansel Wass, 19th Massachusetts Volunteers, president, Roberts was convicted. He was executed at 2 p.m., 30 October 1863, in front of the brigade.

### 9 November 1863

While the 8th Connecticut Infantry was on duty at Portsmouth, Virginia, MITCHELL VANDALL, 27, a Canadian laborer, and FRANCIS WALES, 22, a German laborer, deserted.

Both men had been substitutes, Vandall for James Kimball; Wales, Oliver Derning, entering the service at New Haven, Connecticut, 7 September 1863.

Scant evidence exists in regard to their cases, but it can be determined they deserted together 19 September, and were arrested the next day. They were tried by a general court-martial, presided over by Lieutenant-Colonel Burnham, 16th Connecticut Volunteers, convicted and sentenced to execution by General Order 24, 31 October 1863.

When he received news of his fate, Vandall escaped confinement, causing the execution of both to be postponed. He was quickly returned to his cell, and the execution — by musketry — took place at Fort Reno, Portsmouth, 9 November 1863.

### 13 November 1863

BENJAMIN VALENTINE [Balentine, Volentine, aka Valentine Benjamin and Benjamin Volatine] volunteered for the Union Army in Chicago 1 July 1861. Valentine, 39, a married carpenter from Germany, allegedly deserted from the 44th Illinois Infantry while the unit was on the move to Cape Girardeau, Missouri, 27 May 1862.

He was apparently captured slightly more than a year later because he was picked up on the rolls of Company C, 44th Illinois Infantry, in July or August 1863.

ERASTUS C. DAILY, 35, a New York harnessmaker, apparently joined the same unit 5 August 1862 — shortly after Valentine deserted. Less than a week after his enlistment, Daily deserted on the march near Harradsburg, Kentucky, while the unit was in pursuit of Braxton Bragg. He was apprehended 6 August 1863 at Polo, Illinois.

Both men, neither had known each other in civilian or military life, were executed together 13 or 14 November 1863 at Chattanooga, Tennessee.

Daily poses a problem. According to the Illinois State Archives, "We could find no one under any variant spelling of that name [unless my staff is trying to avoid embarrassing me]". The director of the archives is John Daly.

R | 55 | **U.S.C.T.**

*Lawson Kemp*

*Pv*, Co. *A*, 55 Reg't U. S. Col'd Inf.

Appears on

**Company Descriptive Book**

of the organization named above.

**DESCRIPTION.**

Age *19* years; height *5* feet *9* inches.

Complexion *Blk*

Eyes *Blk* ; hair *Blk*

Where born *Tuscaloosa, Ala.*

Occupation *Farmer*

**ENLISTMENT.**

When *May 15* , 186*3*.

Where *Corinth, Miss.*

By whom *H. C. Kelley* ; term *3* y'rs.

Remarks: *Joined at original organization, Reduced from Sergt for drunkenness & neglect of duty. Shot Nov. 19/63 Final statement given Dec. 29th. No effects. This man was a desperate villian (over)*

*Henderson*

(383*g*)      Copyist.

---

MAY.15   9163261   1891

*I sent him from Ft. Floyd, Tenn., to the Stockdade at Corinth, Miss., for swindling with a request that he be kept until I could prefer charges. Capt. Reever of Co. D, at Corinth, got him out of prison, took him in his own Co., went foraging near Pocahontas, Tenn., when this fellow ravished a white girl for which he was shot next day*

---

**The language regarding Pvt. Lawson Kemp [Co. A, 55th Infantry, USCT], his crime, trial, and punishment was quite terse. Kemp was tried at drum-head and executed the next day.**
*National Archives*

### 19 November 1863

LAWSON KEMP, 19, an Alabama farmer, was a private in the 1st Alabama Infantry [African Descent] — later Company A, 55th Infantry, USCT, joining at Corinth, Mississippi 21 May 1863. Kemp was the first black member of the Union Army executed during the war.

Apparently respected as a soldier when he enlisted, Kemp was promoted to sergeant at the time of his entry into the military. He did, however, have some faults. He was reduced to the ranks 3 June 1863 for drunkenness and neglect of duty, by order of Colonel J. M. Alexander.

While the 55th was on garrison duty at Corinth, Kemp was accused of rape. He was tried at drumhead 19 November, and executed the same day. Or was he?

According to his company's muster rolls, Kemp "died of disease Nov. 19, 1863." The USCT files indicate that he was "shot by sentence of general court-martial" on the same date. There are no records of a trial or orders to execute.

### 27 November 1863

PHILIP RABER, 20, a Virginia [later West Virginia] farmer, was mustered into the 9th Virginia [9th West Virginia] Infantry 30 April 1862, at Guyandotte.

Before the unit was fully organized, Raber deserted — 30 September at Point Pleasant. He was arrested at Petersburg 11 December; court-martialed and sentenced to one-month's hard labor and forfeiture of three-months pay.

That merciful treatment did not teach him a lesson. On 10 April 1863, he deserted from Winchester, Virginia. Captured 5 September, he received a general court-martial. Convicted, he was scheduled for execution by musketry 27 November. Despite a 3:30 a.m. respite, ordered by Colonel C. B. White, the execution was carried out as planned on that day between 2 and 3 p.m.

There are grave doubts that HOMOBONA CARABAJAL [also Carrabo-jal, Carobajal, Carrabajal], 22, a private in Company D, 1st New Mexico Cavalry, was ever executed as the Adjutant General's Office reported in 1885.

Carabajal was, according to his company muster rolls, "obviously H. Molina Carabajal. He might have served in a Civil War engagement although the muster out roll does not so indicate. The very brief notation on the muster roll states that he 'Died, Denver, October 10, 1863.'"

In the same folder, nonetheless, there is a faintly-written document that states Carabajal was an "assassin, suicide, mental, execution suspended until he was better . . . ."

A 13 April 1865 letter, in the same folder, agrees that the man was mentally sick and that his sentence was commuted to life imprisonment. Carabajal was ordered to an asylum in Washington, D.C., 11 September 1865, and discharged from the asylum *and the military* February 1866.

H. Molina Carabajal was accused and convicted of murder. The Adjutant General's Office states that he was hanged 27 November 1863. If he were in a mental hospital and later discharged from the service, who was executed in his place?

PAUL KINGSTON, 34, an Illinois farmer, was a corporal in Company M, 1st Missouri Cavalry, when he was executed at Cape Girardeau 27 November 1863.

Kingston, a three-year volunteer, entered the service 6 September 1861, at Jefferson City, Missouri. Using his service records, we can determine he was attached to Company F from 22 May 1862, until detached 11 August as escort to General Gordon Granger. Kingston deserted 5 February 1863 at Tell City, Indiana "in defiance of . . . Halleck's order attaching him to the same [Company M] . . . ."

Corporal Kingston was tried by general court-martial, found guilty of desertion and the "theft of a pistol," and sentenced to be hanged. Officers of the 1st Cavalry, apparently supportive of the man, petitioned for a mitigation of his sentence. Their request was denied, and Paul Kingston was executed.

The Adjutant General's report lists Kingston as being executed for murder. Nowhere in his records is there any mention of, or allusion to, murder.

## 4 December 1863

CYRUS W. HUNTER, 19, a farmer from Clinton, Maine, was a private in Company G, 3rd Maine Infantry.

He enlisted in the regiment at Augusta 30 April 1861, but later deserted. A general court-martial found him guilty, and he was executed at Brandy Station, Virginia, 4 December 1863.

## 17 December 1863

"In our department," Elbridge J. Copp wrote in his *Reminiscences of the War of the Rebellion 1861-1865,*

> the deserters necessarily went over to the enemy, there being no avenue to the north except by our steamships. One who had made the attempt was found in the bottom of the creek, stuck fast in the mud, and dead, with no less than fifty canteens tied around him as a life preserver that did not work.

JOHN KENDALL, 21, deserted from Company G, 3rd New Hampshire Infantry — Copp's regiment. ". . . in attempting to get across the marshes, [Kendall] became stuck in the mud and was captured."

At Kendall's general court-martial, Brigadier General Thomas G. Stevenson, U. S. Volunteers, presiding, the substitute — for George W. Austin, of

Plainfield, New Hampshire — was accused of desertion on 28 November 1863 and declaring his name to be "Thomas" . . . and a deserter from the enemy — to deceive military authorities. He was found guilty, and his execution was scheduled for 17 December.

On the appointed day at Morris Island, South Carolina, Copp remembered, "Kendall recogniz[ed] some of the men of his company, cried out to them in reckless bravado; his shouts were received in grim silence."

As Lieutenant David Wadsworth's sword descended, twelve rifles cracked, and Kendall fell "forward over his coffin in instant death."

"The whole army was then marched past the body where it lay upon the beach as it fell, and back to their several camps."

### 18 December 1863

GEORGE E. BLOWERS, 23, a farmer from Washington, New York, joined Company A, 2nd Vermont Infantry 15 September 1862, at Burlington. He deserted 1 or 3 July 1863 from a camp near Manchester, Massachusetts.

Blowers was arrested 26 October by the provost marshal, 1st District of Vermont. He "resisted the party who arrested him and is a desperate character . . . While confined in the Jail at this place has been grossly insulting to people visiting the place." One of the other men arrested with him was a Private William Blowers, same company, who may have been a relative. William was not, however, court-martialed, convicted or executed.

This selectivity brings up a question: Who selected the men as examples? Did Blowers' obnoxious behavior in jail draw attention to him and his act of desertion than someone else? Was that why he was selected?

JOHN TAGUE, 22, a Vermont farmer, deserted Company F, 5th Vermont Infantry on or about 28 June 1862. His company rolls listed him as absent without leave from that date; he was not called a deserter until 11 December at Belle Plain, being listed then as having "deserted at the fall of Fredericksburg . . . ." Was it better for military authorities to indicate he deserted following the slaughter at Fredericksburg than at the earlier date? Tague was arrested 21 September 1863 at Woodsboro, Frederick County, Maryland.

Together Blowers and Tague were shot to death at Brandy Station, Virginia, 18 December 1863.

Who was JOHN McMANN, Company B, 11th Infantry, Regulars, who was shot to death 18 December 1863, by General Order 104, Army of the Potomac, 5 December 1863?

According to the order calling for his execution by musketry, John McMann deserted at Harrison's Landing, Virginia, 1 August 1861. But there is no service record for a man by that name in the National Archives.

A search of the records of the Regulars did find an Irish John McMahon, 26, Company H, 3rd Infantry, who deserted 8 May 1861, and a John McMann, 15th Infantry, who deserted 18 July 1863 — but not a John McMann, who deserted 1 August 1861, and was executed 18 December 1863.

On 27 September 1863, the 76th New York Infantry was reinforced with one hundred men. Among the new man was a familiar voice, that of WINSLOW W. ALLEN, formerly a private in Company H. Allen had deserted while the unit was in Washington, in the spring of 1862. After his desertion, he lived under an assumed name [William Newton], married and had one child. Instead of staying in Jefferson County where he was safe, he fell to the temptation of a $300 bounty, and sold himself as a substitute. As fate had it, he was assigned to his old company.

As Allen walked by his old company, his voice was recognized by his former comrades-in-arms. He was quickly arrested, tried, convicted, and sentenced to death.

"So many had been arrested and either returned to duty or punished by imprisonment and loss of pay," A. P. Smith wrote in his *History of the Seventy-Sixth Regiment New York Volunteers*, "that he could not believe he would be sentenced to death. Others who had been sentenced to death had been pardoned, so that after the decision became known to him he still indulged in hope." As the time for execution approached, however, company officers tried to prepare him to "enter 'The undiscovered country, from whose bourne no traveler returns,' "

"He seemed calm and collected, and declared himself ready to die, if such must be his fate," Smith recalled. "So self-possessed was he, that an hour before his execution he sat at the table with his Captain, and ate a hearty dinner, after which he engaged in writing." At the drum signal, summoning the troops to the execution, Allen turned to Captain Swan: ". . . you have been kind to me, which I can only return by my prayers for your welfare." He handed the officer his pocketbook, "Take this, it is all I have, and when I am gone, please lay this, (a fervent prayer for one in his situation, printed on a card), on my breast."

Allen remained calm until he saw the gaping grave; "he seemed suddenly struck with terror, and, seizing the Captain's hand with a vice-like grasp, thus remained until they arrived at the coffin."

After the orders had been read, the Captain bent over him and whispered: "Winslow, I can go no further with you; the rest of your dark journey is alone. Have you any last word for your wife and child?"

"No," Allen responded, "only that I love them all!" Those were his last words. "He had," Smith remembered, "on that day completed his twenty-sixth year. He died without a perceptible movement of a muscle.

"This was the only execution that ever occurred in the Seventy-Sixth Regiment."

WILLIAM H. DEVOE, 44, a New York butcher, was one of the first men to join the 57th New York Infantry, as Gilbert Frederick noted in his *The Story of a Regiment, Being a Record of the Military Service of the Fifty-Seventh New York State Volunteer Infantry in the War of the Rebellion.*

The army, as Frederick remembered it was beginning to "fill up with conscripts and as 'bounty-jumpers' were numerous, it became necessary to adopt extreme measures to check the increasing desertions. Three men from the Second Corps were shot," he noted, "while at Morrisville . . . ." Interestingly enough, records do not show any executions at Morrisville, Virginia. The next man, Devoe, was treated no differently than the other deserters.

He participated at Fair Oaks, Virginia, 1 June 62; Seven Days, 25 June-2 July 1862, but was absent without leave at Antietam, 17 September. He was present before Fredericksburg 11 December, but absent at Fredericksburg Heights 13 December. He left the field at Chancellorsville, Virginia, 3 May 1863, and was court-martialed for misconduct at the same time. Devoe was reported missing in action at Gettysburg, 2 July 1863, and arrived back at his regiment under guard 29 September.

Devoe was tried by general court-martial, Colonel H. B. McKeln, 81st Pennsylvania, presiding, and was found guilty of desertion, and sentenced to be shot to death 18 December 1863 at Stephensburg, Virginia. "It was truly a funeral procession," Frederick recalled, "when the regiment marched to his execution. He sat upon his coffin at the open end of the hollow square and at the command to fire, fell instantly dead."

### 28 December 1863

During the siege of Port Hudson, Louisiana, CHARLES TURNER, 24, a married New York laborer, deserted his company [Company C, 114th New York Infantry] 1 June 1863 "from in front of the enemy . . . . "

Turner was arrested 26 July at Baton Rouge, and kept in the police jail until the time of his court-martial.

Convicted and sentenced to death, Turner was shot to death in New Orleans 28 December 1863.

# ENDNOTES TO CHAPTER SEVEN

1. General Orders II, pp. 13-15.

2. *OR* I, 15, p. 1119.

3. Records of Michigan Military Establishment, RG 59-14, V. 10, p. 48., and Michigan Volunteers, p. 78.

4. Quoted in Donald L. Smith, *The Twenty-Fourth Michigan of the Iron Brigade* [Harrisburg, Penna., 1962], from Sullivan Green mss, O. B. Curtis, *History of the Twenty-Fourth Michigan of the Iron Brigade*, p. 144.

5. General Order 149, Adjutant General's Office, 26 May 1863.

6. *OR* I, 28, Part 2, p. 74.

7. General Orders II, pp. 325-27.

8. Records of the Michigan Military Establishment, RG 59-14, Vol. 5, p. 86.

# CHAPTER EIGHT

## 1864:
## *". . . but for the President's order . . . ."*

*6 January 1864*

JAMES MURPHY [aka Joseph Strobel], 22, a New York locksmith and a substitute for Jonathan Ralston, of Reading, Pennsylvania, in Company I, 55th Pennsylvania Infantry, was charged and found guilty of desertion and leaving his post without being regularly relieved.

Murphy deserted 27 November 1863 while on guard duty at Rifle Pit Picket, near Beaufort, Port Royal Island, South Carolina. He was arrested three days later on St. Helena Island. It was his intent, a general court-martial charged, Colonel R. White, 55th Pennsylvania Volunteers, presiding, to go over to the enemy. Murphy denied the charges, but was found guilty, and sentenced to execution. He was shot to death at Beaufort, 6 January 1864.

*19 January 1864*

JOSEPH [also John] COFFIELD, 25, a member of Company K, 1st New Mexico Cavalry, was a native of Durham, England. When he enlisted in the army 1 July 1862, at Fort Marcy, New Mexico, he listed his civilian occupation as "soldier."

While his unit engaged in operations against the Navajo Indians, Coffield was accused of murder, and convicted.[1] He was then shot by a detachment of his own unit.

Coffield's case seems clear, until one reads his file: "We have no muster roll or service record for Joseph Coffield, Co. K, executed, according to your record, on January 19, 1864."

In another section of Coffield's file, there is a notation that, as of 5 July 1863, he was confined at Fort Canby, New Mexico, awaiting trial. A reference is also made to a Luciano Valencia who "escaped" with Coffield. After Coffield's execution, they didn't know what to do with Valencia.

Sergeant JOHN MARCUM, 27, was mustered into Company F, 5th West Virginia Infantry 14 September 1861.

Two years later, Marcum was tried by general court-martial for the fatal shooting of Andrew J. Farley, an enlisted man in his unit, at Gauley Bridge, West Virginia. Desertion must have played some role in his crime, because his company muster roll indicates that Marcum rejoined the army at Culpepper Court House, Virginia, the same date.

Convicted of murder, Marcum was executed at Gauley Bridge 19 January 1864. According to his muster roll, he was hanged. That fact is reinforced by a casualty sheet. On the other hand, Marcum's file has two casualty sheets: one indicates he was hanged; the other, shot to death.

### 7 February 1864

"It not being warranted by the Army Regulations for a subordinate officer to call a 'Drumhead Court-martial' and execute its sentence," Edward W. Emerson wrote in *Life and Letters of Charles Russell Lowell,*

> except in case of emergency, when too far away to communicate with his superiors, and Colonel Lowell being in daily communication with headquarters at Washington, he expected, on reporting the matter that afternoon, to receive at least a severe reprimand. On the contrary, no mention was made of it at all.

"The matter" was the execution for desertion of WILLIAM E. ORMSLEY [Ormsby], 20, a New York expressman and a private in Company E, 2nd Massachusetts Cavalry. Ormsley, who had been honorably discharged 7 November 1862 from the 3rd U. S. Artillery, had joined the Massachusetts unit 26 April 1863. At the time of his enlistment, he was a resident of San Francisco.

He was reported as a deserter from picket duty at Lewinsville, Virginia, 24 January 1864. According to Emerson, Ormsley took "his horse, arms and accoutrements . . . Very soon after, a scouting party . . . returning from Aldie were attacked in rear by Mosby's men. Making a counter-charge, the soldiers recognized the renegade among the enemy. A rush was made for him, and he was run down and taken."

Colonel Lowell called a drum-head court-martial, which sat all night, and condemned Ormsley to be shot at 10 a.m., the next morning. The trial and execution did not elicit comment from Washington, Emerson surmised, because General [Christopher C.] Augur, and Secretary of War Stanton, "who would naturally be consulted in such a case, were both pleased at Colonel Lowell's action . . ." If the case, Emerson reasoned, had been sent to Washington for action, the "president would probably have pardoned the man, who was young and infatuation of a Southern girl . . . ." Neither Stanton or the general could "command Colonel Lowell for going beyond the authority of the regulations, [they] therefore deemed silence the best means of expressing their approval."

Proceedings of a Drum          Page 1
Head Court Martial convened at
Head Quarters Cavalry Camp Vienna,
Va by virtue of the following order.

Special Order       Head Quarters Cav Camp
No 15.              Vienna, Va. Feb 6th 1864.
              A Drum Head Court-
Martial is hereby ordered to meet this
afternoon at these Head Quarters for
the trial of William B. Ormsby Co C
2nd Mass Cavalry.:
          Detail for the Board.
Major Wm. H. Forbes    2nd Mass. Cav-
  "    Douglas Frazer    13th N.Y.    "
Capt Zabdiel B. Adams   2nd Mass    "
1st Lieut Lewis Dabney   2nd    "      "
          Judge Advocate.

          By Order of
          Col. C. R. Lowell
                    Comdg

Sgd. G. A Stone
    1st Lt & a.a.a.g.

---

One of the few — if not the only — documented records of a drum-head court-martial was that of William Ormsley [Co. C, 2nd Massachusetts Cavalry]. The document, totalling eighteen pages, is much longer than many of the more structured general courts-martial proceeding, causing one to wonder if it had been produced to increase the legitimacy of the sentence.   *National Archives*

The decision made to execute, all that was left was for Chaplain Charles A. Humphreys to prepare him for death.

In *Field, Camp, Hospital and Prison in the Civil War, 1863-1865*, Humphreys notes "The hardest duty that ever fell to my lot as Chaplain was to prepare a deserter to die." In addition to duties as a cleric, Humphreys had been selected to act as defense counsel at the court-martial. "Perhaps one reason why I did not win the case," he surmised, "was that the opposing counsel was Lewis S. Dabney, whose legal acumen made him then Judge Advocate, and later made him one of the leaders of the Bar in Boston."

As Humphreys remembered the situation, Ormsley "leaned still more closely on my faith that, though his country would not forgive hime . . . God *would* forgive him if he was truly pentitent; and the thought appealed to the native nobleness of his nature. . . ."

When the time came for his execution, Ormsley requested permission to speak to the assembled troops:

> Comrades; I want to acknowledge that I am guilty and that my punishment is just. But I want also that you should know that I did not desert because I lost faith in our cause. I believe we are on the right side, and I think it will succeed. But take warning from my example, and whatever comes do not desert the old flag for which I am proud to die.

Ormsley was shot to death on a Sunday morning, and Humphreys "did not feel like holding a service after it, and thought the ceremony of execution had preached more effectively than *I* could . . . ." "The lesson" of Ormsley's execution, Humphreys concluded, was a success. There were no other executions in his Brigade.

JAMES WILSON, 25, a Scottish laborer, entered Union service as a substitute for John Scott, of Huntingdon, Pennsylvania[1], in Company B, 97th Pennsylvania Infantry.

JAMES THOMPSON, 28, an Irish sailor, was another substitute in the regiment, but in Company K.

Both men deserted their unit at Fernandina, Florida: Thompson, 13 December; Wilson, 14 December 1863. They were apprehended and subsequently tried by general court-martial; convicted and sentenced to execution.

Wilson and Thompson were shot to death at Fernandina 7 February 1864.

### 18 February 1864

At a military commission, convened at Camp Shaw, Florida, Mrs. Sarah Hammond came forward and testified that a number of "colored soldiers came to my house yesterday morning . . . ." The defendant in the case was SPENCER LLOYD, 21, Company B, 55th Massachusetts Infantry [Colored], ". . . he is the one I called the black one in my other Evidence. He asked me if he could hug me."

**Judgement in the case of Pvt. John M. Smith [Co. A, 55th Massachusetts Infantry (Colored)] was indeed swift. A military commission on 17 February 1864 found him guilty of raping a white woman. The next morning — at 11 a.m. — General Seymour approved the findings and ordered Smith to be "executed immediately"** . . . which meant the same day.                    *National Archives*

Mrs. Hammond refused. As she testified, Lloyd threatened "if I did not lie still he would take his gun and kill me. He then violated my person . . . After the three others had violated me, I went toward the house . . ."

Along the way, she saw an army officer approaching. She stopped him and explained what had happened. Before he reached the Hammond house, the officer had met "four colored soldiers." Hammond told the officer "those four men with packs on their backs that have just gone down the road, downed me and did what they pleased to me, threatened me with their guns, said they'd shoot me if I made any noise, and that's hard to take."

The officer wheeled his horse and rode rapidly after the men. When he had them in his sight, he followed at a distance until he met the unit's quartermaster. The quartermaster watched the men, while the other officer rounded up a guard detail. The men were arrested, and turned over to the provost marshal in Jacksonville.

An intriguing part of Lloyd's case is that only two men — Lloyd and JOHN W. COOK [Cork], 23, same unit — were tried for the rape of Mrs. Hammond. What happened to the other two men who had been arrested?

The Adjutant General's Office reports that a third man, JOHN M. SMITH, 21, Company A, was hanged for rape along with the others at or near Jacksonville, 18 February 1864. A search of Smith's records, however, reveals that he was not a rapist, rather he was a deserter.

In fact, Smith's service record indicates that, as of 19 October 1863, Smith had been returned from desertion, and allowed to rejoin his company "without trial by court-martial, by order of Gen. Gilmore on condition that he will be required to make good the time lost and forfeit all pay due up to the time of his pardon . . . ." He apparently deserted again, because he is reported "apprehended and returned" 31 October.

The Massachusetts Adjutant General's Office lists him as executed for desertion at Jacksonville, 18 February 1864.

The question still remains: what happened to the others?

### 27 February 1864

PETER GOODRICH, 23, an English sailor and a member of Company I, 97th Pennsylvania Infantry, was scheduled to be executed 7 February 1864, along with James Wilson and James Thompson.

On 14 December 1863, four men: Goodrich, Thompson, Wilson, and John Williams [Company I], recently assigned to the regiment, slipped away from their guard and deserted. The men reached a road leading down the island at Fernandina "by making a detour through the almost impenetrable thicket," as Isaiah Price recalled. Price, author of *History of the Ninety-Seventh Regiment, Pennsylvania Volunteer Infantry, During the War of the Rebellion, 1861-65*, indicated that by the time the deserters reached the water, "a boat, in charge of some negroes in the employ of Mr. H. H. Helper, government agent at Fernandina, who had been fishing, landed on the shore."

Goodrich and the others made a "desperate attempt" to capture the boat, "pointed a pistol at the men who were trying to get off with it and fired, but not hitting the negroes, wounded one of his companions (Thompson), who also had hold of the boat."

In the ensuing confusion, the negroes wrested control of the boat and rowed to the other side. Helper returned with them and approached the deserters. The men, seeing Helper dressed in a gray suit supposed him to be a Confederate, and asked him to take them across. They were sorry, they said, to have "mistaken his men for 'Fernandina niggers.' "

Helper did not try to change their perception, but asked them to surrender their weapons before boarding the boat. He then ordered his men to pull for "the opposite side." Since it was nearly dark, the four men didn't realize — until the last moment — when their pursuers' boat reached them — that they had been captured.

Tried by general court-martial, Major Galusha Pennypacker presided, the four were convicted. Three were sentenced to be shot. Williams, who was the youngest, was sentenced to imprisonment at hard labor for the remainder of his term of service, forfeiture of pay and allowance, and a dishonorable discharge.

Following approval of the sentence by the commanding general 6 February, orders were issued for the execution to take place within twenty-four hours.

"Every precaution had from the first been taken to prevent the escape of the prisoners," Price stated, "who were ironed and doubly guarded." During the night, Goodrich, "being attended to a sink by a corporal, while returning to his cell, one handcuff not having been re-fastened, which had evidently been cut previously, and ran past the guard." The corporal fired after him, but Goodrich made his escape in the dark.

Wilson and Thompson were executed as planned at 3 p.m., 7 February. The next day, three hundred men of the 97th began a search of the island. The search for Goodrich continued for several days, until 12 February, when he was sighted in the woods. There was, as Price put it, "a desperate chase and resistance, [Goodrich] being several times wounded."

His execution was delayed pending orders from department headquarters. These were received and Goodrich "was accordingly executed, at 3 p.m., on the 27th, under similar arrangements and attendance as on the 7th."

### 1 March 1864

Sergeant WILLIAM WALKER, 23, was a river pilot from Georgia. At the time of his execution for mutiny, he was a member of Company E, 21st Infantry, USCT [3rd South Carolina Volunteer Infantry].

Walker was the first — of many — black soldiers to be court-martialed and executed for opposing the inequitable pay structure of the Union Army, and the discrimination against black soldiers.

On 23 August 1863, at Seabrook, South Carolina, Walker made his dissatisfaction known. Ordered by 1st Lieutenant George W. Wood to return to camp, Walker refused, and used, what the army called, "threatening language," such as "I will shoot him (Wood)."

When ordered to go to his tent by Captain Edgar Abeel, 3rd South Carolina, he did not go, saying "I will not be under arrest by you, I will go to the Provost first." Walker was then demoted to the ranks, though his court-martial record continues to refer to him as "sergeant."

On or about 31 October, Walker was ordered to fall in for drill by Sergeant Sussex Brown; he refused by shouting: "God damn you, I will shoot you." Almost three weeks later, when Acting Drum Major William Smith, 76th Pennsylvania Volunteers, attempted to arrest another drummer, Ranty Pope, Walker interceded and prevented Pope's arrest.

The same day, 19 November, Walker took "unlawful" command of his company, and marched them to the guard house to release Private Jacob Smith. Smith was being handcuffed by 2nd Lieutenant John E. Jacobs, when Walker ordered his men to "Take hold of him (Smith), snatch him away, My Bully Boys." That was the final straw, the command realized; Walker was in general mutiny.

Walker was also charged with leaving his tent 20 November to play cards in another tent — in disobedience of orders from Lieutenant-Colonel A. G. Bennett.

"I am a poor Colored Soldier . . . ," Walker wrote to Colonel Hall, provost marshal general, 7 February 1864, "who appeal to your Generosity and Justice . . .

> Sir I have been some three Months A prisoner in the Provost Guard House I an now awaiting Sentence of a *Court-Martial*. Charged with Crimes I am Entirely Guiltless of I have always done my duty as a soldier and a man and I hope to do so in the future my former Good Character has never Been douted . . . I will say no more you can Easily Learn the circumstances Connected with My Case if you are not already acquainted . . .

As a postscript, Walker added:

> . . . If you Should Wish any references with regard to my former Character I refer you Sir to Capt. Worden of the Monitor Montauk. I was his pilot for Six months I also destroyed the rebel Steamer Nashville in the Big Ogeechee River near Fort McAllister by Order of Admiral Dupont . . . .

Regardless of his protestations of innocence, his previous service, and the justice of the cause for which he fought, William Walker was shot to death at Jacksonville, 1 March 1864.

### 7 March 1864

On 7 February 1864, Major-General Benjamin F. Butler made a raid on Richmond to release Union prisoners-of-war held there. "Everything worked precisely as [Butler] expected. The troops reached Bottom's Bridge, 10 miles from Richmond, at 2.30 o'clock . . . but he found a force of the enemy posted there before for two months. They had destroyed the bridge and fallen trees across the road to prevent the passing of the cavalry. Finding the enemy were informed and prepared, we were obliged to retire."[2]

The next day, Butler read a copy of the Richmond *Examiner* "in which it is said that they were prepared for us from information received from a Yankee deserter."

The deserter, whose name was forwarded to Lincoln, was Private William Boyle, New York Mounted Rifles, "under sentence of death for the murder of Lieutenant Disoway . . . ." Boyle, as Brigadier General Isaac J. Wistar contended in a letter to Butler, was allowed to escape by Private WILLIAM ABRAHAM, Company G, 139th New York Infantry, four days prior to Butler's move.

Abraham, Wistar alleged, told Boyle that "large numbers of cavalry and infantry were concentrated here [Fort Magruder] to take Richmond." Boyle supposedly escaped to Richmond, was arrested, and confined in Castle Thunder. "Boyle," Wistar lamented, "would have been hung long ago but for the President's order suspending til further orders the execution of capital sentences." Wistar referred to Lincoln's 26 February 1864 order, General Order 76, which commuted the death sentences of deserters — not murderers — to imprisonment at Dry Tortugas, off Key West, Florida. The order was later issued as a presidential proclamation 20 April.

Abraham was court-martialed quickly, with Colonel H. T. Sanders, 19th Wisconsin Volunteers, presiding. He was charged with "acting and lurking as a spy," and "giving intelligence to the enemy, in violation of the 57th Article of War."

Abraham was found guilty — not of acting as a spy, as the Adjutant General's report states — of giving information to the enemy. He was shot to death at Yorktown, Virginia, 7 March 1864.

One wonders if Boyle was the actual informant for the Confederates. If he were, the intelligence Butler sent to the president, indicating the rebels were prepared two months in advance for the Union move, was inaccurate. If Boyle did convey the troop strength and intended movements four days in advance, why was the Confederate unit in position so long? Such questions are difficult — if not impossible — to answer. It is more logical to assume that Boyle was a scapegoat.

**11 March 1864**

"I wish you to commute the sentence of Private Ely," Colonel R. F. Mayry, 1st Oregon Cavalry, wrote to General Wright, "now under sentence & order to be shot after almost two years service as an exemplary soldier."

FRANCIS ELY, 36, a Canadian miner and member of Company A, 1st Oregon Cavalry, was court-martialed for deserting from Camp 42, Neuf River, 27 August 1863. He was arrested the next day.

Though Colonel Mawry felt that the "proceedings of the court & the approval of commutation on me of execution will have an effect equal to the execution of the sentence . . .," higher command did not.

Francis Ely was shot to death 11 March 1864, at Fort Walla Walla. The Portland *Daily Oregonian*, 17 March, indicated that Ely's life might have been spared "If the telegraph had reached the post . . . as the President by proclamation last week commuted the punishment of all deserters under sentence, and ordered them to be confined at Tortugas during the war."

**20 March 1864**

ROBERT KERR, 34, an unemployed Irish immigrant, enlisted in the 1st California Cavalry at San Francisco 16 August 1861.

Less than a year after his enlistment, Kerr found himself confined at Fort Yuma. "I have been confined five months at this place in Irons," he wrote to Captain William M. Cleave, Company A, 1st Cavalry, California Volunteers, 8 August 1862;

> The first two months Solitary. Since that Time I have been at work. and I am now destitute of every Thing in The line of Clothing. I have never drawn any since last december. Consequently I am in a manner Naked. I have to go bare footed over this Hill which is as great punishment as flesh can stand and cannot get shoes or pants to cloth my nakedness as the commanding officer will not issue prisoners anything. Other prisoners is better situated than me as They have all had officers To provide for them of there own company or Regiment whilst I have been left here Entirely alone a Stranger to my officers and soldiers here and I have been Treated as such for no officer has spoken to me since my stay at this place.

In this transmittal letter, Captain Cleave stated that he had "no official information as this man having been tried and sentenced, though I have no doubt it is so."

Kerr was in confinement for an alleged attack on a Lieutenant Harvey. Major D. Ferguson, 1st Cavalry, California Volunteers, corresponded 8 August

1862 to 1st Lieutenant Benjamin C. Cutler, acting assistant adjutant general, 1st Infantry, California Volunteers, that he was present at the time of the incident. ". . . for on the commission of the offence," he wrote, "Lieut. Harvey summarily chastised [Kerr] and came very near taking his life, unintentionally of course. Drunkenness was the cause of the man's conduct."

Based on the intercession of Major Ferguson, Kerr was released in late September 1862. He apparently served satisfactorily until 29 December 1863, when he "wantonly and maliciously" shot and killed 1st Lieutenant Samuel H. Allyne, Company A, 1st Cavalry, California Volunteers, near San Elizio, Texas.

The general court-martial convened at Mesilla, New Mexico, 28 January 1864 heard the case and convicted Kerr of murder. The sentence of death by musketry was carried out at 2 p.m., 20 March 1864 at Franklin, Texas.

In one of the few instances encountered in the executed men's files, Kerr left a will, giving 'some real estate" in Washington County, Illinois, to his nephew Robert. The boy's father — Robert's brother — Thomas, was appointed executor. Kerr also left $30 in the hands of Colonel Isaac W. Bowie, commander of the 3rd Infantry, California Volunteers, to transmit to another brother, William J., of Disrun, California. "I have written to William J.," Bowie noted to Captain Cutler 27 April 1864, "if he still live there, and where Thomas is, as soon as I learn, I will send the will and money to them." No record exists as to whether the descendents ever replied, or the money reached them.

### 15 April 1864

JOHN EAGEN [also Egin, Egan], 21, a laborer, and HENRY HOLT, 25, a mechanic, were members of the 2nd New Hampshire Infantry. Both were Enlishmen. Eagen had joined Company A, 23 November 1863, for a bounty of $302; Holt's record indicates he joined Company F 17 November.

While the 2nd was guarding prisoners at Point Lookout, Maryland, both men deserted; Eagen, 10 April; Holt, 12 April. Each was apprehended the day after his escape.

Both were tried by general court-martial — almost immediately following their arrest — and convicted. They were shot to death near Yorktown, Virginia 15 April, even though orders were cut for Eagen to be executed 13 April.

In Eagen's file, there is an interesting letter from the Office of the Provost Marshal, Headquarters, Department of Virginia and North Carolina, dated 9 September 1864, to Brigadier General James Barnes, requesting information on Eagen's fate: "It is not positively known here whether his sentence was, or was not carried into effect before being commuted by the President." Did Eagen actually survive? No one knows.

### 17 April 1864

HENRY SCHUMAKER [also Schumacker and Schumacher], 24, a German painter, and HENRY STARK, 24, a German farmer, they joined the 6th Connecticut Infantry as substitutes:  Schumaker for George E. Miller; Stark, for James B. Montgomery, both of Bridgeport.

Schumaker, Stark, and Gustav Hoofan, another "forced" man, deserted their regiment while on picket duty 9 February 1864, but were captured the next day and confined in the provost guard house. While there, they escaped twice. The first time, they were found in Ossanabaw Sound and returned for trial, 4 March. They were convicted of desertion and sentenced to be shot to death.

After sentencing, they were "chained hand and foot to a post inside of the provost quarters; and not withstanding these precautions, together with a strong guard, they succeeded in getting away again."

They "requisitioned" a boat and made their escape. While in Warsaw Sound, near the shore, their boat ran aground and they were picked up by a picket boat from the gunboard *Patapsco*.

Brought back to Hilton Head, South Carolina, the three men continued their struggle for freedom. Only one was successful.

Gustav Hoofan discovered that the orders calling for his death misspelled his name as "Hoffman." The judge advocate had made an error. "Col. Duryee [commander of the 6th] wishing to be merciful, to the full extent consistent with duty, availed himself of this testimonial error and protested his execution." Hoofan was saved, and returned to duty.

With Hoofan free, Schumaker and Stark prepared to meet their fate. "They seemed stolid and indifferent at first," Charles K. Caldwell reminisced in *The Old Sixth Regiment, Its War Record, 1861-5*,

> but upon reflection they gave way to their feelings and desired to have a priest sent to them [they were both Catholics], and Rev. Mr. Hasson, a Catholic priest who was in the department, was sent for and ministered to them. It was for a long time difficult to convince them that their case was hopeless, but Mr. Hasson's arguments finally forced conviction, and after hearing their confession twice, he performed all the rites of the church that were practicable.

On 17 April, the two men, seated on their coffins, were driven to the shooting site at Hilton Head. "They maintained a calm demeanor to all," Caldwell continued, "except as they passed our regiment they took off their caps several times to their old comrades.

". . . After a short prayer by the priest they were blindfolded and their hands tied behind them and made to kneel upon their coffins, facing the center of the square."

On the signal from Captain E. S. Babcock, 9th USCT, the firing party — only six paces from Schumaker and Stark — discharged their weapons. Nine bullets pierced Schumaker; eight, Stark.

"They lay," Caldwell wrote, "just as they had fallen till the whole command marched past them on the way to camp, when they were put into the coffins and buried."

"We had a drum-head court-martial in our regiment when in Florida," Elbridge Copp recalled in his *Reminiscences of the War of the Rebellion 1861-1865*, "for the trial of a deserter. Recruits had been sent to us from the north, and there were always more or less bounty jumpers, called so from having received a large bounty to enlist, then took the first opportunity to desert, finding their way to the North to again enlist, to receive another bounty. We had numerous desertions of this kind . . . ."

Copp felt his commander, Colonel Plimpton of the 3rd New Hampshire Infantry, was a strict disciplinarian; "He determined to put a stop to desertions."

One night, Plimpton secretly put a second picket line outside the first. That night, a recruit escaped from camp and, having passed safely through the line, approached the second, the outside, picket line. "Hulloa, Johnnies," the Union soldier shouted, "I am a Yank and am coming over to your side."

That was fine with the sentry; "Come on," he shouted, and HENRY MILLER [also Heinrich Muller; his spelling, and Hugh Muller], 26, a German barkeep, fell into the trap.

Colonel Plimpton was awakened, and — at midnight — ordered an immediate court-martial. "Short work was made of the trial," Copp wrote, "the evidence was direct and there was no defence."

Henry Miller was found guilty of desertion, and was sentenced to be shot at sunrise 17 April 1864. He was, as Copp put it, "shot and buried within less than six hours of the time he left camp."

Following the execution, Colonel Plimpton reported to the departmental commander, asking that the proceedings of the trial and sentence be approved. A notation in Miller's service record suggests that the department ignored Plimpton's request. Dated 7 June 1864, it states: "Investigation fails to elicit any further information relative to this soldier."

As in the case of William Ormsley, the higher command applauded the actions of its field commanders by ignoring Plimpton's request, thereby approving of it — with silence.

### 22 April 1864

CHARLES CARPENTER and MATHEW RILEY were apparently substitutes in a Vermont regiment. Both were allegedly shot for desertion 22 April 1864, but a records search does not locate either man.

In a check of their records, the Vermont Historical Society finds that a Mathew Riley — the only one in their files — is listed "as having died of wounds received Feb. '64." John Roach, a name that Riley sometimes used, is only listed in a roster. In regard to Charles Carpenter, "There are five . . , none of whom were executed according to the roster."

Were these two men executed? If not them, who?

**25 April 1864**

In a letter to Lincoln, officers of the 19th Massachusetts pleaded for the pardon of THOMAS R. DAWSON, 32, a laborer from England and a private in Company H, 20th Massachusetts Infantry. He had previously served with the 19th.

"Previous to the commission of the violent act for which he has been condemned," they wrote, "he was an excellent soldier, intelligent and obedient. Since his trial, he has been on one occasion, while sick, an inmate of the Regimental Hospital without a guard, and had every opportunity to effect his escape had he so desired to do so."

Dawson had been convicted by general court-martial for desertion and rape. The Rev. William Corby remembered the man in his *Memoirs of Chaplain Life* — in great detail.

Dawson, a Roman Catholic, called for the priest and, in the course of their private conversations, explained his side of what happened. As Corby related:

> [Dawson] with two other soldiers wandered from camp, and coming to a house, they found there wine or liquor of some sort, and needless to say, they indulged freely. He said he became so stupid he knew not what followed. Some men and officers on duty, passing that way, arrested him on a charge of rape made by an old woman [Mrs. Frances West] of about sixty. The other two got away and escaped arrest. His being under the influence of liquor was not, in the eyes of the law, a sufficient excuse, for many reasons, especially because he was out of camp, and besides, he had no reason to be intoxicated.

Father Corby was given the job of going to Washington with the officers' petition. Without delay, the priest got a pass to Washington and arrived there 18 April. When he arrived at the White House, he was met promptly by the president. As Father Corby recalled the conversation, "The good President was inclined to be positive; said it was a 'hard case,' promised to take the matter into consideration, and, across the back of the petition . . . wrote 'See for the 25th of April.' " Though Lincoln's inclination was to be positive, he was not about to grant a pardon, "and said that suspense was more or less inevitable, on account of the movements of the army."

Frustrated by the lack of success of his pleading, the priest finally said: ". . . since Your Excellency sees fit not to grant it, I must leave his life in your hands." As Corby recalled it: "His tender heart recoiled when he realized that a man's life depended on his mercy."

"I will pardon him," Lincoln said, as the priest left the room, then adding almost as a postscript: "if Gen. Meade will, and I will put that on the petition."

Presenting Lincoln's note on the petition to General Meade, Corby met with a rigid position: "Father," General Meade told him, "I know that your mission is one of charity; but sometimes charity to a few means cruelty to many. If our discipline had been severe, or cruel, if you will, in the beginning, we would not have so many causes for execution now. Besides, the President has the final acts of that court-martial in his possession, and he should have given the final and positive decision. I will *not* act."

"Then the man must die," was the only conclusion Corby could reach. The case of Private Dawson had become a personal matter between Meade and Lincoln. "The fact of the matter is," Corby understood,

> at the same time the general in the field, or some of them at least, thought that the kind-hearted President was too good in pardoning so many, and some blame was attached to him on this account. Now, the general-in-chief could not see his way clear to do what had been found fault with in the President.

Dawson had become a pawn in the match between Lincoln and his generals. Corby returned to the regiment with his sad news. But the officers of the unit would not let the matter rest. They — including General Winfield Scott Hancock — urged the priest to telegraph the president. Corby did what was asked of him, "but I was told afterward that, in all probability, the message never reached the President. The secretary of war, very likely, put the dispatch in the fire . . . ."

Dawson, when made aware that his fate was sealed, was confident that everything possible had been done, and went to his death with a firm step. On the gallows, he asked to speak, and he said: "You may break by neck, but you won't break the seal of manhood." Corby felt he wanted to say more, "but, fearing he might become excited, I suggested that he ought to stop there, and he did."

Thomas Dawson, who had fought during the Crimean War in the ranks of the British Army, and been awarded the Victoria Cross and the Cross of Honor, was hanged to death 24 April 1864, at Morrisville, Virginia.

Dawson's hanging was a bungled affair: ". . . the provost marshal misjudged the length of the rope being used. When the trapdoor sprung, [Dawson] fell to a standing position on the ground. A frantic executioner," Corby wrote, "seized the end of the rope and jerked the prisoner upward until death slowly came."

Captain Gregory B. Adams, in his *Reminiscenses of the Nineteenth Massachusetts Regiment*, presumed "that the impressions desired were produced upon the men, but the remarks were that it was too bad to hang men when there were so hard to get, and if they had let him alone a few weeks Johnnie Reb would have saved them the trouble."

# CASUALTY SHEET.

Name: *Jacob Morgan*

Rank: *Private*    Company: *D*  Regiment: *8*

Arm: *Infantry*    State: *Connecticut*

Nature of Casualty: *Shot, for the offence of Desertion, April 28, 1864. — G.O., No. 2, U.S. Forces Norfolk and Portsmouth, April, 27, 1864.*

*... U.S. Sols. executed by U.S. ties, Pages 2 & 3.*

See 12290. A. A.G.O.(EB) 1875.

Sentence of death commuted by President to discharge &c. A.G.O. 55

H.C.M.O. No. 253 A.G.O. Aug. 4/64. Reg. Div.

Nov. 4/85.

Roll of Honor Vol. 25 p.211 shows him "died April 28/64 — Buried at Hampton, Va.

A.G.O. Novbr. 6: 1885.

*Shot to death by musketry at Norfolk, Va., April 28: 1864, for the offence of desertion, by sentence of Genl. Court Martial, promulgated in G.O. No. 2, U.S. Forces, Norfolk & Portsmouth, dated April 27: 1864 " See 12,290. A. A.G.O.(EB) 1875."*

*W. S. Burton*

Clerk.

*Aug. 12 - 85*

Ent. B. & N.

**Pvt. Jacob Morgan [Co. D, 8th Connecticut Infantry] had his death sentence commuted by Lincoln. Unfortunately for Morgan, Lincoln's timing was off:** the soldier had been "shot to death by musketry" on 28 April 1864 at Norfolk, Va. — before the presidential pardon was issued.

*National Archives*

### 28 April 1864

JACOB MORGAN, 37, an English shoemaker who had emigrated to Norwich, Connecticut, enlisted in the 8th Connecticut Infantry 22 February 1864.

On or about 14 March, while his unit was on outpost duty at Deep Creek, near Portsmouth, Morgan deserted. Captured 24 March — he had not left the area — the soldier was tried by general court-martial, convicted and sentenced to be shot. His court-martial transcript was forwarded to Washington for review.

The sentence of death was "commuted by President to discharge, &c.," 8 August 1864. Unfortunately for Morgan, the sentence was carried out at Norfolk, Virginia, 28 April. He is buried somewhere at Hampton, Virginia.

On the same day, in another area of the war, JOHN MYERS [Meyer], a 39-year-old bachelor farmer from Germany, was hanged at Pulaski, Tennessee, 28 April 1864.

Myers had joined the 7th Illinois Infantry 28 October 1861 at Fort Holt, Kentucky. Because of his military prowess, Myers was promoted to sergeant of Company G. On 28 February 1864, the 7th was returned to Pulaski, Tennessee, following a furlough, as the Veteran Volunteer Infantry.

Upon their return, the recruits of Companies C, G and I were merged into Company I, under the command of Captain Henry W. Allen. Shortly after the consolidation, Allen was murdered, and Myers was accused of the crime.

Tried by general court-martial, John Myers was convicted and executed.

### 29 April 1864

JOHN H. THOMPSON, 21, a member of Company C, 1st Ohio Cavalry, was just a few months shy of discharge at the time of his execution. He joined the unit at Columbus, Ohio, 11 September 1861.

Thompson, according to the Adjutant General's Office was convicted of desertion and theft, events that supposedly took place at Louisville, Kentucky, 28 February 1862. According to Thompson's general court-martial, he stood accused only of desertion. There was no record of theft listed. He was shot to death 29 April 1864.

". . . and now the 'subs,' several of whom had already deserted since leaving Fort Lookout, began to sift out faster than ever," Asa W. Bartlett wrote in *History of the Twelfth Regiment, New Hampshire Volunteers in the War of the Rebellion*. "It was evident that something must be done, or the roll of recruits in the Twelfth would diminish *pro rata* with the Second, from which over a hundred had deserted in three days."

General Isaac T. Wistar instituted a general court-martial, at which several deserters were tried, found guilty and sentenced to be shot . . . subject to the approval of the president. "Two," Bartlett recalled, "had already been shot in the Second, and two more apprehended at the same time were executed on the 29th in the presence of the brigade at Williamsburg." The two men were

OWEN McDONOUGH [also McDonald], 29, an English mechanic and member of Company K, and JAMES SCOTT, 22, a Scottish sailor and an unassigned member of the 22nd New Hampshire Infantry. According to company returns, Scott was detailed on a schooner during January/February 1864.

The deaths of these two men marked "the first time," Barlett recalled,

> that the Twelfth had ever witnessed an execution of the extreme penalty of military law, and the scene is quite vivid in the minds of some who saw it. The spot having been selected and two graves dug, the regiments of the brigade were marched out at the hour appointed and formed into three sides of a hollow square, facing inward, with the newly-dug graves in the middle of the open side. Soon the "mark time" beat of the muffled drums is heard, and the condemned men, riding on their rough-made coffins and guarded by twelve soldiers, selected from the Second Regiment, as executioners, slowly approach the square, and entering at one side of the open side, are driven round the whole distance of the other three sides, close to the front of the lines. As they pass along, their countenances are closely scanned by every soldier, eager to read therefrom the emotions of the soul within. One of them, with downcast, sorrowful gaze, looks as if he realised his situation, and that the woeful sorrow for the past, that has brought him here, is early equal to the dread of the terrible present that is now before him. The other acts more like one riding to a circus than his own grave. A brutish grin is on his face, accompanied with an indifference of demeanor that seems half real and half affected. The teams are halted in front of the graves, besides which the coffins are placed, and the victims, dismounting from the cart, remain standing while the provost marshal reads the death warrant and a prayer is made by the chaplain. They are seated upon their coffins, their caps removed (the heedless one, bound to die game, taking his off himself and throwing it for some distance), their eyes bandaged with handkerchiefs, and now the dreadful moment of death-waiting suspense has arrived.

Within seconds, McDonough and Scott fell "over their coffins into eternity." The execution took place 29 April 1864, near Fort Magruder, Virginia, at Williamsburg.

Little is known about the execution of JOHN REILY, JR, 21, a New Orleans boatman and member of Company L, 2nd Missouri Artillery. He joined the unit 4 January 1864, at St. Louis — a little more than three months before he was shot to death.

Reily stood accused of murder, received a general court-martial, and was executed at "Wamens brig" 29 April 1864.

### 9 May 1864

HENRY A. BURNHAM, 29, a New York farmer and a member of Company E, 5th New Hampshire Infantry, was a substitute for Henry C. Johnson, of Mount Lebanon, New Hampshire. At the time of his death, Burnham was still owed $25 of his bounty.

An interesting aspect of Burnham's case is that the general order [4] convicting him of desertion is dated 4 May 1864. A look at his service record indicates he was wounded 3 June at Coal Harbor. The approval for the sentence to execute was dated 26 August 1864. Burnham was allegedly shot to death at Point Lookout, Maryland, 9 May 1864. If the records are accurate, Burnham was executed before he was wounded in action. Was Burnham actually executed? Are the company rolls accurate? If he was not executed at Point Lookout, who was?

### 21 May 1864

"One of the deserters who had returned with the regiment from Massachusetts was shot this morning," Ernest Linden Waitt, in *History of the Nineteenth Regiment Massachusetts Volunteer Infantry, 1861-1865*, quotes in a diary entry for 20 May 1864, "for desertion of the colors in the face of the enemy at Laurel Hill.

> He deserted from our regiment about two years since, joined another, getting a bounty for so doing, and in a short time joined still another, getting another bounty, all of which was taken into consideration. He was pardoned by the president, but on account of his late desertion of the colors, suffered the penalty of death. [5]

JOHN D. STARBIRD [aka Lawrence J. Hoyt], 20, a clerk from Manchester, New Hampshire, and a member of Company K, 19th Massachusetts Infantry, had been a private in Company D, 3rd Battalion of Rifles, Massachusetts Volunteers. Honorably discharged 3 August 1861, Starbird reenlisted as a veteran volunteer the next month. He is listed as being absent without leave 18 April 1862 from Yorktown, Virginia. On 22 March 1864, he was picked up at Stephensburg.

Starbird deserted while his unit was going into action 18 May 1864, at Spotsylvania, Virginia. Two days later, he was tried at drumhead for desertion, convicted and sentenced to death by musketry. The execution took place 21 May 1864.

*S | 19 | Mass.*

*John D. Starbird*

*Pvt.*, Co. *K, 19* Reg't *Mass,*

**Appears on**

**Descriptive List of Deserters Arrested.**

List dated *Nov. 10*, 186*3*, and signed
by Provost Marshal, *3* District of Mass.

**Deserted:**

When *June 29*, 186*2.*

Where *Yorktown*

**Arrested:**

When *Nov. 5*, 186*3.*

Where *Boston, Mass.*

Remarks: *Arrested by officer*
*J. H. Adams.*
*Expenses $30.00*
*This man John D. Starbird*
*enlisted in Sept. 1862 in the 47th*
*Mass. Vols. as Lawrence J. Hoyt.*
*(over)*

Endorsement on list shows that the men named
therein were received at *Hd. Qrs. Milty. Comdr.*
*Boston*, *10th Nov*, 186*3.*

*Thornton*

(516)                                                          Copyist.

*S. | 19 | Mass.*

*John D. Starbird*

*Pvt.*, Co. *K,* 19 Reg't Massachusetts Inf.

Appears on **Returns** as follows:

*Sept. 1861, Recruit from*
*Depot Sept. 27 Camp*
*Benton.*

*Apr. 1862, Absent without*
*leave, Apr. 18"*

*May 1862, Loss, Apr. 17 York-*
*town by desertion,*

*July 1862, Deserted June*
*30 Yorktown, Va,*

*Mar. 1864, Gain Mar. 22 Ste-*
*vensburgh from deser-*
*tion,*

Book mark:

*Sitler*

(546)                                                          Copyist.

The "Descriptive List of Deserters Arrested" and the 19th Massachusetts Infantry "Returns" provide insights in the activities of Pvt. John D. Starbird [Co. K] — and questions. Starbird might have been a bounty-jumper since the "Descriptive List" shows him enlisting in the 47th Massachusetts as Lawrence J. Hoyt, and that he deserted 29 June 1863 at Yorktown, Va. However, the unit returns show him "absent without leave" 18 April, and as a "loss . . . by desertion" as of 17 April. Finally, the returns list him as having deserted 30 June.

*National Archives*

"Those who read this," John G. B. Adams explained in his *Reminiscences of the Nineteenth Massachusetts Regiment*, "and do not understand the situation at the time, may think the killing of Starbird unjust and cruel, but it is not." During that particular time, he continued, "there were in the ranks of every regiment, men who had no interest in the cause. They had enlisted for the bounty, and did not intend to render any service. They not only shirk duty," he decided, "but their acts and conversations were demoralizing good men. The shooting of Starbird," he felt, "changed all this. Men who had straggled and kept out of battle now were in the ranks, and the result to our corps alone was as good as if we had been reinforced by full regiment."

### 10 June 1864
Three members of the 2nd New Jersey Cavalry, executed for rape and theft, are buried in the Mississippi River National Cemetery, Memphis.[6]

JOHN CALLAGHAN [Callahan], 18, an Irish immigrant; THOMAS JOHNSON [Johnston], 22, an English "sadeller"; and JOHN [also Jacob] SNOVER, 40, a New Jersey native, were substitutes. Both Callaghan and Snover were paid $25 bounty, $2 premium, and owed $75 at the time of their deaths. Johnson and Snover had been promoted to corporal soon after they joined the military, but within a few months were reduced to the ranks.

Using existing records, it can be determined that Callaghan had been a deserter. In fact, he had deserted and been apprehended — with $10 being paid for his capture. Those same records do not shed any light on the crimes for which both men were shot to death on 10 June 1864, at Memphis. One can only presume they were all convicted of desertion.

### 17 June 1864
JOHN FLOOD [his records are filed under John Smith], 22, was an Irish laborer who entered the 41st New York Infantry as a substitute 6 November 1863.

While the unit was on duty in Folly Island, South Carolina, Flood "deserted to the enemy from Kiawah Island, 26 April 1864. He was apprehended the same day.

Following a general court-martial, Flood was shot to death at Hilton Head, South Carolina, 17 June 1864.

### 18 June 1864
WALLACE BAKER, 19, a Kentucky farmer,[7] enlisted in Company I, 55th Massachusetts Infantry [Colored], 22 June 1863 at Readville, Massachusetts.

Baker was charged with mutiny, and court-martialed — Lieutenant-Colonel H. N. Hooper, 54th Massachusetts Volunteers, served as president. He was ordered, on 1 May 1864, by 2nd Lieutenant T. F. Ellsworth, of the 55th, to go to his quarters. Baker refused and struck Ellsworth "two violent blows in the face and that [Baker] did then endeavor to take from [the lieutenant] his sword . . . ."

When ordered to go to quarters, Baker shouted "I shan't do it; I'll be damned if I'll go; I'll go to the guard house first . . . ." He was charged with disobedience of orders. He was also accused of "contempt and disrespect to his superior officer," for telling Ellsworth: "You damned white officer, do you think you can strike me, and I not strike you back again? I will do it, I'm damned if I don't . . . ." And finally, Baker was charged with "conduct prejudicial to good order and military discipline," since he refused an order, struck an officer, and used "very abusive language against [Ellsworth] in the presence of his company . . . ."

What was ignored in the terse language of the orders was that Baker was a part of the rising black protest at the inequitable pay structure of black versus white soldiers.

Following Baker's execution 18 June 1864, at Folly Island, South Carolina, Brigadier General A. Schimmelfennig, commanding the Northern District, Department of the South, felt obliged to move the all-white 52nd Pennsylvania Infantry to Morris Island, "they being acquainted with the ground there, and have ordered the Thirty-third Regiment U. S. Colored Troops onto Folly Island . . . ."[8] With tact, Schimmelfenning defused a volatile racial issue.

### 24 June 1864

On 16 June 1864, CORNELIUS THOMPSON, 35 a Mississippi farmer, and a member of Company A, 48th Infantry, USCT, "did deliberately and with malice aforethought, shoot . . . Miss Martha Richardson, a laundress" in his company, the "ball entering the right hip, and passing through the bowels, thereby causing death." The murder happened at the unit's camp at Vicksburg.

Thompson received a general court-martial — Lieutenant-Colonel M. H. Crowell, 48th Infantry, USCT, presided — and was sentenced to execution. He was shot to death in the presence of the division at Vicksburg, 24 June 1864 . . . only eight days after the crime.

### 27 June 1864

". . . The order for the execution . . . evinces considerable demoralization among the renegades," Colonel John S. Ford, 2nd Texas Cavalry, reported.[9]

The execution was for PEDRO GARCIA, 25, a Mexican farmer and substitute in Company E, 1st Texas Cavalry. There is no record that Garcia had been paid by the army, only that a $100 bounty was due him at the time of his death. According to the early guidelines, it would seem that Garcia did not fit the parameters for a military court-martial.

Garcia, however, was reported as deserting "from Scout" 26 May 1864, while part of the Independent Company, Partisan Rangers, attached to the 1st Texas. Prior to his desertion, he attended sick and unserviceable horses.

Pedro Garcia was shot to death at Brownsville, Texas, 27 June 1864.

This photograph indicates that a black soldier, Private William Johnson [23rd Infantry, USCT], was executed in front of Petersburg, Va., 20 June 1864. There is no listing for Johnson's execution on that date. However, a Pvt. Henry Johnson [Co. D, 52nd Infantry, USCT] was hanged on 26 May 1865, along with several other men for the crime of murder. This photograph, showing a single execution, indicates that this was William Johnson — and not Henry — and another man to add to the list of the unlisted soldiers executed by Union authorities.

*Massachusetts Commandery, Military Order of the Loyal Legion and the U. S. Army Military History Institute.*

**28 June 1864**

Three members of the 2nd New Jersey Cavalry were hanged at Fort Pickering, Tennessee, on or about 28 June 1864. According to the *Memphis Bulletin*, the men were executed for rape.[10] There is a possibility that these three men might have been John Callaghan, Thomas Johnson, and John Snover — all members of the 2nd New Jersey Cavalry — who were executed 10 June. Though newspapers during the Civil War period were sometimes late with their news, an eighteen-day lapse seems hardly possible.

**Undated**

WILLIAM JOHNSON, a member of the 23rd Infantry, USCT, was hanged under a flag of truce at Petersburg, about June 1864. His execution, though unrecorded, was quite unusual because it was conducted in view of the Confederates. At least four photographs of this execution exist.[11]

**11 July 1864**

On 8 July 1864, FRANCIS GILLESPIE, 23, a New York farmer and a private in Company B, 15th New York Cavalry, picked up his revolver and fired into the head of 1st Lieutenant William B. Shearer, of his unit, killing him.

Gillesplie joined the 15th at Syracuse, New York, in the fall of 1863 and, previous to the murder, had seen action at Bolivar Heights, Leetown and Martinsburg. His service record does not indicate a violent or undisciplined history. In fact, it resembles the file of any Union veteran of the war, with one exception:

Francis Gillespie was tried by a military commission — Colonel M. McCaslin, 15th West Virginia Infantry, president — and was found guilty of murdering an officer. He was hanged near Cumberland, Maryland, 11 July 1864 . . . three days after the murder.

**15 July 1864**

Though the National Archives could not locate a service file for DANIEL GEARY, a private in Company E, 72nd New York Infantry, a fairly complete reconstruction of the crime, rape — and punishment — he and RANSOM S. GORDON, same unit, received was located in *Inside Lincoln's Army: The Diaries of Marsena Rudolph Patrick, Provost Marshal General, Army of the Potomac.*

Patrick recalled a Mrs. Stiles who attached herself to "our Train" 27 November 1863 and who "actually engaged in plunder a house the Troops broke into —" 24 June 1864. Mrs. Stiles identified Gordon as one of the rapists, and a few days later Geary was captured. "There seemed to be no clew to the perpetrators, at first," Patrick wrote, but the leader could not keep away from the Spot, after the crime, & was the *first* to speak of it as an outrage, before *any* other person knew of it —"

**General Marsena Rudolph Patrick, Provost Marshal General of the Army of the Potomac, seated among his officer cadre. Patrick, a product of "strict Puritanism," took more than a passing interest in the victim of a rape.**
*Massachusetts Commandery, Military Order of the Loyal Legion and the U. S. Army Military History Institute.*

Troops are drawn up to witness the execution of in front of Petersburg, Va., August 1864. According to research and the official listing, the only hanging to take place during the month of August 1864 was that of Pvt. William H. Howe. His execution did not take place at Petersburg . . . but at Fort Mifflin, outside Philadelphia, Pa. This particular photograph points out another unknown . . . and unlisted soldier.

*Massachusetts Commandery, Military Order of the Loyal Legion and the U. S. Army Military History Institute.*

Mrs. Stiles, in Patrick's account "feels terribly and has been here to see me . . . ." Patrick kept the woman in his thoughts for several diary entries,

13 July: "I did not go, as I thought of doing, to see Mrs. Stiles & read to her the Sentence of the Court, that Gordon & Geary be hanged on Friday";

14 July: ". . . I took Chaplain Rammell with me & started off over to see Mrs. Stiles and the Robertson family — I read the Order to her . . ."

2 September: ". . . I mounted & rode out, after dinner, as far as the Stiles House — I did not go in, but seeing Mrs. Stiles near the fence, rode up & asked of their welfare —"

Major-General George Gordon Meade instructed Patrick to obtain a Roman Catholic priest to minister to Geary. The clergyman located was the Rev. William Corby.

Corby,[12] when he arrived at the camp was introduced to the provost-marshal, Richard F. O'Beirne. The priest asked him if he were from Detroit. Yes, the officer said. So am I, the priest replied, and the son of Daniel Corby. As it happened, Corby and O'Beirne had not met since "we were small boys, about fifteen years of age. He was a very exemplary youth, served in the cathedral at Detroit as censer-bearer for many years, and stood in great favor with the Right Reverend Bishop and the clergy of the city . . . ."

After they had concluded their amentities, Corby inquired about Geary. "I found a man who was quite young," the priest wrote, "possibly about twenty, of an excellent frame, healthy and strong. He had a good mind and was somewhat educated. He was not a low, depraved person by any means, but in time of temptation he had fallen. The crime was much, if not entirely, the fault of his accomplice rather than his own."

After meeting with Geary, Corby decided to say mass the next morning, "so as to communicate my penitent on the morning of his execution . . ." He asked O'Beirne to assist him. "It has been a long time since I performed that duty," the provost-marshal replied, "but with the aid of my prayer-book, no doubt I can."

Mass was said early in the morning, and the priest spent the remaining time — until 9 a.m. — with the condemned men. Corby accompanied them to the scaffold, while Geary's brother — a member of the same regiment — held the priest's horse.

"Without much ceremony," the priest recalled,

> the ropes were adjusted about their necks, and, while both continued to pray for God's mercy, a silent signal was given and both dropped dangling at the end of the ropes — dead! As I have observed before, these scenes were harder on the nervous system than the scenes witnessed in the midst of a battle, where there is rattle, dash, and excitement to serve one up for the occasion.

Corby suffered with the "poor brother who witnessed the scene! What anguish! What a wail of grief filled his young heart! But, oh! What lamentations filled the bosom of his heart-broken mother when she beheld the corpse of her loved son, sent to her as the first news of his fate! Let her own words . . . tell what she felt. I give it *verbatim* . . .

> . . . I wish to inform you that my son's remains came to my view two hours previous to the tidings of his death; thus unexpectedly did I see my child's remains come to me. The very day I received these tidings I was preparing to see my boy after three long years of weary servitude; but welcome be the will of God in every shape and way it may appear. . . . I hope you will let me know if my dear child died reconciled with leaving this world and going to meet his God. I am always under the impression that the grief of heart caused me troubled him more than anything else in this world except his own soul. I also have to inform you that his movements in going toward that place of execution, and the spectacle of his bereft and heart-broken brother looking at him for twenty or thirty minutes, as I have been informed by him, stand continually before my eyes . . . .

Gordon, the supposed culprit in the rape case, was listed in the company rolls as "mustered out of service" 19 June 1864 . . . the day after the rape, and almost a month before his execution.

### 5 August 1864
ISAAC B. WHITLOW [aka John Hall], 17, was a Franklin County, Virginia farmer, when he joined Company D, 23rd Ohio Infantry. He was accused of desertion 2 October 1863, at Camp White, Virginia. Convicted, he was shot to death 5 August 1864, at Monacacy, Virginia.

Muster rolls of the 23rd Ohio provide some mystery. John Hall, the alias Whitlow is supposed to have used, was also a Virginia farmer, but listed as being mustered in 23 July 1864, at Cincinnati, a substitute for Edwin Clapp. The probable explanation is that Whitlow and Hall were the same person . . . a bounty-jumper.

### 8 August 1864
"The French have a saying that there is nothing more probable than the improbable," Surgeon Samuel A. Green wrote,[13] "and events often seem to prove the paradox."

As Green remembered the origins of the "improbable," it was the fall of 1861, and a young Boston boy, FRANK McELHENNY, joined the 24th. He came from a disadvantaged home, and "he might have been considered a fair specimen of the North End rough." A year later, young McElhenny fell afoul of the military system while the regiment was stationed in Newbern, North Carolina. He was found guilty of some offenses by a court-martial, and imprisoned in Fort Macon, near Beaufort, for the duration of the war.

After a few weeks in prison, McElhenny escaped, "but the rumor," Green felt, "produced scarcely a ripple, so thoroughly had the whole matter been forgotten."

Two years later, "the scene now changes from North Carolina to Virginia . . .

> One hot and sultry afternoon in the month of July, 1864, on the picket-line in front of Richmond, a man in rebel uniform was seen running towards to Federal lines. At that time, the distance between the two lines was very short, within speaking distances, though it varied in different places. It was late in the day, and the deserting soldier reached the post about ten minutes before the picket guard was to be relieved. Naturally, he was soon surrounded by men anxious to "buzz" him and learn the latest news from the other side. Among the first to approach him was a member of Company F . . . , who approached him and at once said, "How are you, Frank?" The rebel soldier, without being abashed, immediately replied, "My name isn't Frank," which for the instant allayed any suspicion.

Not long after that, another soldier identified the deserter as an old comrade. McElhenny was immediately taken to the rear and turned over to the provost guard. The next day, he was sent to Fortress Monroe, and tried for desertion. He was found guilty, and sentenced to be shot.

> While under guard in camp, [Surgeon Green] had an interview with the unfortunate man and he told me that after escaping from Fort Macon and proceeding to the southern end of the narrow island, he swam across to the mainland, and made his way to Raleigh, where for a short time he worked in a cobbler's shop. Finding this mode of life rather tame, after his army experience, he left for Richmond, where he enlisted under an assumed name, in a company of heavy artillery (Nineteenth Virginia Battalion). Again tiring of military discipline, he made up his mind again to desert, knowing that the National Government had agreed to send all deserters from the rebel army to any place in the North where they wished to go, and he intended to avail himself of the offer.

If McElhenny had selected any other point in the Union line — or any other time of the day — he would not have met members of his former company, "as the regiment went on picket only once in three days . . . In the doctrine of chances, everything was in his favor, and yet he lost. It seems as if keen-eyed justice on that occasion had landed on the point of a needle."

Captain John N. Patridge[14] provided an eyewitness account of the 8 August 1864 execution at Deep Bottom, Virginia: "The most unconcerned appearing man in the entire group was the man with the most at stake — McElhenny. After the reading of the orders, and the commands to fire," McElhenny "fell forward pierced by many bullets . . ." When he was declared dead,

> the brigade was formed in columns of fours and marched past the prostrate form — a warning to the living. After all had passed, the body was placed face downward in the box and lowered into the grave. The grave was then filled and the earth levelled. No mound or head-board marked the spot where the deserter was lying. Such was the ignominious ending.

### 12 August 1864

BARNEY GIBBONS, a private in Company A, 7th Infantry, Regulars, deserted while his unit was on duty at Jacksonville, Florida.

Tried by general court-martial, Gibbons was convicted and sentenced to be shot to death. The sentence was carried out 12 August 1864.

### 26 August 1864

During the devastating battle of Fredericksburg, the 116th Pennsylvania Infantry in the forefront of the attack, and suffered monstrous casualties. One of their number, Lieutenant Christian Folz, was the man who fell closest to the stone wall. The unit's flag had fallen not far from where Folz lay, and a young Pennsylvania farmer of German descent, WILLIAM H. HOWE, retrieved it.

Following the battle, Howe came down with a serious case of dysentery, and tried to gain entrance at the regimental hospital. But the hospital, filled with so many serious cases, turned him away. The young soldier then tried the hospital in Washington; again, he had no success. But he did take the doctor's advice: go home.

Howe traveled from Virginia to Perkiomenville, Pennsylvania, and stayed there, returning to his former work as a cigar-maker.

While Howe remained at home, Lincoln, in an attempt to reinforce the army, offered amnesty to deserters. On 10 March 1863, the president proclaimed that soldiers who were absent without leave could be returned to their units with no punishment — other than forfeiture of pay during the absence — if they reported before 1 April. If they did not, they would be arrested as deserters. William Howe either did not know about the amnesty proposal, or ignored it.

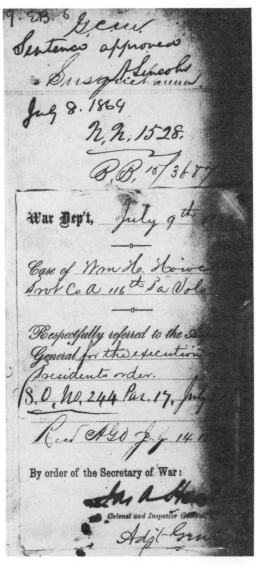

Lincoln's brief notation at the top of this document sealed Pvt. William H. Howe's fate. Nowhere in the records is there any indication that Lincoln looked through the large amount of documents that made up Howe's file. All that exists is his simple phrase: "Sentence approved." *National Archives*

On 21 June 1863, three men — interested in the $5 reward for Howe's capture — spent the afternoon fortifying themselves in preparation for the arrest. In the dark of the night, they approached the house. Shots were fired, and Abraham Bertolet, a former enrolling officer, fell dead.

Howe stood accused of desertion — and now murder. He was apprehended 13 July in Allentown, Pennsylvania. What followed was one of the most bizarre cases of Civil War justice.

William H. Howe was tried by a general court-martial, convened in Philadelphia with Lieutenant-Colonel Henry A. Frink, 11th Pennsylvania Volunteers, as president, and found guilty of both charges, and sentenced to execution. But, the court-martial decision was thrown out due to "informality," and Howe was scheduled for another court-martial.

The "new" court-martial panel, again presided over by Lieutenant-Colonel Frink, found Howe guilty as charged . . . despite evidence brought forth that the testimony of the eyewitnesses, the other enrolling officers, was suspect; the weapon used to kill Bertolet was, in all probability, a revolver [Howe defended himself with a rifle]; that a defense witness at the first trial became a prosecution witness at the second — after he received a promotion to captain.

The decision to execute Howe was not a popular one. Members of the 116th Pennsylvania, from their colonel on down, petitioned Lincoln to commute the man's sentence. This was denied, and on 26 August 1864, William H. Howe walked up to the gallows at Fort Mifflin, Philadelphia, and was hanged.

"The execution," the *Sunday Dispatch* in Philadelphia reported two days after Howe's death,

> was attended with certain features which were not noticed in the daily papers . . . Those entrusted with the unpleasant duty of carrying out the orders from headquarters endeavored to do their duty, in such a manner that which the effect upon the bounty-jumpers and deserters would be a decided one, the prisoner should be treated with all the kindness due to his unfortunate position.

*The Dispatch* listed its charges: Howe was forced to witness the building of the gallows; his minister was not allowed to visit him until two hours before the execution; the execution was staged to produce a maximum effect on the wrong-doers confined at the fort;[15] and "When the body remained suspended about half an hour, preparations were made to take it down." The civilian in charge of the gallows was not affected by the presence of death. "On the contrary," the newspaper reported, "his attention was about equally divided between the dullness of his knife and the mouth of bread he was munching at the time! There was but one sentiment — that of disgust — in the whole assemblage."[16]

This undated photograph shows troops witnessing the execution of a black soldier in front of Petersburg. There is no similarity to the execution site for Pvt. William Johnson, so it would be correct to infere it was a single execution of another black trooper. Since numerous black soldiers were hanged before Petersburg, it is impossible to identify the man. At the same time, there is a nagging thought that this might be yet another photograph of an unknown, unlisted man who was executed.

*Massachusetts Commandery, Military Order of the Loyal Legion and the U. S. Army Military History Institute.*

Howe's execution was the first — and only — instance where research has shown that tickets were sold to anyone who wanted to witness the hanging.

As if history takes care of those persons who have been wronged, the American Legion has placed a marker and an American flag on William H. Howe's grave . . . a short distance from his home in Perkiomenville.[17]

### 31 August 1864

EMANUEL [Manuel] DAVIS, 17, a Louisiana farmer and a drummer in Company A, 48th Infantry, USCT, enlisted for a three-year term 28 September 1863, at Goodrich Landing, Louisiana.

While on garrison duty at Vicksburg, Mississippi, Davis was accused of murder. Following a general court-martial, he was convicted and sentenced to death.

Davis was shot in front of his division 31 August 1864, at Vicksburg.

### 1 September 1864

ROGER JOHNSON, 28, another Mississippi farmer, is listed as being a member of Company H, 6th Heavy Artillery, USCT, when he was shot for murder at Natchez, Mississippi, 1 September 1864. When the crime was committed, however, Johnson was a member of the 5th.

Johnson was convicted of murder, assault with intent to kill, and conduct prejudicial to good order and military discipline. The use of the phrase "conduct prejudicial" is usually employed when the murder victim was an officer. There is no record of whom Johnson murdered.

### 2 September 1864

While the 2nd Tennessee Heavy Artillery was on post and garrison duty 10 July 1863, at Columbus, Kentucky, and Union City, Tennessee, SELDON S. CHANDLER, 39, a resident of Enfield, Connecticut, deserted.

A "soldier" by profession, Chandler had enlisted for the duration 1 November 1862.

He was apprehended a year after he deserted, 21 July 1864, and was court-martialed and convicted.

Seldon Chandler was shot to death near Petersburg, Virginia, 2 September 1864. By that time, his unit had been reorganized as the 4th Heavy Artillery, Regulars.

### 9 September 1864

JAMES WILLIAMS, 29, a South Carolina carpenter, joined the Union Army 10 October 1863, at Natchez, Mississippi. Enlisting for three years, Williams was quickly promoted to corporal.

While his unit, Company G, 6th Heavy Artillery, USCT, was on duty at Natchez and Vidalia, Louisiana, Williams committed murder — in all probability of a civilian. He was confined in a Natchez jail from 6 March 1864 until his trial. He was tried by general court-martial, found guilty, and shot to death 9 September 1864.

The case of WILLIAM C. DOWDY, 22, a Tennessee blacksmith and a private in Company E, 1st Regiment U. S. Volunteers, is a most unusual one: he was convicted of being absent without leave, while aboard the steamer *Effie Deans*, on the Missouri River. He never left the ship.

On 5 September 1864, Captain Justus Fairchild, of Company E, received information from a non-commissioned officer that Dowdy was planning to desert,

> hearing of that I intended to watch him which I did nearly all night. One part of the night I was lying down near the gun on the Starboard side of the boat this man Dowdy & McBride of the same company came from the place where they had been sleeping near the foot of the stairs. That being a place well sheltered from the rain. They passed me and laid down by the side of the gun. then raining very hard just then I got up and the Lieut of the Guard came along with the lantern. I took the lantern and went to where they were laying. I supposed they must have recognized me at this time for they immediately changed their position to the top of the wood pile. I stayed there about 15 minutes longer and then I left them. During the night Dowdy was seen by me in several different places on the boat, evidently with the intention of deserting.

On cross-examination at Dowdy's court-martial, the captain admitted that ". . . it was a little better (at the woodpile than it was up stairs) rain could beat in there as well as up stairs."

The situation of Dowdy and McBride shifting their positions to drier places on the steamer does not fit the usual description of absent without leave — or desertion. If Captain Fairchild felt their actions punishable, why was McBride not tried along with Dowdy?

The answer to that question rests with the other charge lodged against Dowdy: the use of seditious or disrespectful language.

Corporal Alexander Hardy, Captain Fairchild's informant, testified

> I have heard him speak respectfully in some cases and disrespectfully in some . . . When we were in Norfolk about the time we were starting on those raids, about 7 or 8 weeks ago . . . I have heard him say we had no right

to go on those expeditions that we did come in this army for that purpose . . . He is in the habit of using disrespectful language swearing and so on . . . I have heard him say that if anyone wanted to desert he did not care when they went as lief they would go one time as another. have heard him speak several times about men who have deserted the Regt . . . He would not blame the men for leaving for they were not treated as soldiers might be treated in several respects . . . .

Dowdy, it appears, was convicted simply because he complained incessantly about military life, not because he himself planned to desert. His griping was silenced by a firing squad 9 September 1864, two miles north of Florence, Nebraska Territory, on the Iowa side of the Missouri River.

### 15 September 1864

JOHN MITCHELL deserted the 3rd Regiment Mississippi Volunteers, 22 November 1863, while the unit was on garrison and post duty at Haines Bluff, Mississippi.

He was arrested and brought back to his unit, now the 53rd Infantry, USCT, 15 April 1864. Following a court-martial, he was shot to death at Vicksburg, 15 September 1864.

### 16 September 1864

SAMUEL W. DOWNING [aka John W. Ball] was executed by a firing squad 16 September at Alexandria, Virginia. Downing's case provides one of the fullest accounts extant of how bounty-jumpers operated.

At his court-martial, Downing stated he began his bounty-jumping career in July 1863, ten months after he enlisted, at Williamsport, Maryland. He then went to Greencastle, Pennsylvania, where he joined as a substitute 16 August, receiving $500; then on to New York City, receiving $375 as a substitute. In New York, a hot-bed of substitute brokers and bounty-jumpers, he was sent to Rikers Island "where I paid an Arty. Sergt. [$50] to let me go, which he did." Downing paid a boatman $5 to take him back to the city. There he went to another enlistment office 19 August, and became a substitute as John W. Ball for $375. He was again sent to Rikers where he paid the sergeant and the boatman the same amounts for his return to the city.

He left New York and traveled to Harrisburg, Pennsylvania, and became a substitute, using his own name, for $1,500. Sent to Camp Curtin, Downing bought a pass from a sergeant for $10, then went to Philadelphia.

On 7 September, he joined again — for $250. After being sent to the provost barracks, he bribed another sergeant with $30 to let him out. Three days later he was in Frankford, a section in Philadelphia, where he received $450. He returned to the same barracks where he gave the sergeant another $30. Tiring of the City of Brotherly Love, Downing went back to New York City.

On 15 September, he received a payment of $375. This time he was sent to Alexandria, Virginia. He arrived 24 September. To leave camp, he donned an officer's uniform and passed himself out. He changed into civilian clothes, paid $40 for a pass, and returned to New York City.

A week later, he rejoined the army — as a $375 substitute, was sent to Alexandria 8 October, and did it all over again. This time he tried Jersey City, substituting for $350. He was sent to Brandy Station at the end of the month. This time he didn't need to bribe anyone so he could return to New York, he merely walked away.

On 10 November, he went as a substitute for $375 and was sent to Alexandria. To leave, he purchased a $20 pass to Philadelphia.

Ten days later, he rejoined the service for $250, and paid off the sergeant of the guard with $30. He was off to New York again.

In mid-December, Downing was paid $375 and sent again to Alexandria. There he put on a naval officer's uniform, bought a $40 pass and visited Baltimore. Not finding anything interesting there, he traveled to Cincinnati, Ohio. Around the end of December, he joined for $300 and was told to report each day — which he didn't.

From 15 January-15 February, he stayed in Louisville, Kentucky, then went back to Cincinnati where he rejoined for $450, and was sent to a place near Fort Monroe. With $100 he bribed a chief engineer to hide him on a boat returning to Washington.

By mid-March, he was in Columbia, Maryland, and signing up for $250. He bribed the sergeant of the guard with $20, and went to Columbus, Ohio. On 1 April, he substituted for $700 and was sent to Alexandria. He paid the same sergeant $50, and $40 for a pass; then Downing went to Cincinnati. He was arrested there in mid-April.

The arresting officers sent him to Baltimore where he was confined in "the Slave Pens." At the end of June, he passed himself off as a doctor, left confinement, and became a substitute for $500. In Baltimore, the authorities sent him to the Express office — under guard, but he escaped. He remained in Baltimore until 7 July when he went to the provost marshal and "offered myself as a Substitute, but, was arrested by a Detective, who recognized me."

In the course of ten months, Downing picked up $7,750!

Downing, when confronted with the possibility of death, decided to name names: William Jones, a substitute broker in the Bowery; Jones got half the money, and was the reason for Downing's frequent returns to New York, and a Doctor Brown, who helped him in Columbus and Cincinnati, Ohio, and Columbia, Maryland. Records do not indicate that government authorities pursued the information, or took action against Downing's accomplices.

Samuel W. Downing was shot to death 16 September 1864 at Alexandria, Virginia.

Members of the US Colored Troops enjoy a moment of relaxation out-
side the US Provost Marshal's Guard House, Vicksburg, Miss. What thoughts
must have passed through their heads as they guarded other members of the
USCT who were confined for demanding equal pay?
*Massachusetts Commandery, Military Order of the Loyal Legion and the U. S. Army Military*
*History Institute.*

*20 September 1864*

JOHN SWENEY [Swenney, Sweeney], 21, was a laborer from England who deserted the Confederate army and entered Union service in Company C, 1st Maryland Infantry, as a substitute for Obadiah S. Layton.

Sweney deserted the 1st Maryland, and rejoined the Confederacy; only to be captured — and recognized. He was court-martialed, and sentenced to be shot.

Though Charles Camper, in his *Historical Record of the First Regiment Maryland Infantry*, wrote that "It was while the preliminary arrangements for his execution were in progress that the enemy made the attack on the picket lines . . . ," Sweney was executed according to schedule 20 September 1864, near Fort Hughes, opposite the Yellow House.

*21 September 1864*

Sergeant GEORGE W. McDONALD [aka M. M. Dunning] was allegedly executed for desertion and attempted murder 21 September 1864, as a member of Company F, 3rd Maryland Infantry.

The National Archives has no record of the man, under either name.

*25 September 1864*

Sergeant GILES SIMMS, a Mississippi field hand and a member of Company F, 49th Infantry, USCT, and WASHINGTON TONTINE, Company F, 40th Infantry, USCT, were both listed as being executed for mutiny. Simms joined the regiment 3 June 1863, at Milliken's Bend, Louisiana. Three days later, he was wounded in the battle at that site. A year later, he stood in front of a court-martial, accused of having "mutinied and stacked arms . . . ." Tontine's records, on the other hand, were not found in National Archives files. Both were supposedly shot to death at Vicksburg, 25 September 1864.

EDWARD EASTMAN, 19, a farmer from Bolivar County, Mississippi, was a member of Company B, 2nd Missouri Artillery, when he was accused of "leaving his colors to pillage in violation of the 52nd Article of War."

A general court-martial, Major Charles Bichte, 1st Infantry, presided, found him guilty. He was shot to death at Rolla, Missouri, 25 September 1864, for desertion and pillage. His execution was suspended 5 October by order of Major-General Rosecrans.[18] Both actions seem futile, since the man was executed a month earlier.

*30 September 1864*

WILLIAM I. LYNCH, 22, an Albany, New York, bricklayer, "Was arrested by members of his own company and afterwards escaped from Albany Barracks at least three times before the regiment went into the field," the "Descriptive List of Deserters Arrested" indicates for 27 July 1864.

> He escaped from David's Island N. Y. H. July 1862 and
> Sept. 25 1862 was arrested by officer J. Burt and a reward
> of $5 and $2.50 expenses was paid by Maj Sprague Mustg

& Dist Officer at Albany N. Y. He was then conveyed to Ft. McHenry Baltimore where he escaped & reached Albany, even before the officer who took him there. He was again arrested by officer N. Milliman on the 19th Dec. 1862 & $5 was paid by Major Sprauge. He was then taken to Washington D. C. whence he soon made his escape. On the 14th day of August he was brought to these Head Quarters & and on the 20th the same month was transferred to Fort Col, N. Y. H. A reward of $10 was paid for this arrest. Lynch succeeded in making his escape from Ft. Col in a few days. & on the 25th of August 1863 was rearrested and on the 27th of August was again sent to Ft. Col N. Y. H. & a reward of $10 was paid for the arrest. he again escaped & on the 22nd of Oct 1863 was again arrested & a reward of $30 paid for this arrest. The matter in detail was referred to the Pro. Mar. Genl. and an ordered returned that Lynch be sent direct to his regiment for trial. He was accordingly forwarded to his regiment on the 6th of Nov. 1863 he was then tried by court martial and sentenced to be shot. The sentence being approved by the President. The President was then petitioned & Lynch was pardoned & restored to duty. He re-enlisted was given a furlough of thirty days came home was paid his local bounty of $300 in this city & again deserted He was again arrested on or about the 10th inst. in Buffalo by my order and a reward of $30 paid for his arrest.

The provost marshal for the 14th District of New York did not want to have any more to do with this man. "The large amount of money [$90 in rewards; $2.50, expenses; and $300 in bounty] paid by the Government as rewards for his arrest," he wrote, "and the fact that he has never done any duty, make it still more necessary that every precaution should be taken, to make an example of this man, who has so shamefully abused the leniency of the President."

William "Polly" Lynch was sent to the nation's captial "in irons." He did not escape again. He was shot as a deserter from the 62nd New York in Washington, 30 September 1864. It is interesting to note that in a case of such blatant bounty-jumping Lincoln stayed the man's execution and restored him to duty, yet in cases where the evidence was not so clear-cut, amnesty was rejected.

### 7 October 1864

PETER KEIFFE, a 27-year-old Irish immigrant laborer, was a private in Company B, 2nd Arkansas Cavalry, when he was convicted of murdering a civilian in southwest Maryland.

Immediately upon his enlistment 1 July 1863, he was assigned to the 2nd Cavalry, stationed at Benton Barracks, Missouri.

While his unit was at Jefferson City, Keiffe was on a road when he was approached by a civilian, Friday, 5 August 1864, who asked: What regiment do you belong to?

When Keiffe told him, the civilian yelled "there are a damned lot of rebels in that regiment." Keiffe denied it. Then the man "called me a damned liar" and charged the soldier with a knife in his hand.

"I had a small knife in my pocket," Keiffe testified at his court-martial. "I opened its blade and stuck him with it. I then walked on five or six steps and he followed me. I turned around and stuck him again with my knife. I then left him and went into camp. When I arrived in camp." he acknowledged, "I told the boys what I had done, stating that I was justified in acting as I did."

On cross examination, Keiffe indicated the man was still alive and standing when he left him.

There were no witnesses to the confrontation — only a dead civilian. The court-martial panel found Peter Keiffe guilty of murder. He was shot at Springfield, Missouri, 7 October 1864.

### 14 October 1864

CHARLES MERLING [Merlin, Milling], 25, a Welsh sailor, entered Union service as a substitute for Edwin Nicholas and became part of Company H, 2nd Maryland Infantry.

During the siege of Petersburg, Merling attempted to desert, and was apprehended. He was court-martialed, Lieutenant-Colonel William F. Draper, 36th Massachusetts Volunteers, was president, and convicted.

Merling was shot to death near Hancock Station, Virginia, 14 October 1864. The Adjutant General's Office lists the man as a deserter, though his court-martial conviction was for attempted desertion.

### 28 October 1864

JEFFERSON JACKSON, 22, a member of Company B, 9th Missouri State Mounted Cavalry, enlisted 20 January 1862 for the duration.

His service record indicates he was in arrest since 27 August 1864, so that crime he committed — murder, probably of a civilian — had to take place shortly before that time.

His execution was postponed, and the local newspapers suggested that he had committed other murders and was actually a member of the Confederate Army.

Brigadier-General C. B. Fisk, commanding the District of Central Missouri, had better knowledge than did the journalists. In a telegram to Colonel J. V. Dubois, the general called Jackson "one of the best soldiers but in a fit of intoxication committed the deed . . . he is of good family & his mother earnestly desires for him to have more time to prepare for death . . . ."

His mother's wish was granted, and Jefferson Jackson's appearance before a firing squad at St. Joseph, Missouri, was not held until 28 October 1864.

JOHN VELON, 20, a substitute for Samuel Russell and a member of Company G, 5th New Hampshire Infantry, was a Prussian peddler.

Little more than a month after he joined the unit, Velon "deserted his post on picket in front of 1st Div, 2nd Army Corps," 27 September 1864, during the seige of Petersburg. Authorities felt he deserted with the "intention of going to the enemy."

Velon was tried by general court-martial, Lieutenant-Colonel William Wilson presided, found guilty and convicted. He was shot to death near Petersburg 18 October 1864 — he had been in the Union Army slightly more than two months.

### 4 November 1864

There is some confusion as to how HENRY HAMILTON, 23, a private in Company I, 2nd Infantry, USCT, died.

If one relies on the Adjutant General's report, Hamilton was shot to death for mutiny 4 November 1864, at Key West, Florida. His company muster rolls suggest this is the case, since it lists him in arrest February-October 1864. General orders were cut, calling for the man's execution, based on the results of a general court-martial, presided over by Major Benjamin R. Townsend.[20]

On the other hand, a note located in Hamilton's service file — from Assistant Surgeon J. M. Wertz to Brigadier-General Thomas — states: "It becomes my duty to inform you that [Hamilton] died at this Hospital as herein detailed, and that it is desired his remains should be interred with the usual military honors."

Executed soldiers do not receive "usual military honors" when they are buried. Is it possible Dr. Wertz had the wrong man under his care? There was not, however, another Henry Hamilton in the 2nd Infantry, USCT. Did Dr. Wertz merely use a military cliche? What was the man doing in a military hospital? Execution by musketry did not produce a lingering ailment. In all previous cases of military execution, the men were either buried where they fell — or their remains were shipped home for burial, never sent to a hospital for a final opinion.

According to Company I's muster roll, Hamilton's grave — or that of someone else — is located southwest of Key West.

### 10 November 1864

JOSEPH PREVOST [Provost], 25, a Canadian seaman, joined Company A, 1st [New York] Lincoln Cavalry 16 August 1861. As soon as he was mustered out — 31 December 1863 — he reenlisted as a Veteran Volunteer.

Within a few months, Prevost was accused and convicted, by military commission, of the murder of a civilian: Christian Miller, of Morgan County, West Virginia.

Though tried by the military, Prevost was executed "at Cumberland [Maryland] by civil authorities . . ." 10 November 1864. Prevost's was the only recorded execution not conducted by military personnel.

CHARLES LOCKMAN, 31, a former miller from Cammance Kingdom, Saxony, enlisted in the 2nd Colorado Cavalry 18 September 1862. Two years later, he was hanged by members of his own company . . . for the alleged murder of a Private John Groce.

The order to execute was given by Lieutenant William Wise, of Company D, while, official records state, while the unit was "7 miles s.w. of Leavenworth." What is ironic is that neither Lockman's nor Wise's companies were near Kansas either at the time of the crime or execution.

Since Lockman was convicted at drumhead, no records of evidence exist. Did Lockman actually commit murder? Were elements of the 2nd Colorado Cavalry enroute to Leavenworth at the time? Or did an execution take place, then records created?

### 11 November 1864

JOHN CARROLL, 34, a private in Company D, 20th Wisconsin Infantry, is listed in the Adjutant General's report as being executed for rape 11 November 1864, at Mobile Point, Alabama.

Company D's muster roll and the "Certificate of Service," on file at The State Historical Society of Wisconsin, contradict that charge.

According to those records, Carroll was reported absent without leave at New Orleans, since 25 August 1863.

On 31 March 1864, he was arrested and confined by the provost marshal of New Orleans. In W. J. Lemke's *Chaplain Edward Gee Miller of the 20th Wisconsin: His War 1862-1865*, the chaplain's diary for 12 November notes: "John Carroll . . . was shot to death with musketry at 12 o'clock M — for crimes committed in Brownsville, Texas."

Four sources agree that John Carroll died — but for what?

### 25 November 1864

Because of CHARLES WILLIAMS' unique status as an unassigned recruit in the USCT, it is impossible to determine the circumstances of his case, other than to accept the Adjutant General's report that he was shot to death for murder 25 November 1864.

"The man was sent to this post in a filthy condition," Colonel N. B. Bartram wrote Captain Frederick Speed 27 November 1864, "but was provided by Capt. Wage CPM and Mr. Levere Chaplan of the 20th USCT with an opportunity to bathe and some clean clothing . . . ." The implication was quite clear: don't let it happen again.

The man in question, JAMES QUINN, Company A, 11th Heavy Artillery, USCT, enlisted for three years at Providence, Rhode Island, 28 August 1863. He left Camp Parapet, Louisiana, "on the afternoon of June 15, 1864 and remained absent until 9 O'C AM June 16 absenting himself from two roll calls, and sleeping out of his quarters in violation of the 42nd Article of War." Quinn pleaded guilty to both charges at a regimental court-martial, and during September and October he was "in arrest awaiting sentence."

According to the Adjutant General's report, Quinn was executed for murder. His file does not show any evidence of a murder conviction; in fact, his casualty sheet shows the causes of his execution as absent without leave and violation of the 42nd Article of War.

However, a letter from Cornelius W. Harris, 20th Infantry, USCT, states:

> We had a sad lesson showed us on the 25th of November; one of the Twelfth colored privates shot one of the sergeants with a pistol, and killed him dead on the spot: so he was tried and court-martialed, and sentenced to be shot to death by musketry. . . . Poor fellow, he did not know that he had to be shot until three hours before he was tied to the stake of execution. He was from Philadelphia: he ran away from home . . . .[21]

According to Quinn's enlistment record, he was born in Baltimore, Maryland, and, in civilian life, was a seaman. Is it possible that the man Harris wrote about was actually Charles Williams? If so, it would clear up one mystery.

### 2 December 1864

"Merritt burned down to river yesterday and is now on his return," Brigadier-General John D. Stevenson wrote Major-General Philip H. Sheridan, at Harpers Ferry, 1 December 1864. "I have not heard what he did beyond destruction of property. My command in gaps report no attempt of enemy to pass through. I caught yesterday French Bill, a notorious murderer and bushwacker belonging to White's battalion, who was with the party that murdered the surgeon of the Sixth Pennsylvania Cavalry. He is a deserter from the Sixty-first New York Infantry."[22]

Sheridan wired back: "As soon as you have fully ascertained that you have French Bill as your prisoner take him out and hang him. This will be your authority."[23]

Stevenson's response was quick: "I have undoubtedly French Bill. He will be hanged at 2 p.m. tomorrow."[24]

But who was this French Bill? According to the Adjutant General's report, his real name was WILLIAM LOGE, but that is all that is known about him. The muster rolls for the 6th Pennsylvania Cavalry do not list a Loge as a member of that unit.

Captain D. Henry Burknette, in correspondence to Stevenson, suggests French Bill was a member of another unit . . .

> French Bill, of Mobberly's freebooters, was yesterday taken by Keyes men, I understand; if so, he is an important capture, as he is a deserter from the 28th New York Volunteer Infantry . . . Colonel Root, of 15th New York Cavalry, now at Pleasant Valley, will furnish you evidence against French Bill; also a clerk in the employ of Mr. Bush, who was sutler for 28th Regiment. I will bring him to Harpers Ferry.[25]

There was no William Loge in the 28th — or in the records of the National Archives. The best guess is that William Loge was actually a citizen . . . and not a soldier.

French Bill was hanged 2 December 1864 "in accordance with orders."[26]

### 8 December 1864

WILLIAM HENDERSON, 25, a Virginia "hosseler" and a private in Company B, 66th Infantry, USCT, was convicted of murder by a general court-martial, Lieutenant-Colonel George Simpson, 66th Infantry, USCT, presided, at St. Charles, Arkansas, 21 November 1864.

Henderson had enlisted in the unit 17 December 1863, at Vicksburg, Mississippi. His service record is sketchy, but it can be ascertained he did not have a blemish on his record — other than a February 1864 stay in a smallpox hospital.

The murder, probably of another soldier, took place while the unit was on post and garrison duty at Little Rock.

Henderson was shot to death 8 December 1864.

### 10 December 1864

EDWARD ROWE, 21, a Massachusetts clerk, and DANIEL C. SMITH, 21, a New York boatman, joined Company C, 179th New York Infantry, at Elmira, New York, 12 April 1864. They were each paid a $25 bounty.

During the seige of Petersburg, both men deserted 15 October "to the enemy." Quickly apprehended, the men were convicted by general court-martial, and hanged 10 December 1864.

Three months later [16 March 1865], Colonel George D. Ruggles, assistant adjutant general, authorized disinterrment of Smith's remains, to be "sent to commanding officer, 9th Corps." It is likely that Smith's body was returned to his family for proper burial.

### 15 December 1864

On 11 June 1875, a request from C. A. Woodward, chief clerk of the Colored Troops Branch, was made for the "Cause of confinement trial sentence" of ALEXANDER VESS, formerly a private in Company E, 3rd Regiment USCT Heavy Artillery.

Woodward's reply didn't answer his question:

> Co. Desc. Book, Co. "E" repts: "Private Alexander Vess Died Decr 16/64. Executed by hanging, sentence of G. C. M. No additional information. Source and date of Order promulating sentence are not given. The Order promulgating sentence in this case is not on file with General

Orders, Dist of Memphis, Dist of West Tenn, Dept, Army of Tennessee, or Co. and Regt records. Records of Prisoners confined in Fort Pickering, covering date are incomplete and furnish no information in this case.''

Though there is no concrete evidence on Vess [also Vass and Ness], his crime or his trial, the Adjutant General's report states he was hanged for murder 15 December 1864, in pursuance of a general court-martial order.[27] Further research in his file indicates that Vess actually received a drumhead — not a general — court-martial, and was executed by order of Major J. Williams, his regimental commander.

### 16 December 1864

As in the case of Henry Hamilton, as assistant surgeon requested the "usual military honors" for the burial of Private DARIUS STOKES, 23, Company I, 2nd Infantry, USCT, and a Baltimore seaman. Stokes, it must be mentioned, was in the same unit as Hamilton.

Stokes enlisted in the Union Army 10 October 1863; a month later he was promoted to 1st Sergeant. Another month passed, and he was reduced to ranks.

On 10 February 1864, he murdered John Waugh, of his company. Stokes was put under arrest and confined at Key West, Florida, until his general court-martial, Major Benjamin R. Townsend, presided, 26 November, though the general order calling for his execution is dated 15 October.

Darius Stokes was hanged at Key West 16 December 1864.

GEORGE W. [also R.] PRINCE, 31, 5th Sergeant in Company B, 22nd Ohio Infantry, enlisted 1 November 1861, but deserted his unit on or about 18/19 August 1862, at Corinth, Mississippi.

Arrested 19 October 1863, Prince escaped after he was delivered to Cattlettsburg, Kentucky, "or on his way to his regiment . . ." He was finally apprehended at Cincinnati, Ohio, 4 November 1863, and confined at Little Rock, Arkansas.

A general court-martial tried him, and he was found guilty. He was sentenced to death by musketry. Prince appealed his sentence, 22 November 1864, in a letter to Major-General F. Steele, commanding the Department of the Arkansas:

> . . . I cannot willingly and continually pass my few remaining days of living upon this earth without at least making one feeble effort to prolong any life which was dear to me as the life of any other of God's Creations . . .

> . . . I trust that in accordance with other cases Similar to mine if not of a more aggravated nature, . . . during my confinement. Some of them but for a short time. that my Sentance when compared to these Seems to be a very hard one.

Prince received no reply from General Steele. The Larence, Ohio, teamster and furnaceman was shot to death 16 December 1864.

According to the company description book, CHARLES HUMMEL [Commel], 20, a German laborer and saddle maker and a private in Company E, 7th New York Veteran Infantry, was mustered out with his unit 4 August 1865 — eight months after he was allegedly shot to death near Fort Wheaton, near Petersburg, Virginia.

Hummel is listed on the muster roll as being absent without leave since 30 October 1864, but marked present in November and December. There are no records to show that he, in fact, was executed. Hummel was, however, listed in Special Order 600 which called for the executions of CHRISTOPHER SUHR, 24, a German laborer and a member of Hummel's unit, and JOHN THOMPSON, 19, an English boatman and an unassigned recruit in the 5th New Hampshire Infantry.

Suhr, a substitute for Samuel Torey, of New York, deserted 18 October 1864 from picket duty during the seige of Petersburg; Thompson, a substitute for Edward E. Joslyn, of West Lebanon, New Hampshire, deserted 10 June 1864 "before Petersburg . . . to enemy lines while on picket." Suhr had been in Union service three months before his desertion; Thompson, eight.

Tried by general court-martial, Colonel Charles H. T. Collis, 114th Pennsylvania Volunteers presided, both men were convicted and sentenced to death. They were hanged 16 December 1864.

Part of the confusion over Hummel might rest with the case of WILLIAM KANE [aka William Carter], 25, a Canadian sailor and a substitute for T. S. Bondsall, of Baltimore. Kane, a member of Company A, 8th Maryland Infantry, deserted his unit 28 June 1864 during the seige. He was tried by the same general court-martial that convicted Suhr and Thompson. Perhaps he was the third man executed, rather than Hummel, since records show that three were hanged that day.

### 21 December 1864

Five firing squads of twelve men took aim at a group of five convicted deserters. They stood but twenty-five yards from their targets when they fired.

"We looked toward the graves," a New Hampshire soldier wrote,

> but to our astonishment each man yet remained standing, showing conclusively that the detail had fired high. The second or reserve detail was once marched into position . . . and at the same signal the smoke puffed from their carbines, and their fire proved more accurate, but not entirely effective. The prisoners all fell. Three were dead, while two were trying hard to rise again, and one of them even got upon his knees, when a bullet from the

revolver of the provost marshal sent him down. Again he attempted to rise, getting upon his elbow and raising his body nearly to a sitting posture, when a second bullet in the head from the marshal's revolver suddenly extinguished what little life was left and a third shot put out the life of the second prisoner.[28]

Thus ended the military careers of five members of Company G, 1st Connecticut Heavy Artillery. The men: THOMAS DIX, 22, an Irish umbrella maker; HENRY McCURDY [McCardy], 21, a New York joiner who had received a $100 bounty payment, and was owed $200; JOHN SMITH, 23, a Canadian boatsman who had received the same payments as had McCurdy; and JAMES THOMPSON, 21, an Irish laborer, all deserted their unit between 17 and 20 December 1864. JOHN HALL [apparently not his real name[29]], 37, a New York joiner, was accused of murder of another enlisted man. All five were tried by general court-martial on 20 December; orders were cut for their execution the next day, and they were executed.

Hall apparently left a sizable sum of money — $110. He asked that the money be sent to his father by the Rev. Smith, chaplain of the 8th Connecticut.

### 22 December 1864

WILLIAM M. SMITH, a private in Company C, 4th Regiment, U. S. Volunteers, deserted his unit while on duty at Portsmouth, Virginia. Tried by court-martial, he was shot to death 22 December 1864.

### 23 December 1864

Sieges are nerve-wracking experiences for the soldiers assigned to duty during those periods. The uncertainty of what — or when something — will happen can wreak havoc on troop morale. The siege of Petersburg was no exception. Of all the engagements of the Union Army, Petersburg took the greatest toll in the form of repeated desertions — and executions.

JAMES LYNCH [aka John Wood], 21, a St. Johns, New Brunswick, machinist and substitute for David W. Richardson, of Sanbornton, New Hampshire; WILLIAM MILLER [aka James Craig], 20, an Irish dyer and a substitute for Romano Creney, of Chesterfield, New Hampshire; and GEORGE BRADLEY [aka George Bates], 24, a Canadian farmer and substitute for E. A. Shaw, of Concord, New Hampshire, were all members of the 5th New Hampshire Infantry — Lynch and Miller, Company F; Bradley, Company H — when they deserted.

JOHN C. DIXON, 21, a Canadian boot crimper, and a private in Company H, 1st Massachusetts Heavy Artillery, joined at Concord, Massachusetts, 18 August 1864 for a paid bounty of $100; $200 due.

Lynch deserted 10 October; Miller and Bradley, 15 October; and Dixon, 21 November. Each received a general court-martial: Lynch, Miller, and Bradley were tried by a panel with Colonel Charles H. T. Collis as president; Dixon's trial was presided over by Lieutenant-Colonel C. H. Wygant, 124th New York Volunteers.

M | 11   **Cav.** Ind

*John Murray*

Appears with rank of ...... *Pvt* ...... on

**Muster and Descriptive Roll of a Detach-**
**ment of U. S, Vols. forwarded**

for the *11* Reg't *Ind* Cavalry. Roll dated

*La Fayette, Ind Nov 22*, 1864

Where born *Dublin, Ireland*

Age *27* y'rs; occupation *Laborer*

When enlisted *Nov 22*, 1864

Where enlisted *La Fayette, Ind*

For what period enlisted *one* years.

Eyes *Black*; hair *Black*

Complexion *Fair*; height *5* ft. *5 3/4* in.

When mustered in *Nov 22*, 1864

Where mustered in *La Fayette, Ind*

Bounty paid $ ...... 200; due $ ...... 100

Where credited ......

Company to which assigned ......

Valuation of horse, $ ...... 100

Valuation of horse equipments, $ ...... 100

Remarks : *8 C. D. Cam Ap.,*
*Fountain Co.*
*Entitled to Bounty,*
*Not taken up on Co. Rolls*
*of Regt.*

Book mark : ......

*Price*

(389)            *Copyist*

    **John Murray, an unassigned recruit to the 11th Indiana Cavalry, apparently joined the Union Army for the bounty. A look at the "Muster and Descriptive Roll" indivates that he never received it. The roll also indicates he was a native of Dublin, Ireland.**
*National Archives*

Eleven regiments were paraded out to watch as Lynch, Miller and Bradley were hanged near Fort Wheaton, 23 December 1864. Dixon was shot to death the same day on the left of the Halifax Road, near the Lewis House, near Petersburg.

CHARLES BILLINGSBY [also spelled Billingsley; aka Roberts Cooper and Miller Billingsly], 18, an Indiana farmer; JOHN MURRAY [aka John or Jonathan Murry], 27, an Irish laborer; and THOMAS RYAN [aka John Reagen and Patrick Ryan] were executed at Camp Burnside, Indianapolis, 23 December 1864.

Billingsby, according to William R. Hartpence in his *History of the Fifty-First Indiana Veteran Volunteer Infantry*, was a bounty-jumper who enlisted in the 7th Indiana Battery at Indianapolis 23 March 1864. Not long after his enlistment, he deserted. Apprehended at Chattanooga, Tennessee, and court-martialed, Billingsby was paroled. He again deserted and went to Louisville, Kentucky, where he again was caught. Upon questioning, Hartpence relates, Billingsby refused to tell how many times he had deserted, "but substantially admitted a number of times." He also, according to Hartpence, confessed to the murder of a woman and her child.

O. H. Morgan, who signed himself "late Capt, 7th Ind. Battery," wrote the presiding officer of Billingsby's court-martial 17 December 1864 that he read in the newspaper that the man had been tried and convicted of bounty jumping.

> As he is a deserter from my Battery or rather from the Div. Pro. Marshall, while awaiting the publication of the action of a Court Martial in his case. I have concluded to advise you of it. His case is an aggravated one "committing rape on a defenceless woman." while our army was near Dallas Ga., last summer and I hoped he would receive his reward ere this; he deserted the day his trial closed and rumor has it that he went over to the enemy but of that I cannot speak definitely.

Notwithstanding the rumors or supposed confessions, Billingsby was tried only for desertion.

John Murray's case also has allusions to murder. In fact, his casualty sheet lists murder as his convicted crime. His court-martial offense, as specified in General Order 38, District of Indiana, 14 December 1864, is desertion. Hartpence indicates Murray joined Company G, 131st, 13th Cavalry, for one year. He deserted 22 March 1864, the night of his arrival at Camp Carrington, Indiana, and was arrested on a sleeping car enroute to Chicago. Murray's enlistment record, however, lists him as joining 22 November. Was it possible that the man deserted before he enlisted? Or was he too a bounty-jumper?

Thomas Ryan's service records could not be found in the National Archives, under any assortment of spellings or aliases. Hartpence is the only reference. He alleges that Ryan enlisted in the 51st, then deserted by bribing a guard to let him out of camp. He was supposed to have received $433.50 in bounties.

When arrested, he denied being in the military, but he was identified by Colonel A. D. Streight and others. When confronted with this information, he admitted that he had not jumped bounty more than once before. To his friends, Hartpence relates, Ryan confided he had jumped a total of thirty times.

It is possible that all three men were bounty-jumpers — plus a John Doyle who, according to Hartpence, received a presidential pardon. The records do not indicate any extenuating circumstances.

At their execution, held at Camp Burnside, the three were indifferent to the reading of the death sentence. Ryan, in particular, had his mind on something else. Hartpence noted he occasionally glanced "over his shoulder at the bank to his rear, as if he expected something from the quarter."

When a non-commissioned officer blindfolded the men, Ryan, in the middle of the group, "threw his head back, as if he were trying to see under the bandage . . . The hammers of the guns fell so unitedly, that no individual sound was distinguished. As the white smoke curled away from the guns, Ryan fell squarely back on his coffin, and died apparently without moving a muscle.

"This ended a strange and fearful scene," Hartpence decided, "which had not before witnessed an Indiana unit." An impressive feature of the execution, he felt, was the attendance of one hundred bounty-jumpers confined at the Soldiers' Home. They had been invited to witness the executions so they

> might be impressed with the enormity of the crime they stood charged with. They were placed inside of the line of soldiers, where they had a full view of all that occurred. This was a terrible lesson to the "bounty-jumpers," and contributed greatly in breaking up the infamous business in Indiana.

### 26 December 1864

JAMES F. BROWN, 23, a Lancaster, New Hampshire teamster, joined Company G, 3rd New Hampshire Infantry, for a premium of $62 paid; $240 due, 2 December 1863.

Though enlistment records indicate he did not enter until 1863, correspondence in his file presents evidence to the contrary.

On 27 August 1862, Captain G. B. Brunt, 47th New Hampshire Volunteers, provost marshal, responded to a critical letter from the commanding officer of the 3rd New Hampshire Volunteers, by requesting help of the assistant adjutant general, Lieutenant Edward W. Smith:

> I would respectfully call your attention to the following
> — on the 12th of July 1862, there was confined in my
> charge, Private James F. Brown, Co. G, 3rd Regt. N.
> H. V., charges against whom were filed in your office.
> On the 21st of July the above prisoner was sent to Genl.
> Hospital, by order of the Surgeon attending, approved
> by the Medical Director; he was yesterday called for by
> the Judge Advocate of the C. Martial now in session, and
> when called for at Hospital, I was informed that he had
> been sent to Genl Hospital, New York. As we have no
> Hospital accomodations to send prisoners to Genl.
> Hospital, on order of the Surgeon, but supposed they
> would be found there when called for, and returned to
> us as well, unless released as a prisoner by proper authori-
> ty. Considering the sending away of the above prisoner
> improper, I beg leave to lay the matter before you for
> your consideration and wait Instructions.

There were no instructions during the Civil War as to what to do with a hospitalized soldier once he required additional attention, or had recovered. Surgeons took it upon themselves to release men, even those with courts-martial hearings hanging over their heads.

Brown was accused of deserting the 3rd 22/23 June 1863, near Wilcox Landing, Virginia. He was apprehended 11 or 18 December 1864 at Laurel Hill, Virginia, in the 47th New York Volunteers. Apparently Brown had joined that unit as a substitute.

He was tried by general court-martial, Colonel J. C. Abbott, 7th New Hampshire Volunteers, president, and convicted of desertion. He was shot to death at Richmond, 26 December 1864.

In 1885, questions were raised about Brown's execution, and the explanation given was that he "was apparently wounded in the head, arrived 2 Aug [1864] at 51st St. Hospital. From the hospital he seemed to have gone to another unit . . . ."[30]

But what about the discrepancies in the dates? There does not seem to be a logical solution. The 1862 letters coincide with the facts in the case, but not the dates. The answer, perhaps, is buried with the persons who tried Brown.

### 30 December 1864

LARKIN D. RHEA [Ray], 19, an illiterate Tennessee farmer, enlisted in the 7th Kentucky Infantry in Jackson County, Kentucky, 14 August 1861, and was honorably discharged due to "fulfilled enlistment."

During that first enlistment, he deserted near Raymond, Mississippi, 11 May 1863, but was captured the next day in Jackson. Returned to his unit later that month, Rhea was reinstated by general court-martial 1 February 1864. In the spring, he reenlisted.

Though his court-martial file is lost, Rhea was accused of murder, and sentenced to death by hanging. He was executed 30 December 1864.

MICHAEL GENAN [Jenos, aka John Martin], 21, was a substitute for William A. Batchelder, of Andover, New Hampshire, in Company B, 5th New Hampshire Infantry.

A farmer from St. Paul, Canada, Genan deserted his unit 11 October 1864 "to the enemy on picket before Petersburg . . . ."

Apprehended at Lexington, Kentucky, he was tried by a general court-martial, Colonel H. T. Collis, 114th Pennsylvania Volunteers was president, and convicted of desertion.

He was shot to death near Petersburg 30 December 1864, in front of eleven regiments.

# ENDNOTES TO CHAPTER EIGHT

1. General Order 23, Department of New Mexico, 31 December 1863.

2. *OR*, III, 5, p. 926.

3. *OR*, I, 5, p. 144-45.

4. GO 56, Department of Virginia & North Carolina, 4 May 64.

5. The entry date is actually one day off.

6. War Records Office, New Jersey Department of Defense.

7. Very few black soldiers acknowledged being slaves prior to enlistment. The occupations listed usually indicate the labor they performed in their earlier servitude.

8. *OR*, I, 35, Part 1, p. 66.

9. *OR*, I, 34, Part 1, p. 1054-56.

10. Letters, Alan J. Sessarego, Gettysburg, Penna., to the author, dated 14 November 1981 and 8 March 1984.

11. Letters, William Gladstone, Westport, Conn., to the author, dated 10 May 1983 and 11 March 1984.

12. Very Rev. William Corby, C.S.C., *Memoirs of Chaplain Life: Three Years Chaplain in the Famous "Irish Brigade," Army of the Potomac* [Notre Dame, 1894]

13. Quoted in Alfred S. Roe, *The Twenty-Fourth Regiment, Massachusetts Volunteers 1861-1866, "New England Guard Regiment* (Worcester, Mass., 1907) pp. 424-32.

14. *Ibid.*

15. Members of the anti-draft movement from Columbia County, Penna., nicknamed the "Fishing Creek Confederacy," were arrested and brought to Fort Mifflin, principally to witness the execution. Whether Howe's execution was the cause is in doubt, but the anti-draft movement in Columbia County virtually disappeared.

16. If the planned effort of Howe's execution was the threat of similar punishment to other offenders, it was unsuccessful. The morning after his execution, a number of men confined at the fort, escaped to freedom.

17. A detailed account of Howe's trials and punishment can be found in Robert I. Alotta, *Stop the Evil: A Civil War History of Desertion and Murder* (San Rafael, Calif., 1978).

18. Special Order 276, Headquarters, Department of Missouri, 5 October 1864.

19. Special Order 296, 25 October 1864.

20. General Order 132, Division of the Gulf, 18 September 1864.

21. Quoted in Lydia Minturn Post, ed., *Soldiers' Letters, From Camp, Battlefield and Prison*, [New York, 1865]

22. *OR*, I, 43, P 2, p. 72.

23. *Ibid.*

24. *Ibid.*

25. *OR, op. cit.*

26. *OR*, I, 43, P 2, p. 727.

27. General Court-martial Order 259, Adjutant General's Office, 9 July 1864.

28. James I. Robinson, "Military Executions," *Civil War Times Illustrated*, 1966, 5(2), pp. 34-39.

29. In a letter from Captain A. B. Sharpe to Lieutenant H. P. Mitchell, assistant provost marshal, Department of Virginia and North Carolina, 23 December 1864, Sharpe states that Hall "gave the Chaplain his true name and his father's address, and desired him to forward the money to his father . . . ."

30. Soldiers Relief Association Book, 7, p. 44. Casualty sheet signed W. S. Burton, 17 July 1885.

# CHAPTER NINE

## 1865:
### *". . . I do not interfere further . . . ."*

*3 January 1865*

JOHN FOSTER, 19, a Canadian horseman and a substitute for William E. McCall, 13th Ward, 3rd Congressional District, in the 58th Pennsylvania Infantry, deserted during the siege of Petersburg.

WILLIAM G. JOHNSON, 26, a Trenton, New Jersey, laborer, was honorably discharged as a private, 6th U. S. Infantry, 4 October 1863 . . . due to a disability. Thirteen months later, the disability "since removed," Johnson enlisted [16 November 1864] in Company F, 21st Regiment Veteran Reserve Corps, at Philadelphia. Two weeks later, he deserted from Philadelphia. Fact supports his desertion, not "aiding in desertion" as described in the Adjutant General's 1885 report.

John Foster and William G. Johnson were shot to death 3 January 1865.

*5 January 1865*

CHARLES KING, 26, a German machinist, and HENRY REGLEY [also Regly, Rigle or Rugby], 27, a Swiss clerk were enlisted members of Company L, 3rd New Jersey Cavalry, joining in 1864.

> Both were considered by General Sheridan to be spies . . . having been arrested in attempting to desert and having given information to one of the Staff Officers of the location of troops and all changes of troops with great accuracy, supposing the Staff Officer to be a rebel, and afterwards exchanging their own United States uniform for that of the rebel uniform.

King apparently did not spend too much time soldiering, as his company muster roll indicates. He was listed present for duty February, March,

**A look at his certificate of enlistment indicates that Pvt. Charles H. King [Co. L, 3rd New Jersey Cavalry] was a native of Germany. Unfortunately, too few individual service record files contain copies of the certificate.**

*National Archives*

and April of 1864, though a notation for March/April indicates "$30 for apprehension as a deserter to be stopped, also a pistol and belt"; May and June, he was "absent dismounted"; July and August, "absent sick"; September and October, "absent wounded." He was, nonetheless, present November and December.

Regley, on the other hand, had been present for duty October 1864.

Both men were shot at the orders of General Sheridan and Major-General Alfred T. A. Torbett, 5 January 1865, without benefit of court-martial.

At the time of his death, King had "received from the U. S. CLOTHING amounting to $95.36, since 23 December 1863, when his clothing account was last settled. He has received from the U. S. $25 advanced bounty . . . ." He also owed the sutler $18.

### 6 January 1865

LEWIS ROARCH [Roark], 21, a Kentucky laborer, served with the 7th Kentucky Infantry from 19 August 1861 to 16 March 1864. Then he reenlisted for three more years.

In late October or early November 1864, Roarch committed some criminal offense: the Adjutant General's Office report indicates murder; his casualty sheet, desertion.

Whichever the crime, Roarch was executed 6 January 1865. How? A question remains: The Adjutant General indicates he was hanged; his casualty sheet, he was shot.

WATERMAN THORNTON, 40, a Canadian laborer and a private in Company E, 179th New York Infantry, "was captured in Action Sept 30th 1864 at the Peebles House, Va." In a letter dated 4 January 1865, to Major-General Jonathan G. Parker, Thornton stated the circumstances surrounding his alleged desertion.

> After some days retention as a prisoner of war, & changing hands different times, it happened through omission of vigilance on the part of my enemies, that the opportunity of escaping presented itself to me by misrepresenting myself to be a refugee [In an early, almost illegible note, Waterman wrote: ". . . I told I was a Deserter . . . ."], which I much preferred, rather than linger in the loathsome Prisons of the South.

Following two weeks of Confederate confinement, Thornton and a number of other men were escorted through the lines into the interior of Kentucky. "After which I reported myself to the Provost Marshall of Post at Louisa Ky preparatory to being forwarded to my Command," he wrote, "but to my astonishment found myself confronted and falsely accused before the Pro Mar aforesaid by an escaped prisoner who was captured the same day I was made prisoner . . . ."

Thornton had received a $600 bounty when he joined the army 27 August 1864.

Thornton, along with JOHN BENSON, 21, a Canadian laborer and unassigned recruit in the 5th New Hampshire; 2nd Sergeant PETER COX, of Company A, 4th New Jersey Infantry; and MICHAEL WERT, 38, a Pennsylvania laborer and a member of Company G, 184th Pennsylvania Infantry, was hanged near Petersburg, 6 January 1865.

Of the four men, Peter Cox did not have the profile of other Civil War deserters. He enlisted 9 August 1861, and received promotions to corporal, sergeant, and 2nd sergeant. He transferred to Company A, 31 December 1863, and was mustered out near Brandy Station, Virginia, 19 March 1864. He reenlisted as a veteran volunteer the next day.

At the battle of Bull Run, Corporal Cox, along with a company officer, a Lieutenant Wright, and nine other men, went to Colonel E. P. Scammon, commander of the 1st Provincial Brigade, Kanawha Division, "appearing to be indignant at the conduct of the brigade, and asked to be led back to the enemy." Colonel Scammon ordered them to report to "Colonel White, at the bridge . . . I beg that they may be suitably rewarded, and that Captain Durham and Lieutenant Wright be promoted for their gallantry."[1]

While on furlough in Camden, New Jersey, his time expired and he was persuaded by a Canadian to accompany him to Canada.

> I staid there about Five months, and then hired on a Vessell to go to St. Thomas W. I. but instead of going there, the vessell ran into Wilmington N. C. I was in that place near 3 weeks. I gave myself up to the Confederate authorities, and told them I was a Deserter from the Union Army, but that I had no intention of coming in their lines.

Cox was released in Union lines, along with a group of other prisoners, including the men with whom he would die.

John Benson, 21, a Canadian laborer, entered Union service as a substitute for Zebulen Converse, at West Lebanon, New Hampshire, 6 August 1864. He received a bounty of $250.

While a group of recruits were preparing to board the train to join the regiment, Benson and another man

> got permission to get some water, and while we were gone, the cars left us; we were afraid of being put in the Bull Pen, so we went out in the Woods and staid all night, next morning we Started for Norfolk, Va, and when about 15 miles down we met 3 Rebel Scouts. We started

to Run, but the Scouts Shot at us, and Killed a man named Williams who was with me; they then took me prisoner and Robbed me of my Boots and Money, then they took me to Genl Fitz Hugh Lee, whom I told I was a Yankee Deserter . . . .

Benson was sent to Petersburg and then to Richmond, where he was confined in Castles Thunder and Lightning. When released, he reported to the provost marshal at Louisa, Kentucky, and joined the other three men.

Private Michael Wert, 38, Company G, 184th Pennsylvania Infantry, a Pennsylvania laborer, did desert — intentionally — while on picket duty near Petersburg 7 December 1864. Wert was the man Thornton alleged to be a liar — for whatever purpose — at his court-martial.

The four men received separate general courts-martial, with Colonel Charles H. T. Collis, 114th Pennsylvania Volunteers, as president. They were found guilty and hanged 6 January 1865.

## 7 January 1865

Abuses of Secretary Stanton's substitute system have been covered in countless studies of the Civil War, but nowhere do we find a situation like this. In the case of JAMES COLLINS, 21, an Irish boatman, the abuses are unique. Collins was a substitute for a substitute!

Collins joined the 8th Connecticut Infantry 17 November 1864 as a substitute for Henry D. Brainard who himself was a substitute for Charles Miller. Both men were from Hartford.

One month after he joined Company D, Collins deserted his unit at Chapins Farm, Virginia, while the Union was engaged in the sieges against Petersburg and Richmond. He was quickly apprehended and presented to a general court-martial 7 December 1864. One month later, he was shot "in the field," near Fort Harrison, Virginia, "in front of the works," along with WILLIAM DIX [Dicks]. The two bodies were then "carried outside of line."

Dix, 19, a Canadian moulder, was a substitute for J. McMahon, of Bridgeport. Like Collins, Dix had deserted his unit — Company E — but on 9 December. Records do not indicate that the two men knew each other. Their only connection might have been death.

## 13 January 1865

EPHRAIM RICHARDSON, 16, a private in Company C, 21st Missouri Infantry, was the youngest man to be executed by military authorities during the Civil War. Along with ABRAHAM PURVIS, 18, a Missouri farmer and a private in Richardson's unit, Richardson was hanged for murder in the St. Louis jailyard 13 January 1865.

To enter the Union Army 16 November 1862, Richardson needed — and obtained — his guardian's consent. Purvis enlisted 20 February 1864, at St. Louis.

# United States Military Telegraph.

By Telegraph from *Washington*

Dated *Jan 24* 186*4*.

To *Lt Genl Grant*

*If newell W Root of first Conn Heavy artillery is under sentence of death please telegraph me briefly the circumstances*

*A Lincoln*

Abraham Lincoln's review of the situation surrounding the death sentence of Pvt. Newell W. Root [Co. H, 1st Connecticut Heavy Artillery] must have been a hurried study. Lincoln telegraphed General Grant on 24 January 1864; the next day Lincoln wrote that "he would not interfere . . . ."

*National Archives*

The two apparently met in camp and, in an undescribed incident, murdered a civilian. They were arrested in St. Louis 19 November 1864. They were court-martialed, convicted and executed.

### 27 January 1865

NEWELL W. ROOT [aka George W. Harris], 18, was a volunteer with the 1st Connecticut Heavy Artillery at Dutch Gap, Virginia, when he and a pair of friends decided to cross the river to get some grapes.

Once on the other side, they encountered a handful of rebels. Root and his friends told the Confederates they were deserters, though they had not intended to desert when they started across the river. Rumor around the Union Army was that the rebels took better care of deserters than prisoners of war.

The Confederate detachment took them before General George E. Pickett's adjutant general where they repeated their desertion story. The adjutant general sent them to Richmond, where they were confined in Castle Lightning. On 18 October 1864, they were taken to Abbington, and then to Pound Gap where they were released.

Root went to Louisa and reported to the provost telling him he was a "Rebel Deserter. I wanted to get out of the Service. I was sent to Lexington, from thence to Cincinnatti and finally to Washington. When I was there I gave the name of Geo. H. Harris."

Company H's returns indicate Root was "joined" from desertion 8 December 1864, and held in arrest at City Point, Virginia. Following the sentence of death by a general court-martial, Root's file was forwarded to President Lincoln. The president telegraphed Lieutenant General Ulysses S. Grant 24 January 1865: "If Newell W. Root of First Connecticut Heavy Artillery in under sentence of death please telegraph me briefly the circumstances."

The next day, apparently after receiving some information from Grant, Lincoln sent a second telegram: "Having received the report in case of [Root] I do not interfere further in the case."

The court-martial sentence of hanging was carried out 27 January 1865, at City Point, Virginia.

### 5 February 1865

"Within the period of eight months [JAMES DEVLIN] enlisted twice in the Army, and once in the Navy, having twice during the same period, deserted the flag of his country," D. T. Van Buren, assistant adjutant general, wrote, ordering Devlin's execution.

> His case is one of those in which bad men, tempted by enormous bounties, enlist into the service for the sake of making money, with the deliberate purpose of desertion, and in which the profit is proportioned to the number of

successful repetitions of the crime. By common consent,
these infamous men are designated by the expressive ap-
plelation of bounty-jumpers. They might, more proper-
ly be termed traitors and public plunders . . . .[2]

Devlin, alias Pat Diamond and Frank Tully, an Irish butcher, pleaded
guilty to deserting the 43rd New York Volunteers, and the 1st Connecticut
Cavalry. His desertion from the navy was not a specified charge at his court-
martial, presided over by Major Franklin M. Drew, 15th Maine Volunteers.

James Devlin was executed by musketry at Draft Rendezvous, Gover-
nor's Island, New York harbor, 5 February 1865.

### 9 February 1865

JOSEPH H. SHARP [aka Samuel Trangler or Frangler], 30, a Burlington, New Jersey, brickmaker was a substitute in Company A, 12th New
Hampshire Infantry, who joined the regiment at Point Lookout. He deserted
at White House Landing the day the unit arrived.

"Soon after his desertion and safe escape to the North," Asa W. Bartlett
recalled in his *History of the Twelfth Regiment, New Hampshire Volunteers
in the War of the Rebellion*, he reenlisted for a large bounty, "and soon found
himself enrolled as a recruit in the Fifth Maryland, which, most unfortunately
for him, was at that time in the same brigade as the Twelfth."

Sharp tried to remain invisible, but in a few days members of the New
Hampshire regiment recognized him and brought his attention to the regimental commander. Corporal Julius Davis, of Company A, was the one who
reported Sharp's presence, so Colonel Barker and he paid the man a visit.

When they arrived at Sharp's tent, he wasn't there. The colonel's "first
thoughts," Bartlett related, "was that the fellow had got a windward hint of
his discovery and taken another jump, more this time, however, for a longer
lease on life than for another bounty."

The colonel was wrong. Sharp was in another tent. When the colonel
spotted him, he recognized Sharp "as one of his lost black sheep."

Sharp denied being Joseph Sharp. "But when he found he was to be
taken back to his old regiment, where he would be identified by every member
of his company that was still in the ranks," Bartlett wrote, "he broke down
completely and confessed the whole, exclaiming: 'And now, Colonel, I suppose I shall soon be a dead man.' "

Colonel Barker, thinking that Sharp "would only show true repentence
for the past, by a strict compliance with future duty," indicated he would do
all that was possible to help him.

The colonel anticipated that the court-martial verdict would, of course,
be a guilty one, and would "have been followed by a strong recommendation
for mercy and final mitigation of the death sentence . . . ." But Sharp confessed fully; he had deserted several times before — for the bounty, "and that
when arrested he was actually making preparations to desert again, and get one
more bounty before the end of the war.

"He had deserted once too many then," Bartlett concluded, "and he saw, when too late that although he had gained thousands of dollars, he must lose his own life as a penalty for the unlawful and dishonorable means he had employed." Bartlett's assumption that Sharp had gained "thousands of dollars" is perhaps exaggerated. In reviewing the individual soldiers' records, one can see that the military made great effort to show graphically how much an individual "stole." Such information does not appear in Sharp's file.

Sharp was tried by regimental court-martial, presided over by Lieutenant-Colonel J. F. Brown, and convicted. He was shot to death 9 February 1865.

Corporal Davis, because of a reward offered by the War Department to any soldier providing information leading to the arrest and conviction of a deserter, was entitled to a thirty-day furlough and $30 in cash. He received the leave — but not the money.

"Some of the regiment, and especially the recruits," Bartlett felt, "blamed Davis for informing against his comrade, with whom he had been intimate even after Sharp was found by him in the Maryland regiment, and accused him of betraying a friendly confidant solely for selfish gain." As late as 1897, Davis continually denied the accusation.

### 17 February 1865

Justice was quite swift in the Department of Virginia during the 10th Connecticut Infantry's tour in the trenches before Richmond in February 1865.

MICHAEL LANDY, 21, an Irish-Catholic farmer, entered the Union Army as a substitute for Samuel Brown of New Haven. He deserted on picket duty 14/15 February and was arrested the same or next day. His court-martial, presided over by Colonel Dowdy, was held the 16th, and Landy was executed in front of the 3rd Brigade, 1st Division, 24th Army of the Cumberland.

Landy was not alone when he was shot. Records indicate that there was another soldier who shared his fate. Records do not, however, give us any clue to who he was or what was his crime. He remains one of the UNNAMED.

Another deserter during the siege of Petersburg was JOHN HOEFFER [Hofler, Hoefler], 20, a German cigar maker.

Hoeffer, a member of Company E, 12th New York Infantry, entered Union service 8 September 1864, at Schnedectady, New York.

Two months later — to the day — he deserted near Fort Sedgwick. He was arrested not far away 1 January 1865.

Tried by general court-martial, Hoeffer was executed by musketry 17 February 1865.

### 18 February 1865

JOHN BROWN III, a 22-year-old cabinet maker from Scotland, and a substitute for G. Austin, in Company H, 10th Connecticut Infantry, was hanged "before Richmond" 18 February 1865.

Brown was charged with desertion, attempted murder, attempted robbery and violating the 23rd Article of War. Tried before a general court-martial, as detailed in General Court-Martial Order 35, Department of Virginia, 17 February 1865, he was executed. Though the printed order is neat and crisp, the Bureau of Military Justice determined 29 July 1874 that "There is no record of trial of John Brown . . . in file in this bureau."

It is not certain when Brown actually did desert. The rolls of his company indicate 4 January 1865, but the specifications found in the general order state 8 December 1864. He was, as of 1 December 1864, "absent in arrest, confined in the Provost Guard House."

Was Brown a deserter who, after apprehension, escaped confinement? Was he actually tried for the crimes specified?

### 25 February 1865

JOHN PARKER, 19, an Irish farmer, joined the 10th Connecticut Infantry at Bridgeport 14 November 1864. On Christmas Eve that year, he deserted his unit while at work in the provost guard house near Richmond.

Parker was captured New Year's Eve at Bermuda Hundred by Private D. W. Berry, Company H, 24th Massachusetts Volunteers.

At a general court-martial, presided over by Colonel George Brown Dandy [Dandy was breveted brigadier general 29 August 1862], Parker was found guilty of desertion, and was shot to death at 11 a.m., 25 February 1865, near Richmond.

### 28 February 1865

THOMAS JONES, 21, an Irish laborer and substitute for W. B. Bradley of Bridgeport, Connecticut, joined the 10th Connecticut Infantry 22 November 1864.

On 4 January 1865, while the regiment was on duty in the trenches before Richmond, he deserted. He was apprehended shortly thereafter and tried by general court-martial 18 February. At the trial, he was accused and convicted of desertion, attempted robbery and violation of the 23rd Article of War.

Jones was hanged before Richmond 28 February 1865. Or was he? In a letter found in his file, and dated 16 May 1874, the Adjutant General's Office indicates he was executed on the same day as his trial.

### 3 March 1865

FREDERICK MURPHY [aka James Powers], 21, deserted Company F, 6th Cavalry, Regulars, 27 January 1865, near Winchester, West Virginia.

His military career lasted slightly more than three months. An Englishman, he was shot to death at Harpers Ferry, 3 March 1865.

Sergeant CHARLES SPERRY, 29, an Irish painter and member of Company E, 13th New York Cavalry, enlisted 28 March 1863. He advanced in his unit — promoted corporal 20 September 1863; sergeant 12 May 1864 — at a fairly fast rate. He had been taken prisoner 17 October 1863, while on picket duty, but escaped. For some unknown reason, he was arrested in New York City 20 May 1863. Perhaps Sperry had overspent a furlough and had been suspected of desertion. The records do not clarify this.

On 18 June 1864, Sperry left his picket post at Langley, Fairfax County, Virginia. Though he was in charge of the post, he left "without urgent necessity or leave from his superior officer."

While in command of the post, Sperry was also drunk. He wandered from his postition and attacked a young woman. He did "assault, and forcibly and against her will . . . ravish and carnally know one Annie L. Nelson, a maid of about fifteen years of age."

At his general court-martial, Lieutenant-Colonel C. W. Cartwright, 28th Massachusetts Volunteers, presiding, Sperry pleaded guilty to absenting himself from his post, but to none of the other charges. The panel, however, agreed with him to the first charge, and found him guilty also of "drunkenness on duty," "assault and battery, with intent to commit rape," and "rape."

Charles Sperry was shot to death at Old Capitol Prison in Washington, 3 March 1865.

On 15 November 1866 — as an afterthought — Sperry was reduced from sergeant to the ranks.

### 4 March 1865

Was DAVID GEER, 27, a Virginia farmer and private in Company D, 28th Illinois Infantry, actually executed 4 March 1865? That is, at this late date, an unanswerable question.

Geer was accused of murder sometime before 1 June 1864, since his company muster roll indicates he was held at Natchez, Mississippi, "since 1 June 64." Yet the same muster roll states he was on furlough 18 May-8 July 1864. If Geer actually was on furlough at the time of the incident, chances are he murdered a civilian.

A special court-martial was held, and according to General Court-Martial Order 38, Army of the Tennessee, dated 31 October 1864, he was found guilty and sentenced to be shot to death. However, according to Adjutant General's Officer records, the sentence of the special court-martial was commuted to "dishonorable discharge from the service without pay, allowance or bounty."[3]

Whichever the case, someone was "shot to death M[ar]ch 4, '65 at Natchez, Miss. by sentence of G. C. M." Geer's company muster roll indicates it was him.

### 10 March 1865

JAMES KELLY [Kelley], 21, an Irish sailmaker, was a substitute for Charles Long, Reading, Pennsylvania, and an unassigned recruit in the 67th Pennsylvania Infantry.

Kelly deserted 23 December 1864 — seventeen days after he entered the service — from his regiment's camp, during the siege of Petersburg.

Tried by general court-martial, he was convicted and sentenced to execution. Bad weather interfered, and Kelly received a reprieve of several days. On 2 March 1865, the condemned man wrote a letter to his sister, Susan, in Philadelphia, requesting that she "and John Smith go to Washington and do all you can with President Lincoln to have me reprieved." Military authorities at Petersburg never mailed his letter.

Kelly was shot to death, near Fort Cummings, Petersburg, 10 March 1865 — with JOHN NICHOLAS [Nichols; also James Nicholson].

Nicholas, 36, a Canadian farmer and a substitute from Lewistown, New York, joined Company A, 69th New York Infantry, 22 September 1864. During the siege of Petersburg, like Kelly, he deserted; was court-martialed, and executed. The regimental return for the 69th, March 1865, lists Nicholas as "died of disease. Executed by sentence G. C. M."

WILLIAM JACKSON, 23, a Canadian hostler and a substitute for G. Northrup of Bridgeport, Connecticut, in Company A, 10th Connecticut Infantry, supposedly was executed before Richmond 10 March 1865, but his company muster roll lists him as missing or deserted a month after his alleged death.

Was Jackson actually shot, along with JOHN MAHONEY, 21, an Irish laborer and a substitute for John Davis II of New Haven? The only record of his death, other than the 1885 report, is contained in the general order of execution.[4]

An even stranger case is that of WILLIAM T. GRIFFIN [aka George Bolter] executed the same day.

According to testimony by Lieutenant Frank Myers at Griffin's court-martial, the man had enlisted 22 August 1864 [his enlistment record indicates 25 August] in the 8th Delaware Infantry. Interestingly, that unit was not organized until October of that year.

By his own statement, Griffin

> left Wilmington on or about the 1st day of September 1864 and went to Philadelphia and remained there . . . three weeks, I was in the 7th Del and was discharged as 2nd Sergt of the Co. About three weeks before I was discharged the company liked me and voted to elect me 2nd Lieut. I lacked 3 votes of getting it. I was then discharged and they wanted me to get up a Co for one Rear and do as Captain of it.

Griffin, 21, a "brakesman" from Delaware, recruited several men for the 8th Delaware; then, wearing his sergeant's uniform, traveled to Philadelphia.

When he arrived he was put in the guard house, because he was thought to be a deserter from the 7th. He denied being a deserter, but that he had been discharged. He was then advised not to return to Wilmington.

A few minutes after receiving that advice, the officer of the day asked him if he had a pass.

> I told him yes I showed a pass from Capt Culbert to go
> from Wilmington to Philadelphia. They let me out of the
> guard house and I went to the Depot to get on to the
> train . . .

At the railroad station, he met another man who took him back to town, where he was arrested. The man

> . . . took me to New York and left me in a Hotel took
> my money away from me after getting me tight on beer,
> Then he left me and I had no money to go back to Wilm-
> ington again. Then I went to work.

A contradictory view, however, was presented by Lieutenant Myers who stated that

> On or about the later end of August [Griffin] was sent
> to Camp Smithers with a squad of men. He was arrested
> the day afterwards for leaving camp without authority.
> He was then sent back to Camp under guard a day or
> two after that he left camp without authority.

Myers testified he had seen nothing of Griffin until Myers arrested him "in a squad of substitutes at City Point, Va Feb 14th 1865."

Myers, for not having seen or heard from Griffin for such a long period of time, acted as if he was the defendant's confidante.

> Last monday I think it was I had a conversation with him
> he told me he was drafted and was enlisted as a substitute
> under the name of Geo Bolter he said that he had not
> received any bounty nor did he know that he was enlisted
> till a day or two afterwards. He told me that he was
> enlisted at Buffaloo New York.

Private James Murphy, Company B, 8th Delaware Volunteers, also testified that he had seen Griffin in the barracks in mid-February: "He was in a squad I do not know whether they were subs or convalescents." When Murphy asked Griffin if he remembered him, he was assured the defendant did.

... he put out his hand and shook hands with me He told me the boys all know him This is all I know about it . . . . I think he said he wanted to go to his regt and Co for sure I will not be positive about it.

Murphy stated that he knew the accused for eight to nine months.

Though statements made were contradictory, no effort was made at the 24 February 1865 court-martial, to clarify the inconsistencies. The general court-marital, presided over by Colonel Charles H. T. Collis,[5] found him guilty as charged. In most courts-martials during the Civil War period, there is no consistency in testimony. Witnesses made allegations which, if the defendants had been represented, would have been objected to strenuously.

William T. Griffin was shot to death 10 March 1865 at City Point, Virginia.

### 16 March 1865

WILLIAM COOPER joined the Union Army as a substitute for Alexander S. Hawkins at Norwich, Connecticut, 28 December 1864. Cooper, 21, was a seaman from Scotland.

His case is quite interesting, though little is extant of his records: Cooper is charged with desertion on or about 24 November 1864 — a month before he joined the 10th Connecticut Infantry! In fact, his pay was stopped 30 November because he had been apprehended.

Was the Cooper who was shot before Richmond 16 March 1865, the same Cooper who substituted for Hawkins? Was he a bounty jumper? Or was a different Cooper executed?

### 18 March 1865

The execution of Private JOHN SMITH, 34, had been scheduled for 17 March 1865, but because of St. Patrick's Day, a traditional day of celebration in the army, his death was delayed one day.

Smith, a German laborer, entered Company H, 8th New Jersey Infantry, as a one-year substitute for John P. Vorhies, at Morristown, New York, 8 September 1864.

On or about 22 October, Smith deserted "from rear front of Petersburg . . . ." He was captured 31 December, and tried by general court-martial, Lieutenant-Colonel J. Schoonoover, 11th New Jersey Volunteers, presiding. He was convicted and executed by musketry 18 March 1865, at 12:20 p.m., near Petersburg.

JOSEPH JOHNSON [The Adjutant General's Office lists him as J. J. McNealy], a native of Somerset, Maryland, joined Company E, 1st Maryland Infantry, 15 June 1861. His unit surrendered 15 September 1862, and was paroled the next day.

After the exchange, the 1st Maryland was assigned duty on the Potomac until June 1863. While on this assignment, Johnson went absent without leave 24 January to 3 February 1862. He was sentenced by regimental court-martial to forfeit $10 pay. He again deserted — from Baltimore — 2 December. A general court-martial made him forfeit more than pay. Joseph Johnson was shot to death for desertion 18 March 1865.

### 26 March 1865

JAMES WEAVER [aka N. E. Baker], 25, entered Company D, 1st Maryland Infantry, 1 February 1865, as a substitute for Horatio Gettle.

Weaver deserted his unit during the siege of Petersburg; was tried and convicted. He was shot at City Point, Virginia, 26 March 1865.

FREDERICK W. BRANDT, 27, a Prussian miller, was a private in Company E, 81st New York Infantry.

From 31 May-22 September 1864, Brandt was a patient in the hospital at White House Landing. While in the hospital Brandt received a furlough — to return to his unit between 27 August and 10 September. On 27 October 1864, he was listed as absent without leave. He returned three days later. According to his unit's records, after his return Brandt was listed as sick 1, 2, 10, 11, and 20 January 1865.

Brandt must have deserted again, because on 24 March, Brandt was arrested as a deserter. His court-martial was immediate. Two days after his arrest — 26 March 1865 — he was shot to death, before Richmond.

### 27 March 1865

The National Archives do not have records for JEREMIAH ROBERTS, Company D, 55th Pennsylvania Infantry, who was listed by the Adjutant General's Office as being executed for desertion 27 March 1865.

### 31 March 1865

NEWAL [Newell] JANGROW [Jangro, Jangoo], 27, a Canadian shoemaker and a member of Company H, 64th New York Infantry, entered 12 August 1864, at Hart Island, New York.

On 5 February 1865, he deserted from the picket line near Petersburg. Apprehended immediately, he received a general court-martial, and was shot at a camp near where he deserted, 31 March 1865, along with ANTHONY RAYMOND, an unassigned recruit in the 64th.

Raymond, 21, a Canadian lumberman, entered Union service as a substitute "prior to draft" at Remein, New York, 16 August 1864. He attempted to desert to the enemy at Petersburg, 4 February 1865; was arrested, tried by general court-martial, and convicted.

1865

Very few members of the 107th Infantry, USCT, had smiles for the photographer in this photograph. Assigned to guard house duty, one of their tasks was to prevent imprisoned black soldiers from escaping the sentence of death. *Massachusetts Commandery, Military Order of the Loyal Legion and the U. S. Army Military History Institute.*

Before a general court-martial, Lieutenant-Colonel Frank S. Curtis, 127th Illinois Volunteers, presiding, Private JAMES PREBLE, Company K, 12th New York Infantry, was found guilty of "assault with intent to commit rape," and "rape."

Preble, 22, a New York brakeman, joined the army at Buffalo 8 September 1863. On 16 March 1865, the cavalryman assaulted Mrs. Rebecca Drake and Miss Louis Bedard, and attempted to rape both women, at the home of Oliver Bedard, near Kinston, North Carolina. Later, Preble "did by physical force and violence commit rape upon the person of one Miss Letitia Craft," at Bedard's home.

Preble was found guilty on all counts, and was shot to death 31 March 1865, at Goldsboro, North Carolina.

## 20 April 1865

Another black soldier, who joined the protest against the inequities of the Union soldiers' pay scale, was executed at City Point, Virginia, 20 April 1865.

SAMUEL MAPP, 18, a Virginia farmer, joined 17 December 1863, at Fort Monroe. A member of Company D, 10th Infantry, USCT, he was accused of mutiny, disobedience of orders, and threatening the life of a superior officer.

Tried by general court-martial, Lieutenant-Colonel B. F. Pratt, 36th Infantry, USCT, presiding, on 17 March 1865, Mapp was convicted — and shot to death.

## 6 May 1865

While the 1st Heavy Artillery, USCT, engaged in operations in Northern Alabama and East Tennessee, 31 January-24 April 1865, four members of the unit: ALFRED CATLETT, 20, of Richmond; ALEXANDER COLWELL, 26, of North Carolina; CHARLES TURNER, 18, of Charleston, South Carolina — all of Company E; and WASHINGTON JACKSON, 22, of South Carolina and member of Company K, were tried at drumhead for rape.

The four men, all listing themselves as farmers,[6] were shot to death 6 May 1865, at Ashville, North Carolina.

## 12 May 1865

WILLIAM H. HARRISON, 17, an Arkansas laborer, was a member of Company A, 69th Infantry, USCT, when he was hanged for murder 12 May 1865, in the military prison at Little Rock.

Harrison had enlisted 13 August 1864, prior to the organization of the unit. Though he was tried by general court-martial, there are not existing records to document the circumstances — or the victim — of the crime.

The speed of crime to trial to execution is illustrated in this selection of documents from the military service records of Pvt. Henry Anderson [Co. D, 9th Michigan Cavalry]. In (A), General Kilpatrick notifies General Schofield that Anderson committed murder on 9 May 1865. Later that day, Schofield's adjutant general calls for a military commission to try the man (B) and that Schofield *will* approve the sentence. Three days later, Schofield has reviewed, approved and confirmed the findings and sentence. The next day, 13 May, Anderson was executed at Lexington, N. C. *National Archives*

*13 May 1865*

General Hugh Judson Kilpatrick sometimes equated the military commission with drumhead court-martial. The case of HENRY ANDERSON, 21, an Irish soldier and member of Company D, 9th Michigan Cavalry, seems to indicate that.

Anderson allegedly murdered an old man, a civilian, who wouldn't give him money. In order to set an example, Kilpatrick ordered a military commission to try the man. Anderson's execution took place the same day — 13 May 1865.

To make the example sit more firmly in his soldiers' minds, Kilpatrick made an exhibition out of the Irishman's death.

"We remained in camp in the foarnoon," Cornelius Baker wrote in his diary,

> and in the afternoon at half past 2 o clock we were ordered out to see a man of the 9th Mishigan shot    We marched out 2 miles from town to were he was to bee shot and formed out lines pasing his grave and he was brot out in an ambulance on his coffin and the band playing the ded march and the coffin was placed 3 pases from his grave and a chapter was red and a prair oferd up for him by the chaplin of his regiment and after the men were in line and his eyes were tied shut and a voly was fired and the prisoner dropped 15 balls passed threw his body and was an instant corps he was shot for kiling a sitisan for his money at Goalsborough No. Caroliny.[7]

Records for the State of Michigan indicate the execution took place on 3 May,[8] but Anderson's casualty sheet and Baker's entry provide evidence to support the 13 May date.

Though JOHN WILLIS and OTTO PIERCE, were listed as murderers, both men were actually executed for desertion.

Willis enlisted in the 3rd Mississippi Infantry [African Descent] 1 July 1863, at Four Mile Bridge. While the unit was on duty at Milliken's Bend and Goodrich Landing, he deserted 21 August 1863, from Camp Hibbin, Mississippi. When apprehended, his unit had become Company D, 52nd Infantry, USCT.

Pierce, 26, a Mississippi field hand, joined what became Company L, 5th Heavy Artillery, USCT, 1 March 1864, at Vicksburg. He was reported absent without leave — he left camp from noon to 4 p.m., and in disobedience of orders 16 November 1864. He was arrested the same day.

Pierce had been subject to a regimental court-martial 30 April 1864 on an unspecified charge, and sentenced to pay forfeiture and five days solitary confinement.

Both men were hanged 26 May 1865.

WILLIAM WALLACE, 20, a Mississippi servant; MOSES ROLLINS [Mose Rawlings], 20, a Mississippi laborer; EPHRAIM McDOWELL, 21, a Georgia laborer; PETER MOORE, 20, a Tennessee laborer; JAMES MORRISON, 25, a Mississippi laborer; HENRY JOHNSON, 25; and THOMAS FOUR, 29, a Georgia laborer, hanged — along with Willis and Pierce — for murder on the same date. Wallace, Rollins, McDowell, Moore, Morrison, Johnson, and Four were involved in murder while the 52nd Infantry, USCT, was on post and garrison duty at Vicksburg.

Morrison had been appointed corporal 18 November 1864; Wallace had been recommended for the same rank 12 December 1863.

The hanging of these men was the largest execution of the Civil War.

It is probable that a harried government clerk assumed that since the majority of men were executed for murder, all were guilty of the same crime.

WILLIAM COWELL, 20, Company F, 1st Cavalry, USCT, a North Carolina laborer, was hanged near City Point, Virginia, 26 May 1865 — on unspecified charges.

Reports that Cowell had been executed for murder did not surface until 27 August 1868, when the Adjutant General's Office requested a final statement of inventory. The Surgeon General's Office, Record & Pension Division, replied "the desired final papers cannot be furnished by this office . . . ."

Orders, located in Cowell's file, indicate he was to be sent to Headquarters, 25th Army Corps, 25 May 1865 under "strong and secure guard."

What William Cowell did to receive capital punishment — or if he did do something — remains for conjecture.

### 13 June 1865

JOHN LEWIS, 25, Company E, 13th Heavy Artillery, USCT, a Virginia teamster, was tried for murder by a general court-martial, with Brigadier-General Walter C. Whitaker, U. S. Volunteers, presiding.

On 14 May 1865, at Shelbyville, Kentucky, Lewis, "with malice aforethought," shot and killed Thomas C. McGrath, "a peaceable citizen."

Lewis, who had only joined the unit 27 March, was convicted. He was executed at Louisville, 13 June. Accompanying him to the gallows was a civilian, Marshal P. Stewart, who had been convicted of being a guerrilla and a participant in the murder of three Grayson County residents: David Johnson, Grayson Miller, and William McGlossom, 10 February 1865. Stewart had been tried by military commission, General Whitaker presided.

### 16 June 1865

Corporal FRANK HUDSON, 28, an Irish miner, enlisted in the 2nd California Cavalry at Camp Babbitt [Benicia Barracks], California, 14 February 1863. Hudson was promoted to corporal 24 November 1864, though Judge Advocate General reports list him as a private.

No. 1.

# California State Telegraph Company.

The Public are requested to report, by letter, to the Superintendent, at San Francisco, any cause of dissatisfaction.

*TERMS AND CONDITIONS ON WHICH MESSAGES ARE RECEIVED, TRANSMITTED, AND DELIVERED.*

The public are notified that, in order to guard against neglect or mistakes, every message of importance OUGHT to be repeated back, for which service fifty per cent. in addition to the regular tariff will be charged. In case of delay, neglect or mistakes on its own lines, or by its own employees, this Company will refund the amount paid for sending the message, and no more, unless the message be repeated back, and in that case the Company will be responsible for actual damage only, to an amount not exceeding fifty times the sum paid for sending the message; but in no other case will the Company be responsible for interruptions in the working of its telegraphs; nor will it, in any case whatsoever, be responsible for damages sent beyond its own lines, or received from other lines, or for any mistake, fault, omission or misconduct of any other Company or person.

☞ THE FOLLOWING MESSAGE IS TRANSMITTED AND DELIVERED SUBJECT TO THE FOREGOING CONDITIONS, AND NOT OTHERWISE.

**JAS. GAMBLE, Superintendent.** **H. W. CARPENTIER, President.**

Sanfrancisco June 15th 1865

To Brigadier Gen G Wright 6.45P M.

= Commanding Dist of California =
Say to Corporal Hudson of company I. Second (2)
Cavalry at Camp Union that I have received
his letter — That I have again carefully
considered the evidence of the court in his case
and have gone over it with Judge Hoffman
of the U.S. District court and Judge Field of
the United States Supreme Court= They concur
that the evidence fully warrants the sentence
of Death — Tell him that I do not modify
my orders and that the Execution must
take place It will be a mercy to let him
Know that this must be so — That he may
make his last preparations in the short time
that remains to him on Earth

Irvin McDowell
Maj Gen'l
Com'd Dept

III paid 1895
(Insured)

In some cases, such as that of Corp. Frank Hudson [Co. I, 2nd California Cavalry], higher command attempted to discuss the case with legal experts. In Hudson's case, Gen. McDowell discussed the case with a district court judge and an associate justice of the U. S. Supreme Court. *National Archives*

His appointment to the non-commissioned ranks was not to his liking, as he stated in a letter to Major General Irwin McDowell dated 13 June 1865:

> . . . the cause of my desertion was from continued ill usage by the 1st Sergeant of Company G, 2nd Cal. Cav. I was a non commissioned in that Company and repeatedly applied to my Camptain to be reduced to the ranks, stating to him that I thought I could do my duty and get along better as a private soldier.

Hudson left his unit 14 April 1865 while they were stationed at Camp Bidwell. The same evening, 1st Lieutenant Daniel W. Livergood was mortally wounded. The key suspect, of course, was Hudson. He was apprehended 18 April.

"I never was an enemy of Lieut. Levergoods," Hudson continued in his letter to McDowell.

> he had enemies in the Company and they or some of them took advantage of my desertion to accuse me of the crime of Killing him. I did not Kill him nor attempt to injure him in any way.

The lieutenant died of his wounds 16 April.

Hudson's plea fell on deaf ears. By telegram 15 June, McDowell informed Brigadier General G. Wright, commanding the District of California,

> That I have again carefully considered the evidence . . . and have gone over it with Judge Hoffman of the U. S. District court and Judge [Stephen J.] Field of the United States Supreme Court. They concur that the evidence fully warrants the sentence of Death. Tell him that I do not modify my orders and the Execution must take place. It will be a mercy to let him know that this must be so — that he may make his last preparations in the short time that remains to him on Earth.

The next day, 16 June, Frank Hudson was hanged at Camp Union, Sacramento, California, in accordance with General Order 40, Department of the Pacific.

### 21 June 1865

Private HENRY JAY, 20, Company I, 5th Infantry, USCT, a Mississippi laborer, was shot to death 21 June 1865, for the rape of a white woman at Dardannelle, Arkansas.

Jay received a drumhead court-martial.

**23 June 1865**

While Company H, 21st Infantry, USCT, was on garrison duty at Charleston and Mount Pleasant, South Carolina, 10 April 1865, Private SIMON GRANT "willfully" shot to death Private Cuffy Wright, of his Company.

Grant, 22, a South Carolina laborer, enlisted at Hilton Head, 31 August 1864. He was tried by general court-martial; was convicted and hanged at Castle Pinkney, Charleston, 23 June 1865.

**30 June 1865**

About 7 p.m., Christmas Day 1864, Private PATRICK McNAMARA, Company K, 132nd New York Infantry, got into an argument with another soldier in his company, Private James Shaw. The argument ended with McNamara stabbing Shaw twice with a pocket knife. Shaw died two days later. The incident took place at Bachelor's Creek, North Carolina.

McNamara, 25, an Irish laborer, had joined the Union Army 3 August 1862, for a $25 bounty and a $2 premium. He was court-martialed and convicted. He was hanged 30 June 1865 — the day after his unit was mustered out of service.

**21 July 1865**

GEORGE DIXON, 18, joined Company K, 79th Infantry, USCT, 1 April 1863 at Wyandotte, Kansas.

Dixon deserted his unit while on the march from Fort Smith, Arkansas, to Roseville, 12 December 1863. He was returned under arrest 14 February 1864. On 22 June 1865, he was again arrested — this time for murder — and placed in close confinement.

Witnesses for Dixon's defense were unable to attend his court-martial. He was subsequently convicted, and hanged 21 July 1865.

**28 July 1865**

WILLIAM A. WILSON, 18, a Vienna, Illinois farmer, enlisted in the 12th Illinois Cavalry 8 August 1861. He was a native of Marion, North Carolina.

While with his unit, the 12th Illinois Cavalry, at the battle of Shiloh, 6 April 1862, Wilson was wounded and sent to the hospital. He never returned.

Married, Wilson probably went home from the hospital. He was declared a deserter 28 April 1863.

According to Adjutant General's Office records — on file in the Illinois State Archives — that is the end of Wilson's story. However, according to the 1865 report, the story on Wilson is quite different.

Wilson's service record at the National Archives indicates the man enlisted 14 December 1863 at Camp Yates. He was declared a deserter 8 July 1865 while his unit was on a march from Alexandria, Virginia, to Hempstead, Texas.

Quickly apprehended, Wilson was tried by general court-martial and sentenced by General Order 9, Division of the Gulf, Headquarters Cavalry, dated 25 July 1865, to be shot to death.

The execution of Wilson allegedly took place 28 July 1865 at Alexandria. The question remains: was Wilson executed? Or was it someone else?

### 30 July 1865

WILLIAM JACKSON and DANDRIDGE BROOKS, both members of Company G, 38th Infantry, USCT, were hanged by order of a general court-martial for rape 30 July 1865.

Jackson, 24, a laborer, enlisted 20 August 1864, at Newport News, Virginia; Brooks, 22, a teamster, 21 June 1864, at Point Lookout, Maryland. Both were native to Virginia.

Both men, at the time of the offense which occurred in late April 1865, had been sergeants. They were reduced to ranks 1 May.

Tried by general court-martial, and convicted, Jackson and Brooks were hanged at Brownsville, 30 July 1865.

### 11 August 1865

Sergeants WILLIAM KEASE and DOCTOR MOORE, of Company I, 116th Infantry, USCT, were tried by general court-martial for mutiny — which took place before 12 May 1865.

Kease, 23, a Kentucky farmer, and Moore, 29, a Kentucky engineer, were the only black soldiers who admitted to having been slaves. At their enlistments, Kease stated he had been owned by Timothy Hughes; Moore, Wilas Roberts.

The men apparently mutinied while the unit was on duty at Petersburg, but were not tried until the unit moved to Rome, Texas. The general court-martial found them guilty. They were executed by musketry at Ringgold Barracks, Texas 11 August 1865.

### 18 August 1865

There is no service record for AARON COLLINS, Company H, 6th Cavalry, USCT, who the Adjutant General's Office lists as being executed for murder 18 August 1865.

### 21 August 1865

ALEXANDER McBROONE was a farmer from Carson, Tennessee, when he enlisted in the 1st Arkansas Infantry 4 February 1863, at Fayetteville, Arkansas.

The 25-year-old private was reported as a deserter 24 days later. Over a year later, 18 April 1864, he was arrested and confined at Fort Smith. By General Order 23, Department of the Arkansas, 18 February 1865, he was found guilty and sentenced to be executed by musketry. That sentence was carried out 21 August at Fort Smith.

McBroone's brother Maxwell was also a member of the same unit. On 15 August, while McBroone was in confinement, Maxwell was killed in action against the enemy.

### 6 September 1865

JOHN W. HARDUP and HIRAM OLIVER were allegedly executed for murder 6 September 1865.

Hardup, 18, an Ohio laborer, was a member of Company A, 43rd Ohio Infantry, who enlisted 24 October 1861, at Camp Chase, Ohio.

His service record indicates he deserted the unit 23 June 1862 at Clear Creek, Mississippi. He was arrested and put in prison in Steubenville, Ohio. There is no record of murder.

Oliver, on the other hand, is a mystery. There is no service record for him in the National Archives.

### 9 September 1865

Corporal Cruz Torres was murdered in the Raton Mountains, 14 July 1865, by JUAN MADRID [Juan Madrill, Juan de Dois].

Madrid, 33, a native laborer from New Mexico, had entered Union service 2 July 1861, and had served throughout the war in Company C, 1st Cavalry — reenlisting after his discharge 29 February 1864.

Madrid was hanged at Fort Union, 9 September 1865.

### 13 October 1865

Though listed as having been executed for rape and murder, Corporal JOHN SHEPPARD, Company I, 38th Infantry, USCT, was convicted of rape, plunder and pillage.

Sheppard, 20, a Virginia laborer, became a Union soldier 31 January 1865, as a substitute for Mahlon Buckman. He was promoted to corporal 15 March, but placed in arrest 16 May. He was reduced to ranks 8 August.

Following a general court-martial, Sheppard was hanged at Fort Monroe, 13 October 1865.

### 20 November 1865

While the 103rd Infantry, USCT, was on garrison duty at various posts in South Carolina, JAMES GRIPEN [Gripon] and BENJAMIN RUDDING were accused of rape.

Gripen, 20, a South Carolina butler, had enlisted 25 June 1865, at Beaufort, South Carolina. Rudding cannot be described. There is no service record for him.

Both men, according to the Adjutant General, were court-martialed, convicted; and hanged 20 November 1865, at Hilton Head.

*1 December 1865*

The 3rd Infantry, USCT, was on duty at Tallahassee, Lake City, and other points in Florida, when DAVID CRAIG, JOSEPH GRIEN, JAMES ALLEN, JACOB PLOWDER [Plowdon], NATHANIEL JOSEPH, and HOWARD THOMAS stood accused of mutiny.

It is possible that some — if not all — of the men might not have been executed. In David Craig's file, a letter from H. C. Marehand, Greensburg, Florida, dated 10 December 1865, to Senator E. Cowan, was requested that the execution be suspended because Craig "had been excused to take the guns from some of the mutineers, and in doing so was arrested." There is a notation on the letter: "Telegraph to Genl Foster to suspend sentence & transmit record here." Unfortunately, the letter and suspension were nine days late. Craig and the rest were shot to death at Fernandina, Florida, 1 December 1865.

Craig, 21, was a Pennsylvania laborer. He enlisted as a substitute for Edward Houston, Pittsburgh, Pennsylvania, 16 July 1863. Allen, 23, was an Indiana farmer, who enlisted at Philadelphia, 1 August 1863. Plowder, 44, a Pennsylvania farmer, enlisted at Philadelphia 8 July 1863, and was promoted to corporal 29 September 1863; then reduced to ranks 7 December. Joseph, 20, a Jamaican seaman, enlisted at Portsmouth, New Hampshire, 10 September 1864. Howard, 19, an Eastern Shore, Maryland, farmer, enlisted at Philadelphia, 20 July 1863. He had been subjected to a regimental court-martial, because he received a pay stoppage for November and December of that year. There is no service record for Grien.

The mutiny for which they were charged, convicted and executed is not described in the records, except in the letter to Senator Cowan: "In the mutiny, the Colonel of the Regiment had his finger shot off."

The 3rd Infantry, USCT, ironically, did not witness the shooting death of these five men. The unit mustered out 31 October 1865.

Greensburgh Dec. 10./65

Hon. E. Cowan

Dear Sir

Yesterday I received a
letter from David Craig (colored) Co. K.
3 U.S.C.T dated 28 November in which he
states that he was sentenced to be shot to
death on the 1st day of December at Fort Clinch
Fernandina Florida —

I will be obliged if you make immediate
inquiry at the War Department to ascertain the
truth of this matter, and if this sentence has
not been executed, to endeavor to have it postponed until I can get the necessary petition
letter &c. showing his innocent & unofficious character prior to his enlistment —

Having raised the boy from his infancy
our family have taken a deep interest in
his welfare.

The peculiar circumstances under which he
was induced to enlist by some of the white
folks of Pittsburgh make his fate the more
unfortunate —

He was a minor at the time of enlistment without father or mother —

He writes me that at the time of the mutiny he had been ordered to take the guns
from some of the mutineers, and in doing so
was arrested — In the meantime the Colonel of
the Regiment had his fingers shot off

Yours truly

M. C. Marehouse

U. S. Rep. E. Cowan noted in the margin of a letter from a Mr.
Marehouse that records relative to the case of Pvt. David Craig [Co. K, 3rd
Infantry, USCT] should be forwarded to Washington for review and that the
sentence should be suspended until such a review was completed. His note went
unanswered.                                          *National Archives*

# ENDNOTES TO CHAPTER NINE

1. *OR*, 12, part 2, p. 407.

2. General Order 9, Headquarters, Department of the East, 1 February 1865.

3. Special Order 476, Adjutant General's Office, dated 4 September 1865.

4. General Order 44, Department of Virginia, 4 March 1865.

5. Collis, who presided over more military executions than any other officer, was breveted brigadier general, 28 October 1864, and was in 1893 recipient of the Medal of Honor for his actions at Fredericksburg.

6. Former slaves usually listed the type of work they performed as their occupation. There is little or no evidence to indicate that the black men executed were free men.

7. Quoted in John W. Rowell, *Yankee Cavalrymen: Through the Civil War with the 9th Pennsylvania Cavalry* (Knoxville, 1971).

8. Records of the Michigan Military Establishment: RG 59-14, Vol. 39, p. 31, and Michigan Volunteers, 9th Cav., p. 7.

# CHAPTER TEN

## 1866:
### "... a most humane intention ...."

**9 February 1866**

Private BENJAMIN McCLOUD, 32, Company E, 37th Infantry, USCT, a North Carolina farmer, was not executed 9 February 1866 for mutiny.

In McCloud's service file, a notation from the Record and Pension Office, dated 13 April 1893, states:

> ... the records on file and from the testimony in the Pension Bureau ... is erroneous. He escaped from his guard while awaiting execution of the sentence ... and it does not appear that he was ever retaken by the military authorities of the U. S. up to the date of his alleged death in 1884.

**2 March 1866**

FORTUNE WRIGHT, a private in Company A, 96th Infantry, USCT, should never have been executed.

Wright was stationed at Camp Parapet, near Carrolton, when he visited New Orleans. He was walking down the street when a "colored woman, disipated and immoral," accosted him. She put her hand on his shoulder and "acting her willingness to prostitute her person."

She asked Wright for a dime for her services. He indicated he had a wife, "and what dimes he got he gave to her." The woman then became abusive, calling him a "God damned liar." Wright, angry with the situation, told her to stop or he would slap her. She continued, and Wright slapped her. At about that time, two white men came on the scene. Not having any knowledge of what transpired, the two "abused and roughly interfered with" Wright. The soldier didn't want to get involved with the men because "they were white men, and he was a negro."

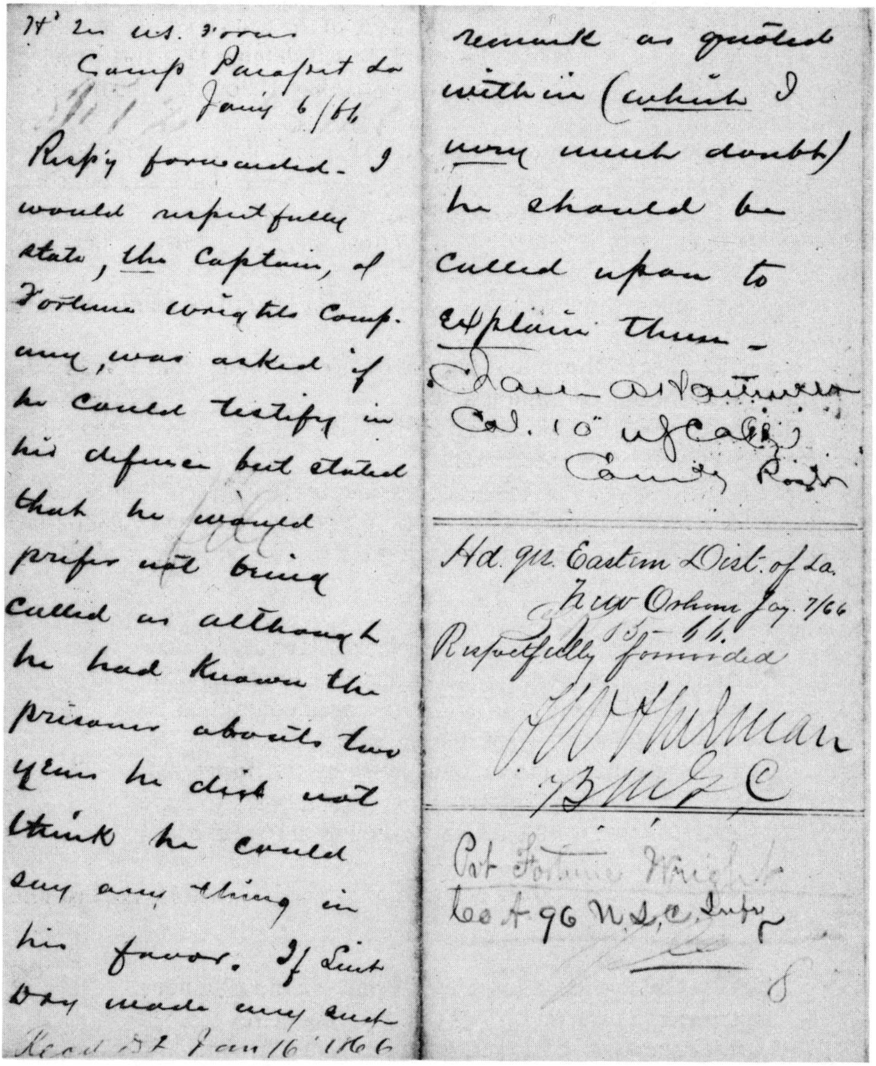

Hd Qrs. U.S. Forces
Camp Parapet La
Jany 6/66
Resp'y forwarded - I would respectfully state, the Captain, of Fortune Wrights Company, was asked if he could testify in his defence but stated that he would prefer not being called as although he had known the prisoner about two years he did not think he could say any thing in his favor. If Lieut Day made any such remark as quoted within (which I very much doubt) he should be called upon to explain them -
Chas. A. Hartwell
Col. 10 U.S.C.H.A.
Comdg Post

Recd DT Jan 16 1866

Hd. Qrs. Eastern Dist. of La.
New Orleans Jany 7/66
[illegible] 15 66
Respectfully forwarded
T. W. Sherman
Bvt. M. G. C.

Pvt Fortune Wright
Co A 96 U.S.C. Infy

In the case of Fortune Wright [Co. A, 96th Infantry, USCT], the facts support self-defense, but there appeared to be a strong bias to overturning the decision of his court-martial panel. Notes in his military service record indicate questions about the veracity of his captain and why he did not testify at the trial. Further exploration found notes that demonstrate Wright was actually deserving of clemency. *National Archives*

Wright started back to his camp, when one of the men, Dr. Octavius Undecimen Tresgerant, "struck him on the back of the head a very severe blow with a walking stick he . . . held in his hand. In self defence [Wright] wheeled around and caught the cane or stick and said what have I done for you to strike me with this stick."

Dr. Tresgerant said, "Let go this stick you dam black Sun of a bitch," and grabbed Wright by the collar. Tresgerant then wheeled back and punched Wright in the face. The other man came up and loudly ordered Tresgerant: "Kill him. Kill the damned black Sun of a bitch. there is no law for him. Kill him."

Both men jumped on Wright, and the soldier withdrew a knife he carried and, in self defense, stabbed Tresgerant.

Tresgerant died of the injury, but not before he pleaded that Wright was not at fault, and should go unmolested.

The Fortune Wright case caused a stir in New Orleans, from the ranks, from the officers, and from the citizenry.

Lieutenant-Colonel O. Fariola, commanding the regiment, appeared to be the guiding force in the appeal process. On 4 January 1866, he wrote to Major Wickham Hoffman, assistant adjutant general of Louisiana, stating the reasons a reprieve should be granted.

> . . . I can say that some of the ablest lawyers of New Orleans think that the defence has not used all of its means and that an error may have been committed by the court. This last opinion is sustained, as it seems, by a statement made rather reluctantly by the Judge Advocate, Lieutenant Thomas Dry, who appears to have stated that "he would not have voted as the Court did."

Fariola then enumerated the grounds on which he based his application for pardon:

> 1st — The President has always evinced a most humane intention to exercise his right of granting mercy to even great culprits, and has yet, quite recently commuted the death sentence of a man who was convicted of murder at New Orleans, under, I think, more Aggravated circumstances.
> 2nd — A large number of loyal citizens of New Orleans, and among them some of the first members of the bar, earnestly desire the pardon . . ., and are preparing a petition to that effect, which cannot fail to have great weight with the President when the standing of the petitioners is considered.

> 3rd — Myself, as the commanding officer of [Wright],
> and with me, my whole regiment, will most respectfully
> apply for the same favor, as the only reward, of whatever
> kind, we will ever have applied for, or received, until now,
> for several years of faithful services.
> 4th — It is reported that Dr. Tresgerant himself, on his
> death-bed, requested that the man who had stabbed him
> be unmolested: These last words may go to show that
> in Dr. Tresgerant the community lost a noble heart, could
> they not show too, that he felt himself somewhat respon-
> sible for the fatal occurence?

The appeal process did nothing more than prolong Wright's hope. He
was finally hanged 2 March 1866. Lincoln did not intervene in any manner.
It is quite apparent that military authorities in New Orleans ignored the
mandate of General Order 28, 15 May 1862. The order stated

> As the officers and soldiers of the United States have been
> subjected to repeated insults from the women (calling
> themselves ladies) of New Orleans, in return for the most
> scrupulous non-interference and courtesy on our part, it
> is ordered, that hereafter, when any female shall, by
> word, gesture, or movement, insult or show contempt for
> any officer or soldier of the United States, she shall be
> regarded and held liable to be treated as a woman of the
> town plying her avocation.

The "Woman Order," though severely criticized far and wide, including
the London *Times*, was never revoked. If the order had been brought into the
court-martial, Wright might have been able to show that the attack on him by
Tresgerant was uncalled for, and his actions were nothing more than self-defense.

### 23 March 1866

Private Thomas Kershaw, Company L, 10th Heavy Artillery, USCT, was
murdered by a member of his own company, LEWIS WILSON, at Fort Pike,
14 January 1866.

Wilson, 25, a Tennessee laborer, entered Union service 25 March 1865,
at New Orleans.

Following the murder, Wilson was arrested 24 January 1866, and confined in the New Orleans police jail. Following a general court-martial, he was
shot to death at the Parish Prison, New Orleans, 23 March 1866.

Lewis Wilson was the second executed man to leave a will.

### 8 June 1866

ROBERT RODGERS, 20, a Marietta, Ohio, laborer, and a member of
Company B, 77th Ohio Infantry, was the last Union soldier to be executed.

Head Quarters Dist. Rio Grande,
Pro. Mar. Office
Brownsville, Texas, April 27th /66.

Lieut Col. D. D. Wheeler,
   Asst. Adjt. Genl,

Colonel,
        I have the honor to report that
the prisoner Rogers made his escape
from the Military Prison last night.
        As soon as I was notified
of his escape I sent parties up and
down the river to search for him,
but none of the parties come able
to find any trace of him.
        I have since found that Rogers
crossed the river last night — and that
he is now in Matamoros.
        After a careful examination of
the prison and finding the prisoners
chains in his room, it appears that
Rogers filed or sawed off his irons,
climbed over the partition of the room where
he was confined, went into the yard
of the prison where there were two (2) sentinels on duty, and made his escape over

Being a guard at the provost marshal's office was almost as dangerous as being a prisoner, as three "sentinels" in Brownsville, Tex., learned. When Robert Rodgers [Co. B, 77th Ohio Infantry] allegedly escaped confinement, the three who were on duty were arrested. Luckily for them, they never had to stand court-martial; the man had not escaped, but had been hiding under the floor of the prison.                                       *National Archives*

Rodgers, convicted of murdering a civilian, had enlisted in the army 27 December 1861, at Marietta, Ohio. While there he was held by civilian authorities for "stabing" a citizen, but reenlisted 9 October 1862. He was discharged 19 December 1863 "by virtue of re-enlistment as Veteran Volunteer . . . ." Rodgers was reported missing in action at Marks Mills, Arkansas, 25 April 1864. He was a prisoner of war, from November 1864 to 22 February 1865. Confined at Brownsville, Texas, he was paroled at Red River Lodge, Louisiana 26 February.

With a capital offense hanging over his head, Rodgers requested the assistance of an attorney, Frank E. MacManus. MacManus, who didn't know the man at all, attempted to visit him in the military prison at the post in Brownsville.

"I am in effect," MacManus wrote to Major-General G. W. Getty, commanding the District of the Rio Grande, 28 February 1866,

> denied admittance to the prison in time to be of any use to this unfortunate man, upon a question of mere form. The Provost-Marshal of the Post, and his Lieutenant are absent on business or pleasure; and the Acting Provost-Marshal General, as a matter of etiquette, refuse to give an order which should properly emanate from the former! This man's trial, if it has not already commence tomorrow. I respectfully submit for your Consideration, General, whether under a wise administration, military or civil, subordinates can thus be permitted to kill the spirit of the law by a pretended adherence to mere formula.

Before this event, MacManus acknowledged, he had good rapport with the officers of the post. But now, the officers had been transferred and replaced by "gentlemen who are no less strangers to their official duties than to me."

MacManus had received a general pass from Major-General Godfrey Weitzel, "as in Consequence of the reluctance manifested by Capt. Ayers, Act'g P. M. G. and Lieut. Potter Prison-Keeper, to accord me that privilege."

After Weitzel was relieved, MacManus presented his pass, "and was refused admittance on the ground that Genl. Weitzel was no longer in command.

> I urged that Col. Wheeler, A. A. G., by whom it was signed, still held the same position, and that his order entitled me to admittance without further question by a subordinate."

Based on his logic, he was "admitted once as a *favor*, and requested to give up the order for the inspection of Capt. Ayers, the new Act'g P. M. G."

MacManus did so "cheerfully, because in my previous intercourse with U. S. officers, I had generally found them to be gentlemen." But, when Mac-Manus asked for his pass back, *"as my property*, Capt. Ayers at first denied having received the paper at all, but afterward declared it was *mislaid*!"

Ayers finally allowed MacManus a pass, but only with a series of involved steps, taking close to two hours. "I respectfully submit, General," Mac-Manus complained, "that this paltry system of tergiversation is unworthy of any man, who, in the uniform of an officer of the United States, is permitted to represent them in even the meanest capacity.

> It is notorious that the prison is daily visited by any persons of more than questionable character without the slightest hindrance. Perhaps the fact of my *not* being the associate or partner of detectives, thieves or smugglers furnishes the real ground of my exclusion. If a more valid objection exists — if I am unfit to be trusted within the filthy precincts of that den, it should be made known — the cause of my exclusion or guarded admittance should be made public.

"Personally or pecuniarly," he concluded, "I have no interest in going there, but it is the inalienable right of every American citizen or soldier accused of crime to be aided by counsel in making his defense, and it is my *duty* to respond to this call."

There is nothing in Rodger's file to indicate that General Getty ever responded to MacManus' plea — or if the attorney represented Rodgers.

Two months later, while Rodgers was awaiting execution, Captain J. H. Evans, 116th Infantry, USCT, provost marshal, reported on 27 April 1866 to Lieutenant-Colonel D. D. Wheeler, assistant adjutant general, that

> . . . the prisoner Rogers made his escape from the Military Prison last night. . . . I have since learned that Rogers crossed the river last-night — and that he is now in Matamoras. After a careful examination of the Prison and finding the prisoners chains in his room, it appears that Rogers filed or sawed off his irons, climbed over the partition of the room where he was confined, went into the yard of the prison . . . were two (2) sentinels on duty, and made his escape over a brick wall about ten (10) feet high. . . . I have arrested the three (3) sentinals on duty at the time when Rogers made his escape.

Another month passed, and an anonymous request from the prison was sent to Colonel C. H. Whittelsey, assistant adjutant general, Department of Texas, requesting "that a day be fixed for the execution of [Rodgers] . . .

> On the night of the 26th of April 1866, Rodgers was sup-
> posed to have made his escape from prison. In the morn-
> ing of the day fixed for his execution he could not be
> found. It has just transpired that although he did escape
> from his room, he did not escape from the prison but
> concealed himself under the floor of one of the rooms
> of the prison, and for the last month has been engaged
> in tunnelling his way out. A plan for the escape of a very
> large number of men sentenced by the Civil Courts to
> the penitentiary and to be hung was divulged by one of
> their number to-day. The escape was to take place to-
> night. . . . An examination of the prison disclosed where
> Rodgers had been concealed, disclosed his implements
> of work, and his tunnel not less than 80 feet long, leading
> through the prison wall, under two sidewalks, the street,
> a yard and a building. The tunnel was completed, and
> Rodgers, when discovered, had escaped from the tunnel
> which opened under the building, and has attempted to
> secret himself under the floor of the building, having
> crawled not less than thirty feet under this floor. There
> is no doubt as to his identification.

Robert Rodgers' attempts to survive were fruitless. On 8 June 1866, the last man to be officially executed by the Union Army was hanged.

# CHAPTER ELEVEN

## The Afterword

During the Civil War, more than 275 men were executed for military offenses by the Union Army, whether they were guilty or not. It was not until 1885 — nineteen years after the last execution — that the Adjutant General's Office published its list. That list, used by historians since Dyer's day, is inaccurate and misleading. Why?

In the course of the research for this book, the author spent countless hours digging into original military service files, many of which had not been opened since the National Archives put them into place. They were filled with tantalizing information — information which could, or should, have been picked up more than a century ago.

The first reaction was a hint of cover-up. But such a reaction is based on mid-Twentieth century thinking, not on the realities and expediencies of the post-Civil War era. The Adjutant General's Office, charged with the responsibility of keeping records on all military executions, fell short in that duty. By reading individual files, I could sense the hurried pace in developing the 1885 report. Many of the files examined — when opened by me — were opened for the first time by a modern historian.

Each file begins with an official casualty sheet, followed by company muster rolls, enlistment documents, and miscellaneous material, such as court-martial proceedings, correspondence, and orders. Not all files are complete. In several cases, the files could not be located.

In a number of cases, a second or third casualty sheet was filed among the miscellaneous documents — with dates and cause of death differing from the first. The cause of death listed in the topmost sheet was, in most cases, the one listed in the Adjutant General's report. After confronting this frustrating discrepancy several times, it dawned on the author how that report might have been compiled, and why it is not accurate.

A civil servant, some anonymous person, was given the task of compiling the list. His first step was to go through the orders on file in the Adjutant General's Office, and decide who had been executed — on orders. Then he turned to the service records of the men who had been ordered executed. He took, unfortunately, the easy way out.

Without checking through the files, and the miscellaneous bits of paper, he assumed that the top sheet was the most factual. For the scores of historians who have used this document as reference, the clerk's assumption was not always correct. As a result, the 1885 report from the Adjutant General's Office is flawed and misleading.

The total number of men executed cannot be determined at this time and, one wonders, can an accurate accounting ever be made. At this time, all we can do is discard that number. We can determine without a shadow of a doubt that at least 275 men were executed. Beyond that, it is only conjecture.

Did all the men who were actually executed receive justice? The answer to that is yes and no . . . with strong emphasis on the no.

There appear to be elements of ethnic, religious and racial bias in the subjects for execution. In the initial manuscript search, only one or two instances of religious bias were encountered. At that time, the only evidence of a religious affiliation was found in a personal reminiscence written by a chaplain or an officer, usually referring to who gave the man or men the last rites. These random mentions were insufficient to develop a conclusion. Religious bias, if it existed to any extent, was not a major determinant in execution cases. Yet it appears that Roman Catholics suffered greater punishment than persons who professed other faiths. On the other hand, there are indications that ethnicity and race were greater determinators.

Of all men executed, 54.31 percent either were foreign-born or black. It is evident that the ethnics executed represented a greater proportion than they did in the army as a whole. According to the statistics developed by James M. McPherson,[1] 26 percent of all white soldiers in the Union Army were foreign-born, 9 percent were black. The number of foreign-born men executed is thus 28 percent higher than the average for the entire army. The black soldiers represent an even greater distortion:  133 percent higher than the army population proportion.

These observations led to the conclusion that, based on the comparison of the ratios, an ethnic or racial factor did influence who was chosen to set the example — by execution. The reason why, however, is elusive. There is no documentary evidence that states unequivocally that a man's race or place of birth was used against him in a court-martial. But, based on the statistical data, the appearance of this disproportion suggests it as a distinct possibility.

Were the executed soldiers any different from the rank and file?

Except for the racial and ethnic differences, the soldiers executed were no different from the average Billy Yank. Though similar, their presence before a firing squad or upon a gallows made them stand out vividly in the personal recollections of both officers and men. From August 1863 until March 1865, a week did not go by without one or more men being executed. On some days, as many as seven men were executed. The apparent reason for this regular execution pattern was the success of the retrieval process for deserters.

Estimates of the wartime desertion rate indicate that 200,000 Union soldiers left their units without permission; 80,000 were caught.[2] Using the figures developed in this research, only .19 percent of the returned deserters were executed. Such a small number of men brought to justice indicates a desire — not to fulfill the mandates of military justice — to set an example of some, but not others. Since accurate records of retrieved Civil War deserters do not exist, it is impossible to develop a statistical analysis of their ethnic and racial backgrounds. One can only assume that the total number of returned deserters reflected the total population mix of the Union Army, and not the ethnic/racial composition of those executed. If this presumption is true, the contention that ethnicity and race had a role in who would be used as examples gains additional validity.

Proponents of the separation of military justice from civilian courts of law state that military justice is faster. An analysis of the lapsed times — from offense to order of death sentence and from order to actual execution — supports that contention. Justice in the Union Army was swift and efficient. But was is it justice? In a number of cases, it was too swift and too efficient to be labeled justice.

This swiftness, and the military's own rules on appeals, denied innocent men their rights — and their lives. Field commanders, acting on their own authority, violated the Articles of War, by executing men — then writing the orders. The military also looked the other way at Lincoln's proclamation commuting death sentences to imprisonment. Men were executed in defiance of that order.

One cannot help but wonder if the actions of some of these officers did as much to tarnish the reputation of the military as did the crimes for which these men were executed.

If men were executed without due process, why was there not a public outcry?

The lack of public reaction can possibly be traced to the only source of information available to Civil War America: the daily newspaper. Newspaper coverage of military crimes and military executions was supportive of the military. Pro-justice media coverage, coupled with lacks of education and sophistication on the part of the "criminals" and their families, reduced or eliminated any negative reaction among the general public.

When one considers the number of innocent men executed for military crimes, the acts of injustice appear to be few and far between. But is justice served when even one individual is wrongly convicted, or the system is modified for military expediency? That question provokes us to review the mutiny cases against members of the United States Colored Troops. The treatment afforded these men, a majority of whom were former slaves, was deplorable. It points out that the federal government did not know what to do with slaves once they were freed — a fact that was reinforced during Reconstruction. If the Union Army was a staging ground for future national leaders, as it was for white officers, it would have been the ideal time to nurture the blacks who would some-day return to the South and rebuild it. Unfortunately, it was another opportunity lost.

The last — and the largest — executions for mutiny taking place during the Civil War took place 1 December 1865, when six members of the 3rd Infantry, United States Colored Troops, were shot to death. These men died almost a year after the federal government acknowledged their right to equal pay, and nine months after Lee surrendered to Grant.

Justice during the Civil War was indeed swift; it was indeed efficient, but the question still remains: Was it truly justice?

## ENDNOTES TO CHAPTER ELEVEN

1. James M. McPherson, *Ordeal by Fire, The Civil War and Reconstruction* [New York, 1982], p. 358.

2. *Ibid.*, p. 358.

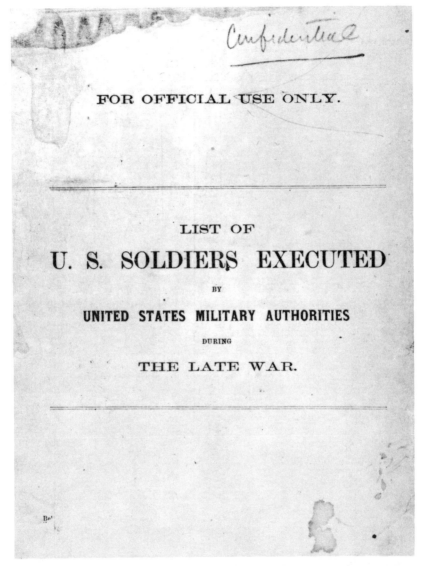

*Confidential*

FOR OFFICIAL USE ONLY.

LIST OF

# U. S. SOLDIERS EXECUTED

BY

## UNITED STATES MILITARY AUTHORITIES

DURING

THE LATE WAR.

The official version . . . "List of U. S. Soldiers Executed by United States Military Authorities During the Late War." Note the handwritten "confidential" label and printed "For Official Use Only" designation. Was this done to keep prying eyes from uncovering the truth about the execution of Union soldiers during the Civil War?     *National Archives*

2

*List of U. S. soldiers executed by United States*

| Name. | Rank. | Co. | Regiment. | Date of execution. |
|---|---|---|---|---|
| **ARKANSAS.** | | | | |
| Keiffe, Peter | Private... | B | 2d Cavalry | Oct. 7, 1864 |
| McBroone, Alexander D | ...do ..... | B | 1st Infantry | Apr. 21, 1865 |
| **CALIFORNIA.** | | | | |
| Hudson, Frank | Private... | I | 2d Cavalry | June 16, 1865 |
| Kerr, Robert | ...do ..... | A | 1st Cavalry | Mar. 20, 1864 |
| Kleinkoff, Peter | ...do ..... | E | 4th Infantry | July 17, 1863 |
| Smith, Charles | Corporal | K | 1st Infantry | Nov. 26, 1862 |
| **COLORADO.** | | | | |
| Lockman, Charles | Private... | F | 2d Cavalry | Nov. 10, 1864 |
| Philbrooks, Darius A | 1st sergt. | K | 1st Cavalry | Apr. 8, 1862 |
| **CONNECTICUT.** | | | | |
| Brown, John, 2d | Private... | H | 10th Infantry | Feb. 18, 1865 |
| Collins, James | ...do ..... | D | 8th Infantry | Jan. 7, 1865 |
| Cooper, William | ...do ..... | E | 10th Infantry | Mar. 11, 1865 |
| Dix, Thomas | ...do ..... | G | 1st Heavy Artillery | Dec. 21, 1864 |
| Dix, William | ...do ..... | E | 8th Infantry | Jan. 7, 1865 |
| Elliott, Edward | ...do ..... | I | 14th Infantry | Sept. 18, 1863 |
| Hall, John | ...do ..... | G | 1st Heavy Artillery | Dec. 21, 1864 |
| Jackson, William | ...do ..... | A | 10th Infantry | Mar. 10, 1865 |
| Jones, Thomas | ...do ..... | H | ...........do | Feb. 18, 1865 |
| Landy, Michael | ...do ..... | A | ...........do | Feb. 17, 1865 |
| Layton, George, *alias* Charles Eastman | ...do ..... | K | 14th Infantry | Sept. 18, 1863 |
| Mahoney, John | ...do ..... | K | 10th Infantry | Mar. 10, 1865 |
| McCurdy, Henry | ...do ..... | G | 1st Heavy Artillery | Dec. 21, 1864 |
| Morgan, Jacob | ...do ..... | D | 8th Infantry | Apr. 28, 1864 |
| Newton, Frank L | ...do ..... | F | 13th Infantry | June 16, 1862 |
| Parker, John | ...do ..... | G | 10th Infantry | Feb. 24, 1865 |
| Root, Newell W., *alias* George H. Harris | ...do ..... | H | 1st Heavy Artillery | Jan. 27, 1865 |
| Rowley, John | ...do ..... | D | 7th Infantry | Sept. 3, 1864 |
| Schumaker, Henry | ...do ..... | C | 6th Infantry | Apr. 17, 1864 |
| Smith, John | ...do ..... | G | 1st Heavy Artillery | Dec. 21, 1864 |
| Stark, Henry | ...do ..... | E | 6th Infantry | Apr. 17, 1864 |
| Thompson, James | ...do ..... | G | 1st Heavy Artillery | Dec. 21, 1864 |
| Vandall, Mitchell | ...do ..... | K | 8th Infantry | Nov. 9, 1863 |
| Wales, Francis | ...do ..... | D | ...........do | ...do ...... |
| **DELAWARE.** | | | | |
| Griffin, William T., *alias* George Bolter | Private... | C | 8th Infantry ... ...... | Mar. 10, 1865 |
| **ILLINOIS.** | | | | |
| Benjamin, Valentine | Private... | C | 44th Infantry | Nov. 13, 1863 |
| Daily, Erastus C | ...do ..... | D | 88th Infantry | ...do ...... |
| Dickman, Robert | ...do ..... | G | 18th Infantry | Oct. 2, 1861 |
| Geer, David | ...do ..... | D | 28th Infantry | Mar. 4, 1865 |
| McLean, Henry | ...do ..... | G | 2d Light Artillery | Aug. 25, 1863 |
| Myers, John | Sergeant | C | 7th Infantry | Apr. 28, 1864 |
| Wilson, William A | Private... | G | 12th Cavalry | July 28, 1865 |
| **INDIANA.** | | | | |
| Billingsby, Charles, *alias* Cooper, *alias* Roberts | Private... | | 7th Battery | Dec. 23, 1864 |
| Blazer, David | ...do ..... | | 4th Battery | June 1863 |
| Gay, Robert | ...do ..... | D | 6th Cavalry | Mar. 27, 1863 |
| Murray, John | ...do ..... | Unas'd. | 11th Cavalry | Dec. 23, 1864 |
| Reynolds, Hiram | ...do ..... | H | 82d Infantry | Aug. 17, 1863 |
| Ryan, Thomas, *alias* Reagan | ...do ..... | Unas'd. | 51st Infantry | Dec. 23, 1864 |
| Stout, Reuben | ...do ..... | K | 60th Infantry | Oct. 23, 1863 |
| Woods, John P | ...do ..... | F | 19th Infantry | June 12, 1863 |
| **KANSAS.** | | | | |
| ...l, John | Private... | I | 2d Cavalry | July 11, 1862 |
| ...le, John W | ...do ..... | G | 1st Infantry | July 14, 1861 |
| Dr...ll, Alexander | ...do ..... | H | 7th Cavalry | Mar. 18, 1862 |
| Ray...nd, Joseph | ...do ..... | C | ...........do | Nov. 24, 1861 |
| **KENTUCKY.** | | | | |
| Anderson, James | Private... | H | 27th Infantry | Sept. 4, 1863 |

3

*military authorities during the late war.*

| Mode of execution. | Offense. | Authority. |
| --- | --- | --- |
| Shot......... | Murder......................... | G. O., No. 168, Dept. of the Missouri, Sept. 14, 1864. |
| ....do ......... | Desertion ...................... | G. O., No. 23, Dept. of Arkansas, Feb. 18, 1865. |
| | | |
| Hanged ..... | Murder ,........................ | G. O., No. 40, Dept. of the Pacific, June 1, 1865. |
| Shot.......... | ....do .......... | G. O., No. 4, Dept. of New Mexico, Feb. 29, 1864. |
| ....do ......... | Desertion and attempted murder... | G. O., No. 149, War Dept., Adjt. Gen.'s Office, May 26, 1863. |
| ....do ......... | Mutiny........................ | By order of Colonel J. R. West. |
| | | |
| Hanged ..... | Murder ......................... | By order of Lieutenant William Wise, 2d Colorado Cavalry. |
| Shot.......... | Violation 9th Article of War ........ | G. O., No. 25, Dept. of New Mexico, Apr. 4, 1862. |
| | | |
| Hanged ..... | Desertion ...................... | G. C. M. O., No. 35, Dept. of Virginia, Feb. 17, 1865. |
| Shot.......... | ....do........ | G. O., No. 179, Dept. Virginia and North Carolina, Dec. 30, 1864. |
| ....do ......... | ....do........ | G. C. M. O., No. 47, Dept. of Virginia, Mar. 9, 1865. |
| ....do ......... | ....do........ | G. O., No. 172, Army of the James, Dec. 20, 1864. |
| ....do ......... | ....do........ | G. O., No. 179, Dept. Virginia and North Carolina, Dec. 30, 1864. |
| ....do ......... | ....do........ | G. O., No. 88, Army of the Potomac, Sept. 11, 1863. |
| Hanged ..... | Murder ....................... | G. O., No. 172, Army of the James, Dec. 20, 1864. |
| Shot.......... | Desertion ...................... | G. O., No. 44, Dept. of Virginia, Mar. 4, 1865. |
| Hanged ..... | ....do........ | G. O., No. 35, Dept. of Virginia, Feb. 17, 1865. |
| Shot.......... | ....do........ | G. O., No. 32, Dept. of Virginia, Feb. 16, 1865. |
| ....do ......... | ....do........ | G. O., No. 88, Army of the Potomac, Sept. 11, 1863. |
| ....do ......... | ....do........ | G. O., No. 44, Dept. of Virginia, Mar. 4, 1865. |
| ....do ......... | ....do........ | G. O., No. 172, Army of the James, Dec. 20, 1864. |
| ....do ......... | ....do........ | G. O., No. 2, U. S. Forces Norfolk and Portsmouth, Apr. 27, 1864. |
| Hanged ..... | Theft........................ | S. O., No. 103, Dept. of the Gulf, June 14, 1862. |
| Shot.......... | Desertion ...................... | G. O., No. 34, Dept. of Virginia, Feb. 17, 1865. |
| Hanged ..... | ....do........ | G. C. M. O., No. 3, Army of the Potomac, Jan. 18, 1865. |
| ....do ......... | ....do........ | G. O., No. 97, Dept. Virginia and North Carolina, Aug. 23, 1864. |
| Shot.......... | ....do........ | G. O., No. 50, Dept. of the South, Apr. 15, 1864. |
| ....do ......... | ....do........ | G. O., No. 172, Army of the James, Dec. 20, 1864. |
| ....do ......... | ....do........ | G. O., No. 50, Dept. of the South, Apr. 15, 1864. |
| ....do ......... | ....do........ | G. O., No. 172, Army of the James, Dec. 20, 1864. |
| ....do ......... | ....do........ | G. O., No. 24, Dept. Virginia and North Carolina, Oct. 31, 1863. |
| | | Do. |
| | | |
| Shot......... | Desertion ...................... | G. C. M. O., No. 11, Army of the Potomac, Mar. 1, 1865. |
| | | |
| Shot.......... | Desertion...................... | G. O., No. 24?, Dept. of the Cumberland, Oct. 20, 1863. |
| ....do ......... | ....do........ | Do. |
| Hanged ..... | Murder ..................... | Regimental court-martial. |
| Shot.......... | ....do........ | G. C. M. O., No. 38, Army of the Tennessee, Oct. 31, 1864. |
| ....do ......... | Desertion ...................... | G. O., No. 105, Dept. of the Cumberland, May 9, 1863. |
| Hanged ..... | Murder ..................... | G. C. M. O., No. 159, War Dept., Adjt. Gen.'s Office, Apr. 14, 1864. |
| Shot.......... | Desertion ...................... | G. O., No.9, Headquarters Cavalry, Div. of the Gulf, July 25, 1865. |
| | | |
| Shot.......... | Desertion ...................... | G.-O., No. 38, District of Indiana, Dec. 14, 1864. |
| ....do ......... | ....do........ | G. O., No. 108, Dept. of the Cumberland, June 19, 1863. |
| ....do ......... | ....do........ | G. O., No. 23, Dept. of the Ohio, Mar. 21, 1863. |
| ....do ......... | ....do........ | G. O., No. 38, Dist. of Indiana, Dec. 14, 1864. |
| Hanged ..... | Murder ..................... | G. O., No. 188, Dept. of the Cumberland, Aug. 11, 1863 |
| Shot.......... | Desertion ...................... | G. O., No. 38, Dist. of Indiana, Dec. 14, 1864. |
| ....do ......... | Murder ..................... | G. O., No. 279, War Dept., Adjt. Gen.'s Office, Aug. 8, 1863. |
| ....? ......... | Desertion ...................... | G. O., No. 60, Army of the Potomac, June 8, 1863. |
| | | |
| Hanged ..... | Rape........................ | G. O., No. 55, Headquarters 2d Kansas Cavalry, July 9, 1862. |
| Shot.......... | Murder ..................... | Orders, No. 8, Army of the West, July 12, 1861. |
| ....do ......... | | |
| ....do ......... | | |
| | | |
| Shot.......... | Desertion ...................... | G. O., No. 130, Dept. of the Ohio, Aug. 13, 1863. |

4

| Name. | Rank. | Co. | Regiment. | Date of execution. |
|---|---|---|---|---|
| **KENTUCKY—Continued.** | | | | |
| Calhoun, Samuel H. | Private... | A | 2d Infantry | Feb. 5, 1862 |
| Carmen, Frazier | ...do ..... | F | 27th Infantry | Sept. 4, 1863 |
| Coffey, Christopher | ...do ..... | C | ........do........ | ...do........ |
| Coffey, John W. | ...do ..... | C | ........do........ | ...do........ |
| Gatewood, Richard | ...do ..... | C | ........do........ | ...do........ |
| Minix, William | ...do ..... | A | 1st Infantry | Dec. 20, 1861 |
| Pointer, James A. | ...do ..... | H | 9th Infantry | June 16, 1863 |
| Rhea, Larkin D. | ...do ..... | C | 27th Infantry | Sept. 4, 1863 |
| Roarch, Lewis | ...do ..... | D | 7th Infantry | Dec. 24, 1864 |
| Schockman, John | ...do ..... | I | ........do........ | Jan. 6, 1865 |
| Stivers, Lewis | ...do ..... | B | 1st Infantry | June 23, 1863 |
| | | | 7th Infantry | Sept. 21, 1862 |
| **LOUISIANA.** | | | | |
| Scott, Francis | Private... | F | 1st Infantry | Aug. 14, 1863 |
| **MAINE.** | | | | |
| Hunter, Cyrus H. | Private... | G | 3d Infantry | Dec. 4, 1863 |
| Jewett, Thomas | ...do ..... | D | 5th Infantry | Aug. 14, 1863 |
| Laird, William H. | ...do ..... | G | 17th Infantry | July 15, 1863 |
| Lunt, William W. | ...do ..... | I | 9th Infantry | Dec. 1, 1862 |
| **MARYLAND.** | | | | |
| Downing, Samuel W., *alias* John W. Ball | Private... | H | 4th Infantry | Sept. 16, 1864 |
| Jones, Albert | ...do ..... | K | 3d Infantry | Sept. 18, 1863 |
| Kane, William, *alias* William Carter | ...do ..... | A | 8th Infantry | Dec. 16, 1864 |
| Kuhnes, Joseph | ...do ..... | I | 2d Infantry | Mar. 7, 1862 |
| McNealy, J. J., *alias* Joseph Johnson | ...do ..... | | 1st Infantry | Mar. 18, 1865 |
| McDonald, George W., *alias* M. M. Dunning | Sergeant. | | Cavalry | Sep. 23, 1864 |
| Merling, Charles H | Private... | H | 2d Infantry | Oct. 14, 1864 |
| Sweney, John | ...do ..... | C | 1st Infantry | Sept. 20, 1864 |
| Weaver, James, *alias* N. E. Baker. | ...do ..... | D | ........do........ | Mar. 26, 1865 |
| Williams, Charles | ...do ..... | D | 4th Infantry | Sept. 25, 1863 |
| **MASSACHUSETTS.** | | | | |
| Baker, Wallace | Private... | I | 55th Infantry (col'd) | June 18, 1864 |
| Cook, John W | ...do ..... | B | ........do........ | Feb. 18, 1864 |
| Dawson, Thomas R. | ...do ..... | H | 20th Infantry | Apr. 20, 1864 |
| Dixon, John C. | ...do ..... | I | 1st Heavy Artillery ... | Dec. 23, 1864 |
| Hill, William F. | ...do ..... | K | 20th Infantry | Aug. 28, 1863 |
| Lloyd, Spencer | ...do ..... | B | 55th Infantry (col'd) | Feb. 18, 1864 |
| Lynch, William | ...do ..... | G | 2d Cavalry | June 16, 1863 |
| McElheny, Frank | ...do ..... | F | 24th Infantry | Aug. 8, 1864 |
| Ormsley, William E. | ...do ..... | B | 2d Cavalry | Feb. 7, 1864 |
| Roberts, John | ...do ..... | H | 15th Infantry | Oct. 30, 1863 |
| Smith, John M | ...do ..... | A | 55th Infantry (col'd) | Feb. 18, 1864 |
| Smith, John | ...do ..... | 1st Co. | Sharpshooters | Aug. 28, 1863 |
| Starbird, John D. | ...do ..... | K | 19th Infantry | May 20, 1864 |
| **MICHIGAN.** | | | | |
| Anderson, Henry | Private... | D | 9th Cavalry | May 13, 1865 |
| Beardsley, Henry C. | ...do ..... | G | 5th Infantry | Oct. 17, 1863 |
| Milika, Julius | ...do ..... | E | 10th Infantry | May 15, 1863 |
| **MISSOURI.** | | | | |
| Eastman, Edward | Private... | B | 2d Artillery | Nov. 25, 1864 |
| Jackson, Jefferson | ...do ..... | B | 9th M. S. M. Cavalry. | Oct. 28, 1864 |
| Kingston, Paul | ...do ..... | M | 1st Cavalry | Nov. 27, 1863 |
| Purvis, Abraham | ...do ..... | C | 21st Infantry | Jan. 13, 1865 |
| Reily, John, jr. | ...do ..... | L | 2d Artillery | Apr. 29, 1864 |
| Richardson, Ephraim | ...do ..... | C | 21st Infantry | Jan. 13, 1865 |
| **NEW HAMPSHIRE.** | | | | |
| Benson, John | | Unas'd | 5th Infantry | Jan. 6, 1865 |
| Bradley, George, *alias* George W. Bates. | Private... | H | ........do........ | Dec. 23, 1864 |
| Brown, James F. | ...do ..... | G | 3d Infantry | Dec. 26, 1864 |
| Burnham, Henry A | ...do ..... | E | 5th Infantry | May 9, 1864 |
| Eagen, John | ...do ..... | A | 2d Infantry | Apr. 15, 1864 |
| Genan or Jenos, Michael, *alias* John Martin | ...do ..... | B | 5th Infantry | Dec. 30, 1864 |
| Holt, Henry | ...do ..... | F | 2d Infantry | Apr. 15, 1864 |

5

*military authorities during the late war.*—Continued.

| Mode of execution. | Offense. | Authority. |
|---|---|---|
| Shot | Murder | G. O., No. 7, Dept. of the Ohio, Feb. 4, 1862. |
| ......do | Desertion | G. O., No. 130 Dept. of the Ohio, Aug. 13, 1863. |
| ......do | ......do | Do. |
| ......do | ......do | Do. |
| ......do | ......do | G. O., No. 13, Dept. of Western Virginia, Nov. 15, 1861. |
| ......do | ......do | G. O., No. 140, Dept. of the Cumberland, June 12, 1863. |
| ......do | ......do | G. O., No. 130, Dept. of the Ohio, Aug. 13, 1863. |
| ......do | ......do | G. O., No. 178, Dept. of the Gulf, Dec. 20, 1864. |
| Hanged | Murder | G. O., No. 180, Dept. of the Gulf, Dec. 29, 1864. |
| ......do | ......do | G. O., No. 153, Dept. of the Cumberland, June 22, 1863. |
| Shot | Desertion | |
| ......do | Murder | |
| | | |
| Shot | Murder | G. O., No. 58, Dept. of the Gulf, Aug. 10, 1863. |
| | | |
| Shot | Desertion | G. O., No. 103, Army of the Potomac, Nov. 20, 1863. |
| ......do | ......do | G. O., No. 73, Army of the Potomac, Aug. 7, 1863. |
| ...?..do | ......do | G. O., No. 57, Dept. of the East, July 7, 1863. |
| ......do | ......do | G. O., No. 171, War Dept., Adjt. Gen.'s Office, Oct. 29, 1862. |
| | | |
| Shot | Desertion | G. O., No. 83, Dept. of Washington, Sept. 14, 1864. |
| ......do | ......do | G. O., No. 88, Army of the Potomac, Sept. 11, 1863. |
| Hanged | ......do | G. C. M. O., No. 50, Army of the Potomac, Dec. 12, 1864. |
| ......do | Murder | G. O., No. 87, Army of the Potomac, Mar. 4, 1862. |
| Shot | Desertion | G. O., No. 12, Army of the Potomac, Mar. 11, 1865. |
| ......do | Desertion and attempted murder | G. O., No. 74, Middle Department, Sept. 19, 1864. |
| ......do | Desertion | G. C. M. O., No. 36, Army of the Potomac, Sept. 18, 1864. |
| ......do | ......do | G. C. M. O., No. 32, Army of the Potomac, Aug. 31, 1864. |
| ......do | ......do | G. O., No. 12, Army of the Potomac, Mar. 11, 1865. |
| ......do | ......do | G. O., No. 90, Army of the Potomac, Sept. 17, 1863. |
| | | |
| Shot | Mutiny | G. O., No. 90, Dept. of the South, June 16, 1864. |
| Hanged | Rape | G. O., No. 6, Dist. of Florida, Feb. 17, 1864. |
| ......do | Desertion and rape | G. C. M. O., No. 40, War Dept., Adjt. Gen.'s Office, Mar. 15, 1864. |
| Shot | Desertion | G. C. M. O., No. 51, Army of the Potomac, Dec. 17, 1864. |
| ......do | ......do | G. O., No. 86, Army of the Potomac, Aug. 24, 1863. |
| Hanged | Rape | G. O., No. 6, Dist. of Florida, Feb. 17, 1864. |
| Shot | Mutiny | G. O., No. 46, Dept. of the East, June 6, 1863. |
| ......do | Desertion | G. O., No. 91, Dept. Virginia and North Carolina, Aug. 6, 1864. |
| ......do | ......do | G. O., No. 10, Cavalry Camp, Vienna, Feb. 7, 1864. |
| ......do | ......do | G. O., No. 98, Army of the Potomac, Oct. 24, 1863. |
| Hanged | Rape | G. O., No. 6, Dist. of Florida, Feb. 17, 1864. |
| Shot | Desertion | G. O., No. 86, Army of the Potomac, Aug. 24, 1863. |
| ......do | ......do | G. C. M. O., No. 18, Army of the Potomac, May —, 1864. |
| | | |
| Shot | Murder | Military Commission, General Kilpatrick. |
| ......do | Desertion | G. O., No. 95, Army of the Potomac, Oct. 8, 1863. |
| ......do | ......do | G. O., No. 100, Dept. of the Cumberland, May 4, 1863. |
| | | |
| Shot | Desertion and pillage | G. O., No. 174, Dept. of the Missouri, Sept. 23, 1864. |
| ......do | Murder | G. O., No. 190, Dept. of the Missouri, Oct. 6, 1864. |
| Hanged | ......do | G. O., No. 122, Dept. of the Missouri, Oct. 21, 1863. |
| ......do | ......do | G. O., No. 3, Dept. of the Missouri, Jan. 9, 1865. |
| Shot | ......do | G. O., No. 41, Dept. of the Missouri, Mar. 19, 1864. |
| Hanged | ......do | G. O., No. 3, Dept. of the Missouri, Jan. 9, 1865. |
| | | |
| Shot | Desertion | G. C. M. O., No. 1, Army of the Potomac, Jan. 2, 1865. |
| Hanged | ......do | G. C. M. O., No. 51, Army of the Potomac, Dec. 17, 1864. |
| Shot | ......do | G. O., No. 173, Army of the James, Dec. 24, 1864. |
| ......do | ......do | G. O., No. 56, Dept. Virginia and North Carolina, May 4, 1864. |
| ......do | ......do | G. O., No. 43, Dept. Virginia and North Carolina, Apr. 14, 1864. |
| Hanged | ......do | G. C. M. O., No. 32, Army of the Potomac, Dec. 24, 1864. |
| Shot | ......do | G. O., No. 43, Dept. Virginia and North Carolina, Apr. 14, 1864. |

6

*List of U. S. soldiers executed by United States*

| Name. | Rank. | Co. | Regiment. | Date of execution. |
|---|---|---|---|---|
| **NEW HAMPSHIRE—Continued.** | | | | |
| Kendall, John | Private | G | 3d Infantry | Dec. 17, 1863 |
| Lynch, John, *alias* John Wood | do | F | 5th Infantry | Dec. 22, 1864 |
| McDonough, Owen | do | K | 3d Infantry | Apr. 29, 1864 |
| Miller, Henry | do | F | 3d Infantry | Apr. 16, 1864 |
| Miller, William, *alias* James Craig | do | F | 5th Infantry | Dec. 22, 1864 |
| Murray, William F | do | G | 2d Infantry | Aug. 2, 1861 |
| Scott, James | do | A | do | Apr. 29, 1864 |
| Sharp, Joseph H., *alias* Samuel Trangler | do | A | 12th Infantry | Feb. 9, 1865 |
| Thompson, John | do | H | 5th Infantry | Dec. 16, 1864 |
| Velon, John | do | G | do | Oct. 28, 1864 |
| **NEW JERSEY.** | | | | |
| Callaghan, John | Private | H | 2d Cavalry | June 10, 1864 |
| Connelly, Joseph | do | H | 4th Infantry | Oct. 9, 1863 |
| Cox, Peter | do | A | do | Jan. 6, 1865 |
| Johnson, Thomas | do | D | 2d Cavalry | June 10, 1864 |
| King, Charles | do | L | 3d Cavalry | Jan. 6, 1865 |
| Krubert, Christopher | do | B | 13th Infantry | June 19, 1863 |
| Regley, Henry | do | L | 3d Cavalry | Jan. 6, 1865 |
| Smith, John | do | H | 8th Infantry | Mar. 18, 1865 |
| Snover, John | do | M | 2d Cavalry | June 10, 1864 |
| **NEW MEXICO.** | | | | |
| Coffield, Joseph | Private | K | 1st Cavalry | Jan. 19, 1864 |
| Carrabojal, Homoboma | do | D | do | Nov. 27, 1863 |
| Madrid, Juan | do | C | do | Sept. 8, 1865 |
| **NEW YORK.** | | | | |
| Abraham, Thomas | Private | G | 139th Infantry | Mar. 7, 1864 |
| Aierdain, Jacob | Corporal | G | 119th Infantry | Sept. 17, 1863 |
| Allen, Winslow N | Private | H | 76th Infantry | Dec. 18, 1863 |
| Brandt, Frederick W | do | E | 81st Infantry | Mar. 26, 1865 |
| Butler, Bradford | do | I | 157th Infantry | Aug. 1, 1863 |
| Devlin, Jas., *alias* Pat. Diamond, *alias* Fr'k Tully | | E | 43d Infantry | Feb. 3, 1865 |
| Devoe, William H | Private | B | 57th Infantry | Dec. 18, 1863 |
| Flood, John, *alias* John Smith | do | E | 41st Infantry | June 19, 1864 |
| Geary, Daniel | do | E | 72d Infantry | July 15, 1864 |
| Gillespie, Francis | do | B | 15th Cavalry | July 11, 1864 |
| Gordon, Ransom S | do | E | 72d Infantry | July 15, 1864 |
| Hamill, Henry | do | D | 131st Infantry | Apr. 25, 1863 |
| Hoefler, John | do | E | 124th Infantry | Feb. 17, 1865 |
| Hummel, Charles | do | H | 7th Infantry | Dec. 16, 1864 |
| Jangrow, Newal | do | D | 64th Infantry | Mar. 3, 1865 |
| Johnston, William H | do | K | 1st Cavalry | Dec. 13, 1861 |
| Kessler, John | do | E | 103d Infantry | Dec. 5, 1862 |
| Lynch, William I | do | F | 63d Infantry | Sept. 30, 1864 |
| McMahon, John | do | K | 99th Infantry | June 13, 1862 |
| McNamara, Patrick | do | A | 132d Infantry | June 30, 1865 |
| Nichols, John | do | K | 69th Infantry | Mar. 14, 1865 |
| Preble, James | do | A | 12th Cavalry | Mar. 31, 1865 |
| Prevost, Joseph | do | A | 1st Lin. Cavalry | Nov. 30, 1864 |
| Raymond, Anthony | do | B | 64th Infantry | Mar. 3, 1865 |
| Rowe, Edward | do | C | 179th Infantry | Dec. 10, 1864 |
| Smalz, Adam | do | E | 66th Infantry | Oct. 2, 1863 |
| Smith, Daniel C | do | C | 179th Infantry | Dec. 10, 1864 |
| Smith, William | do | E | 78th Infantry | Sept. 18, 1863 |
| Sperry, Charles | Sergeant | B | 13th Cavalry | Mar. 3, 1865 |
| Suhr, Christopher | Private | H | 7th Infantry | Dec. 16, 1864 |
| Thornton, Waterman | do | D | 179th Infantry | Jan. 6, 1865 |
| Timlin, John | do | B | 145th Infantry | Sept. 25, 1863 |
| Treece, Cornelius | do | K | 78th Infantry | do |
| Turner, Charles | do | C | 114th Infantry | Dec. 28, 1863 |
| Van, George | do | D | 12th Infantry | Sept. 18, 1863 |
| **OHIO.** | | | | |
| Connel, Michael | Private | E | 24th Infantry | Mar. 5, 1862 |
| Hardup, John W | do | A | 43d Infantry | Sept. 6, 1865 |
| Prince, George W | do | B | 22d Infantry | Dec. 16, 1864 |
| Rodgers, Robert | do | C | 77th Infantry | June 3, 1866 |
| Thompson, John H | do | C | 1st Cavalry | Apr. 28, 1864 |
| Whitlow, Isaac B., *alias* John Hall | do | D | 23d Infantry | Aug. 5, 1864 |

7

*military authorities during the late war*—Continued.

| Mode of execution. | Offense. | Authority. |
|---|---|---|
| Shot | Desertion | G. O., No. 111, Dept. of the South, Dec. 14, 1863. |
| Hanged | do | G. C. M. O., No. 51, Army of the Potomac, Dec. 17, 1864. |
| Shot | do | G. O., No. 45, Dept. Virginia and North Carolina, Apr. 18, 1864 |
| do | do | Drum-head court-martial, Apr. 15, 1864. |
| Hanged | do | C. C. M. O., No. 51, Army of the Potomac, Dec. 17, 1864. |
| do | Murder | G. O., No. 25, Dept. Northeast Virginia, Aug. 1, 1861. |
| Shot | Desertion | G. O., No. 45, Dept. Virginia and North Carolina, Apr. 18, 1864. |
| do | do | G. O., No. 26, Dept. of Virginia, Feb. 4, 1865. |
| Hanged | do | G. C. M. O., No. 50, Army of the Potomac, Dec. 12, 1864. |
| Shot | do | G. C. M. O., No. 39, Army of the Potomac, Oct. 15, 1864. |
| | | |
| Shot | Rape and theft | G. C. M. O., No. 119, War Dept., Adjt. Gen.'s Office, May 26, 1864. |
| do | Desertion | G. O., No. 94, Army of the Potomac, Oct. 2, 1863. |
| do | do | G. C. M. O., No. 1, Army of the Potomac, Jan. 2, 1865. |
| do | Rape and theft | G. C. M. O., No. 119, War Dept., Adjt. Gen.'s Office, May 26, 1864. |
| do | Spy | By order of General Sheridan. |
| do | Desertion | G. O., No. 63, Army of the Potomac, June 13, 1863. |
| do | Spy | By order of General Sheridan. |
| do | Desertion | G. C. M. O., No. 12, Army of the Potomac, March 11, 1865. |
| do | Rape and theft | G. C. M. O., No. 119, War Dept., Adjt. Gen.'s Office, May 26, 1864. |
| | | |
| Shot | Murder | G. O., No. 33, Dept. of New Mexico, Dec. 31, 1863. |
| Hanged | do | G. O., No. 104, Dept. of New Mexico, Sept. 30, 1863. |
| do | do | G. O., No. 23, Dept. of New Mexico, Sept. 2, 1865. |
| | | |
| Shot | Acting as a spy | G. C. M. O., No. 26, Dept. Virginia and N. Carolina, Feb. 29, 1864. |
| do | Desertion | G. O., No. 88, Army of the Potomac, Sept. 11, 1863. |
| do | do | G. O., No. 104, Army of the Potomac, Dec. 5, 1863. |
| do | do | G. C. M. O., No. 51, Army of Virginia, Mar. 25, 1865. |
| do | do | G. O., No. 71, Army of the Potomac, July 21, 1863. |
| do | do | G. O., No. 9, Dept. of the East, Feb. 1, 1865. |
| do | do | G. O., No. 104, Army of the Potomac, Dec. 5, 1863. |
| do | do | G. O., No. 91, Dept. of the South, June 17, 1864. |
| Hanged | Rape | G. C. M. O., No. 194, War Dept., Adjt. Gen.'s Office, July 8, 1864. |
| do | Murder | G. O., No. 44, Dept. of West Virginia, July 10, 1864. |
| do | Rape | G. C. M. O., No. 194, War Dept., Adjt. Gen.'s Office, July 8, 1864. |
| Shot | Pillaging | S. O., No. 37, Advanced Brig. on Bayou Boeuff, La., Apr. 25, 1863. |
| do | Desertion | G. C. M. O., No. 7, Army of the Potomac, Feb. 9, 1865. |
| Hanged | do | S. O., No. 50, Army of the Potomac, Dec. 12, 1864. |
| Shot | do | G. C. M. O., No. 9, Army of the Potomac, Feb. 20, 1865. |
| do | do | G. O., No. 52, Army of the Potomac, Dec. 11, 1861. |
| Hanged | Murder | G. O., No. 136, War Dept., Adjt. Gen.'s Office, Nov. 15, 1862. |
| Shot | Desertion | G. C. M. O., No. 35, Army of the Potomac, Sept. 15, 1864. |
| Hanged | Murder | G. O., No. 54, Dept. of Virginia, June 1, 1862. |
| do | do | G. O., No. 71, Dept. of North Carolina, May 31, 1865. |
| do | Desertion | G. C. M. O., No. 11, Army of the Potomac, Mar. 1, 1865. |
| Shot | Rape | G. O., No. 22, Dept. of North Carolina, Mar. 26, 1865. |
| Hanged | Murder | G. O., No. 72, Dept. of West Virginia, Sept. 10, 1864. |
| Shot | Desertion | G. C. M. O., No. 9, Army of the Potomac, Feb. 20, 1865. |
| Hanged | do | G. C. M. O., No. 49, Army of the Potomac, Dec. 6, 1864. |
| Shot | do | G. O., No. 92, Army of the Potomac, Sept. 27, 1863. |
| Hanged | do | G. C. M. O., No. 49, Army of the Potomac, Dec. 6, 1864. |
| Shot | do | G. O., No. 88, Army of the Potomac, Sept. 11, 1863. |
| do | Rape | G. O., No. 31, Dept. of Washington, Feb. 27, 1865. |
| Hanged | Desertion | G. C. M. O., No. 50, Army of the Potomac, Dec. 12, 1864. |
| do | do | G. C. M. O., No. 1, Army of the Potomac, Jan. 2, 1865. |
| Shot | do | G. O., No. 90, Army of the Potomac, Sept. 17, 1863. |
| do | do | G. O., No. 88, Army of the Potomac, Sept. 11, 1863. |
| do | do | G. O., No. 80, Dept. of the Gulf, Dec. 7, 1863. |
| do | do | G. O., No. 88, Army of the Potomac, Sept. 11, 1863. |
| | | |
| Hanged | Murder | G. C. M. O., No. 8, Dept. of the Ohio, Aug. 4, 1865. |
| Shot | Desertion | G. O., No. 74, Dept. of Arkansas, Nov. 8, 1864. |
| Hanged | Murder | G. C. M. O. No. 21, Dept. of Texas, May 28, 1866. |
| Shot | Desertion and theft | G. C. M. O., No. 176, War Dept., Adjt. Gen.'s Office, Apr. 21, 1864. |
| do | Desertion | S. O., No. 30, U. S. Forces in the Field, Dept. of West Virginia, Aug. 4, 1864. |

8

*List of U. S. soldiers executed by United States*

| Name. | Rank. | Co. | Regiment. | Date of execution. |
|---|---|---|---|---|
| **OREGON.** | | | | |
| Ely, Francis | Private | A | 1st Cavalry | Mar. 11, 1864 |
| **PENNSYLVANIA.** | | | | |
| Barnett, John T | Private | A | 11th Cavalry | Sept. 18, 1863 |
| Clark, Charles | do | H | 1st Light Artillery | Mar. 2, 1863 |
| Dormady, William | do | H | do | do |
| Folancy, John, *alias* Geacinto Lerchzie | do | I | 118th Infantry | Aug. 29, 1863 |
| Foster, John | do | Unas'd | 58th Infantry | Jan. 3, 1865 |
| Goodrich, Peter | do | I | 97th Infantry | Feb. 27, 1864 |
| Grover, William | do | A | 46th Infantry | June 19, 1863 |
| Haley, James | do | B | 116th Infantry | Oct. 16, 1863 |
| Howe, William H | do | A | do | Aug. 26, 1864 |
| Kelley, James | do | Unas'd | 67th Infantry | Mar. 9, 1865 |
| Kuhne, George, *alias* G. Week | do | Unas'd | 118th Infantry | Aug. 29, 1863 |
| Lai, Emil, *alias* E. Duffie | do | Unas'd | do | do |
| Lanahan, John | do | A | 40th Infantry | Dec. 23, 1861 |
| McKee, William | do | A | do | June 19, 1863 |
| Murphy James | do | I | 55th Infantry | Jan. 6, 1864 |
| Oliver, Hiram | do | Not given | | Sept. 6, 1865 |
| Rionese, John, *alias* George Rionese | do | I | 118th Infantry | Aug. 29, 1863 |
| Roberts, Jeremiah | do | D | 55th Infantry | Mar. 27, 1865 |
| Smitz, William | do | F | 90th Infantry | Oct. 2, 1863 |
| Thompson, James | do | K | 97th Infantry | Feb. 7, 1864 |
| Walter, Charles, *alias* C. Zene | do | Unas'd | 118th Infantry | Aug. 29, 1863 |
| Wert, Michael | do | G | 184th Infantry | Jan. 6, 1865 |
| Wilson, James | do | B | 97th Infantry | Feb. 7, 1864 |
| **RHODE ISLAND.** | | | | |
| Davis, William | Private | G | 2d Cavalry | Aug. 30, 1863 |
| Smith, Richard | do | F | do | do |
| **TEXAS.** | | | | |
| Garcia, Pedro | Private | E | 1st Cavalry | June 27, 1864 |
| **VERMONT.** | | | | |
| Blowers, George E | Private | A | 2d Infantry | Dec. 18, 1863 |
| Carpenter, Charles | | Unassigned recruit | | Apr. 2, 1864 |
| Riley, Mathew, *alias* John Roach | | Unassigned recruit | | do |
| Tague, John | Private | A | 5th Infantry | Dec. 18, 1863 |
| **WEST VIRGINIA.** | | | | |
| Marcum, John | Sergeant | F | 5th Infantry | Jan. 19, 1864 |
| Raber, Philip | Private | K | 9th Infantry | Nov. 27, 1863 |
| **WISCONSIN.** | | | | |
| Carroll, John | Private | D | 20th Infantry | Nov. 11, 1864 |
| **U. S. VOLUNTEERS.** | | | | |
| Dowdy, William C | Private | E | 1st Regiment | Sept. 9, 1864 |
| Smith, William M | do | C | 4th Regiment | Dec. 22, 1864 |
| **VETERAN RESERVE CORPS.** | | | | |
| Johnson, William G | Sergeant | F | 21st Regiment | Jan. 3, 1865 |
| **U. S. COLORED TROOPS.** | | | | |
| Allen, James | Private | E | 3d Infantry | Dec. 1, 1865 |
| Brooks, Dandridge | do | G | 38th Infantry | July 30, 1865 |
| Catlett, Alfred | do | E | 1st Heavy Artillery | May 6, 1865 |
| Collins, Aaron | do | H | 6th Cavalry | Aug. 18, 1865 |
| Colwell, Alexander | do | F | 1st Heavy Artillery | May 6, 1865 |
| Cowell, Willis | do | E | 1st Cavalry | May 26, 1865 |
| Craig, David | do | K | 3d Infantry | Dec. 1, 1865 |
| Davis, Emanuel | do | A | 48th Infantry | Aug. 31, 1864 |
| Dixon, George | do | K | 19th Infantry | July 21, 1865 |
| Four, Thomas | do | D | 52d Infantry | May 26, 1865 |
| Grant, Simon | do | H | 21st Infantry | June 23, 1865 |
| Grien, Joseph | do | I | 3d Infantry | Dec. 1, 1865 |

9

*military authorities during the late war.*—Continued.

| Mode of execution. | Offense. | Authority. |
|---|---|---|
| Shot......... | Desertion ................................. | G. O., No. 8, Dept. of the Pacific, Feb. 2, 1864. |
| Shot......... | Desertion and highway robbery.... | G. O., No. 256, War Dept., Adjt. Gen.'s Office, Aug. 1, 1863. |
| Hanged .... | Murder .................................. | G. O., No. 10, Dept. of Virginia, Feb. 18, 1863. |
| ....do........ | .....do....... | Do. |
| Shot......... | Desertion ................................ | G. O., No. 84, Army of the Potomac, Aug. 23, 1863. |
| ....do........ | .....do....... | G. O., No. 181, Dept. Virginia and North Carolina, Dec. 31, 1864. |
| ....do........ | .....do....... | G. O., No. 17, Dept. of the South, Feb. 2, 1864. |
| ....do........ | .....do....... | G. O., No. 63, Army of the Potomac, June 13, 1863. |
| ....do........ | .....do....... | G. O., No. 95, Army of the Potomac, Oct. 8, 1863. |
| Hanged .... | Desertion and murder............... | G. O., No. 26, Dept. of the Susquehanna, Apr. 9, 1864. |
| Shot......... | Desertion ................................ | G. C. M. O., No. 11, Army of the Potomac, Mar. 1, 1865. |
| ....do........ | .....do....... | G. O., No. 84, Army of the Potomac, Aug. 23, 1863. |
| ....do........ | .....do....... | Do. |
| Hanged .... | Murder .................................. | G. O., No. 54, Army of the Potomac, Dec. 13, 1861. |
| Shot......... | Desertion ................................ | G. O., No. 63, Army of the Potomac, June 13, 1863. |
| ....do........ | .....do....... | G. O., No. 1, Dept. of the South, Jan. 1, 1864. |
| Hanged .... | Murder .................................. | G. C. M. O., No. 8, Dept. of the Ohio, Aug. 4, 1865. |
| Shot......... | Desertion ................................ | G. O., No. 84, Army of the Potomac, Aug. 23, 1863. |
| ....do........ | .....do....... | G. C. M. O., No. 53, Dept. of Virginia, Mar. 26, 1865. |
| ....do........ | .....do....... | G. O., No. 92, Army of the Potomac, Sept. 27, 1863. |
| ....do........ | .....do....... | G. O., No. 17, Dept. of the South, Feb. 2, 1864. |
| ....do........ | .....do....... | G. O., No. 84, Army of the Potomac, Aug. 23, 1863. |
| ....do........ | .....do....... | G. C. M. O., No. 1, Army of the Potomac, Jan. 2, 1865. |
| ....do........ | .....do....... | G. O., No. 17, Dept. of the South, Feb. 2, 1864. |
| Shot......... | Mutiny.................................... | Order of Colonel H. Robinson, 1st Louisiana Cavalry. |
| ....do........ | .....do....... | Do. |
| Shot......... | Desertion ................................ | G. O., No. 44, U. S. Forces on the Rio Grande, June 21, 1864. |
| Shot......... | Desertion ................................ | G. O., No. 104, Army of the Potomac, Dec. 5, 1863. |
| ....do........ | .....do....... | G. O., No. 28, Dept. of the East, Apr. 12, 1864. |
| ....do........ | .....do....... | Do. |
| ....do........ | .....do....... | G. O., No. 104, Army of the Potomac, Dec. 5, 1863. |
| Hanged .... | Murder .................................. | G. O., No. 20, Dept. of West Virginia, Dec. 9, 1863. |
| Shot......... | Desertion ................................ | G. O., No. 14, Dept. of West Virginia, Oct. 15, 1863. |
| Shot......... | Rape...................................... | G. C. M. O., No. 263, War Dept., Adjt. Gen.'s Office, Aug. 30. 1864. |
| Shot......... | Violation 7th and 21st Art. of War. | G. O., No. 64, Headquarters 1st U. S. Volunteers, Sept. 8, 1864. |
| ....do........ | Desertion ................................ | G. O., No. 166, Dept. Virginia and North Carolina, Dec. 9, 1864. |
| Shot......... | Aiding desertion...................... | G. O., No. 181, Dept. Virginia and North Carolina, Dec. 31, 1864. |
| Shot......... | Mutiny.................................... | G. C. M. O., No. 39, Dept. of Florida, Nov. 13, 1865. |
| Hanged .... | Rape...................................... | G. C. M. O., No. 288, War Dept., Adjt. Gen.'s Office, June 7, 1865. |
| Shot......... | .....do....... | Drum-head court-martial, S. O., No. 43, May 4, 1865. |
| Hanged .... | Murder................................... | G. C. M. O., No. 62, Dept. of Kentucky, July 31, 1865. |
| Shot......... | Rape...................................... | Drum-head court-martial, S. O., No. 43, May 4, 1865. |
| Hanged .... | Murder................................... | G. C. M. O., No. 60, Dept. of Virginia, May 19, 1865. |
| Shot......... | Mutiny.................................... | G. C. M. O., No. 39, Dept. of Florida, Nov. 13, 1865. |
| Hanged .... | Murder................................... | G. O., No. 25, Dept. and Army of the Tennessee, July 14, 1864. |
| ....do........ | .....do....... | G. O., No. 73, Dept. of Arkansas, July 14, 1865. |
| ....do........ | .....do....... | G. C. M. O., No. 16, Dept. of the Mississippi, May 10, 1865. |
| ....do........ | .....do....... | G. O., No. 92, Dept. of the South, June 14, 1865. |
| Shot......... | Mutiny.................................... | G. C. M. O., No. 39, Dept. of Florida, Nov. 13, 1865. |

10

*List of U. S. soldiers executed by United States*

| Name. | Rank. | Co. | Regiment. | Date of execution. |
|---|---|---|---|---|
| **U. S. COLORED TROOPS—Continued.** | | | | |
| Gripen, James | Private | F | 104th Infantry | Nov. 20, 1865 |
| Hamilton, Henry | do | I | 2d Infantry | Nov. 4, 1864 |
| Harrison, William H | do | A | 60th Infantry | May 12, 1865 |
| Henderson, William | do | B | 69th Infantry | Dec. 7, 1864 |
| Howard, Thomas | do | E | 3d Infantry | Dec. 1, 1865 |
| Jackson, Washington | do | E | 1st Heavy Artillery | May 6, 1865 |
| Jackson, William | do | G | 38th Infantry | July 30, 1865 |
| Jay, Henry | do | I | 57th Infantry | June 21, 1865 |
| Johnson, Henry | do | D | 52d Infantry | May 20, 1865 |
| Kease, William | do | A | 116th Infantry | Aug. 11, 1865 |
| Kemp, Lawson | 1st serg't. | E | 55th Infantry | Nov. 19, 1863 |
| Lewis, John | Private | D | 13th Heavy Artillery | June 13, 1865 |
| Mapp, Samuel | do | E | 10th Infantry | Apr. 20, 1865 |
| McCloud, Benjamin | do | E | 37th Infantry | Feb. 9, 1866 |
| McDowell, Ephraim | do | D | 52d Infantry | May 29, 1865 |
| Mitchell, John | do | B | 53d Infantry | Sept. 15, 1864 |
| Moore, Doctor | Sergeant | I | 116th Infantry | Aug. 11, 1865 |
| Moore, Peter | Private | D | 52d Infantry | May 20, 1865 |
| Morrison, James | Corporal | D | do | do |
| Nathaniel, Joseph | Private | K | 3d Infantry | Dec. 1, 1865 |
| Pierce, Otto | do | E | 5th Heavy Artillery | May 26, 1865 |
| Plowder, Jacob | do | A | 3d Infantry | Dec. 1, 1865 |
| Quinn, James | do | D | 11th Heavy Artillery | Nov. 25, 1864 |
| Rawling, Mose | do | H | 52d Infantry | May 26, 1865 |
| Roger, Johnson | do | D | 6th Heavy Artillery | Sept. 1, 1864 |
| Rudding, Benjamin | do | P | 104th Infantry | Nov. 20, 1865 |
| Sheppard, John | do | F | 26th Infantry | Oct. 13, 1865 |
| Simms, Giles | Sergeant | I | 49th Infantry | Sept. 25, 1864 |
| Stokes, Darius | Private | A | 2d Infantry | Dec. 16, 1864 |
| Thompson, Cornelius | do | F | 48th Infantry | June 24, 1864 |
| Tontine, Washington | do | E | 49th Infantry | Sept. 25, 1864 |
| Turner, Charles | do | E | 1st Heavy Artillery | May 6, 1865 |
| Vess, Alexander | do | D | 3d Heavy Artillery | Dec. 16, 1864 |
| Walker, William | do |  | 21st Infantry | Mar. 1, 1864 |
| Wallace, William | do | D | 52d Infantry | May 26, 1865 |
| Williams, Charles | Unassigned recruit | | | Nov. 25, 1864 |
| Williams, James | Private | G | 6th Heavy Artillery | Sept. 1, 1864 |
| Willis, John | do | H | 52d Infantry | May 26, 1865 |
| Wilson, Lewis | do | L | 10th Heavy Artillery | Mar. 23, 1865 |
| Wright, Fortune | do | A | 96th Infantry | Mar. 2, 1866 |
| **REGULARS.** | | | | |
| Chandler, Seldon S | Private | K | 4th Artillery | Sept. 2, 1864 |
| Gibbons, Barney | do | A | 7th Infantry | Aug. 12, 1864 |
| Lanahan, Michael | do | B | 2d Infantry | Jan. 6, 1862 |
| McMann, John | do | F | 11th Infantry | Dec. 18, 1863 |
| Murphy, Frederick, *alias* James Powers | do | K | 6th Cavalry | Mar. 3, 1865 |
| Tansey, John | do | K | 3d Cavalry | Apr. 6, 1862 |
| **MISCELLANEOUS.** | | | | |
| Loge, William, *alias* French Bill | | | | Dec. 2, 1864 |

AGO, Wash. aug. 1, 1885
(see search room copy
for date)

11

*military authorities during the late war.—Continued*

| Mode of execution. | Offense. | Authority. |
|---|---|---|
| Hanged | Rape | G. O., No. 63, Dept. of South Carolina, Nov. 17, 1865. |
| Shot | Mutiny | G. O., No. 132, Dept. of the Gulf, Sept. 18, 1864. |
| Hanged | Murder | G. O., No. 39, Dept. of Arkansas, May 6, 1865. |
| Shot | do | G. O., No. 81, Dept. of Arkansas, Dec. 3, 1864. |
| ...do | Mutiny | G. C. M. O., No. 39, Dept. of Florida, Nov. 13, 1865. |
| ...do | Rape | Drum-head court-martial, S. O., No. 43, May 4, 1865. |
| Hanged | ...do | G. C. M. O., No. 268, War Dept., Adjt. Gen.'s Office, June 7, 1865. |
| Shot | ...do | Drum-head court-martial. |
| Hanged | Murder | G. C. M. O., No. 18, Dept. of the Mississippi, May 10, 1865. |
| Shot | Mutiny | G. C. M. O., No. 1, Military Div. of the Southwest, July 14, 1865. |
| ...do | Rape | Drum-head court-martial. |
| Hanged | Murder | G. C. M. O., No. 35, Dept. of Kentucky, June 4, 1865. |
| Shot | Mutiny | G. C. M. O., No. 55, Dept. of Virginia, Apr. 9, 1865. |
| ...do | ...do | G. C. M. O., No. 9, Dept. of North Carolina, Feb. 1, 1866. |
| Hanged | Murder | G. C. M. O., No. 18, Dept. of the Mississippi, May 10, 1865. |
| Shot | Desertion | G. O., No. 20, Army of the Tennessee, Aug. 4, 1864. |
| ...do | Mutiny | G. C. M. O., No. 1, Military Div. of the Southwest, July 14, 1865. |
| Hanged | Murder | G. C. M. O., No. 18, Dept. of the Mississippi, May 10, 1865. |
| ...do | ...Do | |
| Shot | Mutiny | G. C. M. O., No. 39, Dept. of Florida, Nov. 13, 1865. |
| Hanged | Murder | G. C. M. O., No. 18, Dept. of the Mississippi, May 10, 1865. |
| Shot | Mutiny | G. C. M. O., No. 39, Dept. of Florida, Nov. 13, 1865. |
| ...do | Murder | G. O., No. 149, Dept. of the Gulf, Oct. 15, 1864. |
| Hanged | ...do | G. C. M. O., No. 18, Dept. of the Mississippi, May 10, 1865. |
| Shot | ...do | G. C. M. O., No. 15, Dept. Virginia and N. Carolina, July 14, 1864. |
| Hanged | Rape | G. O., No. 63, Dept. of South Carolina, Nov. 17, 1865. |
| ...do | Rape and murder | G. C. M. O., No. 268, War Dept., Adjt. Gen.'s Office, June 7, 1865. |
| Shot | Mutiny | G. O., No. 20, Army of the Tennessee, Aug. 4, 1864. |
| Hanged | Murder | G. O., No. 149, Dept. of the Gulf, Oct. 15, 1864. |
| Shot | ...do | G. O., No. 9, Dist. of Vicksburg, June 20, 1864. |
| ...do | Mutiny | G. O., No. 20, Army of the Tennessee, Aug. 4, 1864. |
| ...do | Rape | Drum-head court-martial, S. O., No. 43, May 4, 1865. |
| Hanged | Murder | G. C. M. O., No. 259, War Dept., Adjt. Gen.'s Office, July 9, 1864. |
| Shot | Mutiny | G. O., No. 8, Dist. of Florida, Feb. 28, 1864. |
| Hanged | Murder | G. C. M. O., No. 18, Dept. of the Mississippi, May 10, 1865. |
| ...do | ...do | G. O., No. 109, Dept. of Washington, Nov. 16, 1864. |
| Shot | ...do | G. C. M. O., No. 15, Dept. Virginia and N. Carolina, July 14, 1864. |
| Hanged | ...do | G. C. M. O., No. 18, Dept. of the Mississippi, May 10, 1865. |
| Shot | ...do | G. C. M. O., No. 20, Dept. of Louisinna., Mar. 6, 1866. |
| Hanged | ...do | G. O., No. 74, Dept. of Louisiana, Dec. 16, 1865. |
| Shot | Desertion | G. C. M. O., No. 31, Army of the Potomac, Aug. 26, 1864. |
| ...do | ...do | G. O., No. 124, Dept. of the Missouri, July 19, 1864. |
| Hanged | Murder | G. O., No. 1, Army of the Potomac, Jan. 2, 1862. |
| Shot | Desertion | G. O., No. 104, Army of the Potomac, Dec. 5, 1863. |
| ...do | ...do | G. O., No. 20, Middle Military Division, Feb. 22, 1865. |
| ...do | Murder | G. O., No. 26, Dept. of New Mexico, Apr. 5, 1862. |
| Hanged | Desertion and murder | S. O., No. 107, Military District of Harper's Ferry, Dec. 2, 1864. |

# APPENDIX TWO: Descriptive List of Soldiers Executed

Note: [ ] indicates unlisted personnel.

## 1861

John W. Cole; 1st Kansas; shot 14 July; murder of enlisted man.

William F. Murray; 2nd New Hampshire; hanged 2 August; murder of civilian.

[Sergeant Joyce; 2nd Kentucky; shot 28 August; mutiny.]

Robert Dickman; 18th Illinois; hanged 2 October; murder of enlisted man.

Joseph Raymond; 7th Kansas Cavalry; shot 24 November; stealing.

William H. Johnston; 1st New York Cavalry; shot 13 December; desertion.

Richard Gatewood; 1st Kentucky; shot 20 December; desertion, assaulting a sentinel.

John Lanahan; 46th Pennsylvania; hanged 23 December; murder of commanding officer.

[unnamed; 8th Illinois; hanged (no date); murder.]

## 1862

Michael Lanahan; 2nd Infantry Regulars; hanged 6 January; murder.

Samuel H. Calhoun; 2nd Kentucky; shot 5 February; murder.

Michael Connel; 24th Ohio; executed 5 March; desertion.

William Kuhnes; 2nd Maryland; hanged 7 March; murder of an officer.

Alexander Driscoll; 7th Kansas Cavalry; shot 18 March; murder.

John Tansey; 3rd Cavalry Regulars; (no service record).

Darius A. Philbrooks; 1st Colorado; shot 8 April; striking a superior officer.

John McMahon; 99th New York; hanged 13 June; murder of enlisted man.

Frank Newton; civilian [discharged from 13th Connecticut]; hanged 16 June; stealing.

John Bell; 2nd Kansas Cavalry; hanged 11 July; rape.

Lewis Stivers; 7th Kentucky; shot 21 September; murder.

Charles Smith; 1st California Cavalry; shot 28 November; mutiny.

William W. Lunt; 9th Maine; shot 1 December; desertion and highway robbery.

John Kessler; 103rd New York; shot 5 December; murder of an officer.

## 1863

William Dormady; 1st Pennsylvania Light Artillery; hanged 2 March; murder and quiting post to plunder and pillage.

Charles Clark; 1st Pennsylvania Light Artillery; hanged 2 March; murder and quiting post to plunder and pillage.

Robert Gay; 6th Indiana Cavalry; shot 27 March; desertion.

Henry Hamill; 131st New York; shot 26 April; desertion, plunder and pillage.

[John W. Summers; 2nd Kansas Cavalry; shot 13 May; desertion.]

Julius Milika; 10th Michigan; shot 15 May; desertion.

[Claudeus C. Frizell; Missouri militia; hanged 27 May; unknown offense.]

John P. Woods; 19th Indiana; shot 12 June; desertion.

William Minix; 9th Kentucky; shot 14 June; desertion.

[Pendergast; 2nd Massachusetts Cavalry; unknown; unknown.]

James Lynch; 2nd Massachusetts Cavalry; shot 16 June; mutiny.

William Grover; 46th Pennsylvania; shot 19 June; desertion.

William McKee; 46th Pennsylvania; shot 19 June; desertion.

Christopher Krubert; 13th New Jersey; shot 19 June; desertion.

David Blazer; 4th Indiana Light Artillery; shot 23 June; desertion.

John Schockman; 1st Kentucky; shot 23 June; desertion.

William H. Laird; 17th Maine; shot 15 July; desertion.

Peter Kleinkoff; 4th California; shot 17 July; desertion, assault with intent to commit robbery, and assault with intent to commit murder.

Bradford Butler; 157th New York; shot 1 August; desertion.

Hiram Reynolds; 82nd Indiana; shot 12 August; murder of enlisted man.

Thomas Jewett; 5th Maine; shot 14 August; desertion.

Francis Scott; 1st Louisiana; shot 14 August; murder of commanding officer.

Henry McLean; 2nd Illinois Light Artillery; shot 25 August; desertion.

William F. Hill; 20th Massachusetts; shot 28 August; desertion.

John Smith; Massachusetts Sharpshooters; shot 28 August; desertion.

John Folancy; unassigned 118th Pennsylvania; shot 29 August; desertion.

Emil Lai; unassigned 118th Pennsylvania; shot 29 August; desertion.

George Kuhne; unassigned 118th Pennsylvania; shot 29 August; desertion.

John Rionese; unassigned 118th Pennsylvania; shot 29 August; desertion.

Charles Walter; unassigned 118th Pennsylvania; shot 29 August; desertion.

William Davis; 2nd Rhode Island Cavalry; shot 30 August; mutiny.

Richard Smith; 2nd Rhode Island Cavalry; shot 30 August; mutiny.

James M. Anderson; 27th Kentucky; shot 4 September; desertion.

Frazier Carmen; 27th Kentucky; shot 4 September; desertion.

Christopher Coffey; 27th Kentucky; shot 4 September; desertion.

John W. Coffey; 27th Kentucky; shot 4 September; desertion.

James A. Pointer; 27th Kentucky; shot 4 September; desertion.

Jacob Aierdain; 119th New York; shot 17 September; desertion.

Edward Elliott; 14th Connecticut; shot 18 September; desertion.

George Layton; 14th Connecticut; shot 18 September; desertion.

John T. Barnett; 11th Pennsylvania Cavalry; shot 18 September; highway robbery, assault with intent to commit murder, and desertion.

Albert Jones; 3rd Maryland; shot 18 September; desertion.

William Smith; 78th New York; shot 18 September; desertion.

Cornelius Treece; 78th New York; shot 18 September; desertion.

George Van; 12th New York; shot 18 September; desertion.

Charles Williams; 4th Maryland; shot 25 September; desertion.

John Timlin; 145th New York; shot 25 September; desertion.

Adam Schmalz; 66th New York; shot 2 October; desertion.

William Smitz; 90th Pennsylvania; shot 2 October; desertion.

Joseph Connelly; 4th New Jersey; shot 9 October; desertion.

Henry C. Beardsley; 5th Michigan; shot 16 October; desertion.

James Haley; 116th Pennsylvania; shot 16 October; descrtion.

Reuben Stout; 60th Indiana; shot 23 October; desertion.

John Roberts; 15th Massachusetts; shot 30 October; desertion.

Mitchell Vandall; 8th Connecticut; shot 9 November; desertion.

Francis Wales; 8th Connecticut; shot 9 November; desertion.

Benjamin Valentine; 44th Illinois; shot 13 November; desertion.

Erastus C. Daily; 44th Illinois; shot 13 November; desertion.

Lawson Kemp; 1st Alabama (African Descent), later 55th Infantry, USCT; might not have been executed on the charge of rape.

Philip Raber; 9th Virginia, later 9th West Virginia; shot 27 November; desertion.

Homobona Carabajal; 1st New Mexico Cavalry; not executed for murder.

Paul Kingston; 1st Missouri Cavalry; hanged 27 November; desertion and theft of a pistol.

Cyrus W. Hunter; 3rd Maine; shot 4 December; desertion.

John Kendall; 3rd New Hampshire; shot 17 December; desertion.

George E. Blowers; 2nd Vermont; shot 18 December; desertion.

John Tague; 5th Vermont; shot 18 December; desertion.

John McMann; 11th Infantry Regulars; shot 18 December; no records found, though he is cited for desertion.

Winslow W. Allen; 76th New York; shot 18 December; desertion.

William H. Devoe; 57th New York; shot 18 December; desertion.

[3 unnamed members of Second Corps, executed at Morrisville, Virginia, for desertion.]

Charles Turner; 114th New York; shot 28 December; desertion.


## 1864

James Murphy; 55th Pennsylvania; shot 6 January; desertion and leaving his post without being regularly relieved.

Joseph Coffield; 1st New Mexico Cavalry; shot 19 January; murder.

John Marcum; 5th West Virginia; either hanged or shot 19 January; murder of an enlisted man.

William E. Ormsley; 2nd Massachusetts Cavalry; shot 7 February; desertion.

James Wilson; 97th Pennsylvania; shot 7 February; desertion.

James Thompson; 97th Pennsylvania; shot 7 February; desertion.

Spencer Lloyd; 55th Massachusetts (Colored); hanged 18 February; rape.

John W. Cook; 55th Massachusetts (Colored); hanged 18 February; rape.

John M. Smith; 55th Massachusetts (Colored); hanged 18 February; desertion.

Peter Goodrich; 97th Pennsylvania; shot 27 February; desertion.

William Walker; 21st Infantry, USCT; shot 1 March; mutiny.

William Abraham; 139th New York; shot 7 March; giving intelligence to the enemy in violation of the 57th Article of War.

Francis Ely; 1st Oregon Cavalry; shot 11 March; desertion.

Robert Kerr; 1st California Cavalry; shot 20 March; murder of an officer.

John Eagen; 2nd New Hampshire; no records to show that he was executed 15 April for desertion.

Henry Holt; 2nd New Hampshire; shot 15 April; desertion.

Henry Schumaker; 6th Connecticut; shot 17 April; desertion.

Henry Stark; 6th Connecticut; shot 17 April; desertion.

Henry Miller; 3rd New Hampshire; shot 17 April; desertion.

Charles Carpenter; unassigned Vermont; no records to show he was shot 22 April for desertion.

Mathew Riley; unassigned Vermont; no records to show he was shot 22 April for desertion.

Thomas R. Dawson; 20th Massachusetts; hanged 25 April; desertion and rape.

Jacob Morgan; 8th Connecticut; shot 28 April; desertion.

John Myers; 7th Illinois; hanged 28 April; murder of commanding officer.

John H. Thompson; 1st Ohio Cavalry; shot 29 April; desertion.

Owen McDonough; 2nd New Hampshire; shot 29 April; desertion.

James Scott; unassigned 2nd New Hampshire; shot 29 April; desertion.

John Reily, Jr.; 2nd Missouri Artillery; shot 29 April; murder of an unknown person.

Henry A. Burnham; 5th New Hampshire; doubt as to whether he was actually executed 9 May for desertion.

John D. Starbird; 19th Massachusetts; shot 21 May; desertion.

John Callaghan; 2nd New Jersey Cavalry; shot 10 June; desertion.

Thomas Johnson; 2nd New Jersey Cavalry; shot 10 June; desertion.

John Snover; 2nd New Jersey Cavalry; shot 10 June; desertion.

John Flood; 41st New York; shot 17 June; desertion.

Wallace Baker; 55th Massachusetts (Colored); shot 18 June; mutiny.

Cornelius Thompson; 48th Infantry, USCT; shot 24 June; murder of a civilian.

Pedro Garcia; 1st Texas Cavalry; shot 27 June; desertion.

[3 members of 2nd New Jersey Cavalry; hanged 28 June; rape.]

[William Johnson; 23rd Infantry, USCT; hanged "about June" for an undetermined offense.]

Francis Gillespie; 15th New York Cavalry; hanged 11 July; murder of an officer.

Daniel Geary; 72nd New York; hanged 15 July; rape.

Ransom S. Gordon; 72nd New York; hanged 15 July; rape.

Isaac B. Whitlow; 23rd Ohio; shot 5 August; desertion.

Frank McElhenny; 24th Massachusetts; shot 8 August; desertion.

Barney Gibbons; 7th Infantry Regulars; shot 12 August; desertion.

William H. Howe; 116th Pennsylvania; hanged 26 August; desertion and murder.

Emanuel Davis; 48th Infantry, USCT; shot 31 August; murder of an unidentified person.

Roger Johnson; 6th Heavy Artillery, USCT; shot 1 September; murder (of an officer), assault with intent to kill, and conduct prejudicial to good order and military discipline.

Seldon S. Chandler; 2nd Tennessee Heavy Artillery, later 4th Heavy Artillery, Regulars; shot 2 September; desertion.

James Williams; 6th Heavy Artillery, USCT; shot 9 September; murder of a civilian.

William C. Dowdy; 1st Regiment U. S. Volunteers; shot 9 September; absent without leave, and the use of seditious or disrespectful language.

John Mitchell; 3rd Regiment Mississippi Volunteers, later 53rd Infantry, USCT; shot 15 September; desertion.

Samuel W. Downing; numerous units; shot 16 September; desertion.

John Sweney; 1st Maryland; shot 20 September; desertion.

George W. McDonald; 3rd Maryland; no records to prove his existence or that he was executed for desertion and attempted murder on 21 September.

Giles Simms; 49th Infantry, USCT; shot 25 September; mutiny.

Washington Tontine; 40th Infantry, USCT; shot 25 September; mutiny.

Edward Eastman; 2nd Missouri Artillery; shot 25 September; leaving his colors to pillage in violation of the 52nd Article of War.

William I. Lynch; 62nd New York; shot 30 September; desertion.

Peter Keiffe; 2nd Arkansas Cavalry; shot 1 October; murder of a civilian.

Charles Merling; 2nd Maryland; shot 14 October; attempted desertion.

Jefferson Jackson; 9th Missouri State Mounted Cavalry; shot 28 October; murder of a civilian.

John Velon; 5th New Hampshire; shot 18 October; desertion.

Henry Hamilton; 2nd Infantry, USCT; shot 4 November; mutiny.

Joseph Prevost; 1st (New York) Lincoln Cavalry; hanged 10 November; murder of a civilian.

Charles Lockman; 2nd Colorado Cavalry; hanged 10 November; murder of an enlisted man.

John Carroll; 20th Wisconsin; shot 11 November; undetermined offense — either desertion, rape or other crimes.

Charles Williams; unassigned recruit, USCT; shot 25 November; murder.

James Quinn; 11th Heavy Artillery, USCT; shot 25 November; absent without leave, and sleeping out of quarters in violation of the 42nd Article of War.

William Loge; no unit; hanged 2 December; desertion and murder.

William Henderson; 66th Infantry, USCT; shot 8 December; murder of an enlisted man.

Edward Rowe; 179th New York; hanged 10 December; desertion.

Daniel C. Smith; 179th New York; hanged 10 December; desertion.

Alexander Vess; 3rd Regiment Heavy Artillery, USCT; hanged 15 December; murder.

Darius Stokes; 2nd Infantry, USCT; hanged 16 December; murder of an enlisted man.

George W. Prince; 22nd Ohio; shot 16 December; desertion.

Charles Hummel; 7th New York Veteran Infantry; doubts exist whether he was shot 16 December for desertion.

Christopher Suhr; 7th New York Veteran Infantry; hanged 16 December; desertion.

John Thompson; unassigned 5th New Hampshire; hanged 16 December; desertion.

William Kane; 8th Maryland; hanged 16 December; desertion.

Thomas Dix; 1st Connecticut Heavy Artillery; shot 21 December; desertion.

Henry McCurdy; 1st Connecticut Heavy Artillery; shot 21 December; desertion.

John Smith; 1st Connecticut Heavy Artillery; shot 21 December; desertion.

James Thompson; 1st Connecticut Heavy Artillery; shot 21 December; desertion.

John Hall; 1st Connecticut Heavy Artillery; shot 21 December; desertion.

William M. Smith; 4th Regiment, U. S. Volunteers; shot 22 December; desertion.

James Lynch; 5th New Hampshire; hanged 23 December; desertion.

William Miller; 5th New Hampshire; hanged 23 December; desertion.

George Bradley; 5th New Hampshire; hanged 23 December; desertion.

John C. Dixon; 1st Massachusetts Heavy Artillery; shot 23 December; desertion.

Charles Billingsby; 7th Indiana Battery; shot 23 December; desertion.

John Murray; 13th Indiana Cavalry; shot 23 December; desertion.

Thomas Ryan; 51st Indiana; shot 23 December; desertion.

James F. Brown; 3rd New Hampshire; doubt exists whether he was executed 26 December for desertion.

Larkin D. Rhea; 7th Kentucky; hanged 30 December; desertion.

Michael Genan; 5th New Hampshire; shot 30 December; desertion.

### 1865

John Foster; 58th Pennsylvania; shot 3 January; desertion.

William G. Johnson; 6th U. S. Infantry; shot 3 January; desertion.

Charles King; 3rd New Jersey Cavalry; shot 5 January; attempting to desert and giving information.

Henry Regley; 3rd New Jersey Cavalry; shot 5 January; attempting to desert and giving information.

Lewis Roarch; 7th Kentucky; either hanged or shot 6 January for murder or desertion.

Waterman Thornton; 179th New York; hanged 6 January; desertion.

John Benson; unassigned 5th New Hampshire; hanged 6 January; desertion.

Peter Cox; 4th New Jersey; hanged 6 January; desertion.

Michael Wert; 184th Pennsylvania; hanged 6 January; desertion.

James Collins; 8th Connecticut; shot 7 January; desertion.

William Dix; 8th Connecticut; shot 7 January; desertion.

Ephraim Richardson; 21st Missouri; hanged 13 January; murder of a civilian.

Abraham Purvis; 21st Missouri; hanged 13 January; murder of a civilian.

Newell W. Root; 1st Connecticut Heavy Artillery; hanged 27 January; desertion.

James Devlin; 43rd New York and 1st Connecticut Cavalry; shot 5 February; desertion.

Joseph H. Sharp; 12th New Hampshire; shot 9 February; desertion.

Michael Landy; 10th Connecticut; shot 17 February; desertion.

[unnamed, executed with Landy; shot 17 February.]

John Hoeffer; 12th New York; shot 17 February; deserter.

John Brown II; 10th Connecticut; hanged 18 February; desertion, attempted murder, attempted robbery, and violation of the 23rd Article of War; though there is doubt he was executed.

John Parker; 10th Connecticut; shot 25 February; desertion.

Thomas Jones; 10th Connecticut; shot 26 February; desertion, attempted robbery, and violation of the 23rd Article of War.

Frederick Murphy; 6th Cavalry Regulars; shot 3 March; desertion.

Charles Sperry; 13th New York Cavalry; shot 3 March; absent from post, drunkenness on duty, assault and battery with intent to commit rape, and rape.

David Geer; 28th Illinois; doubt exists as to whether he was shot 4 March for murder, or dishonorably discharged.

James Kelly; 67th Pennsylvania; shot 10 March; desertion.

John Nicholas; 69th New York; shot 10 March; desertion.

William Jackson; 10th Connecticut; doubt exists if he was executed 10 March for desertion.

John Mahoney; 10th Connecticut; shot 10 March; desertion.

William T. Griffin; 8th Delaware; shot 10 March; desertion.

William Cooper; 10th Connecticut; doubt exists as to whether he was executed 16 March for desertion.

John Smith; 8th New Jersey; shot 18 March; desertion.

Joseph Johnson; 1st Maryland; shot 18 March; desertion.

James Weaver; 1st Maryland; shot 26 March; desertion.

Frederick W. Brandt; 81st New York; shot 26 March; desertion.

Jeremiah Roberts; 55th Pennsylvania; no records exist, but Adjutant General's Office indicates he was executed 27 March, for desertion.

Newal Jangrow; 64th New York; shot 31 March; desertion.

Anthony Raymond; unassigned 64th New York; shot 31 March; desertion.

James Preble; 12th New York; shot 31 March; assault with intent to commit rape, and rape.

Samuel Mapp; 10th Infantry, USCT; shot 31 March; mutiny, disobedience of orders, and threatening the life of a superior officer.

Alfred Catlett; 1st Heavy Artillery, USCT; shot 6 May; rape.

Alexander Colwell; 1st Heavy Artillery, USCT; shot 6 May; rape.

Charles Turner; 1st Heavy Artillery, USCT; shot 6 May; rape.

Washington Jackson; 1st Heavy Artillery, USCT; shot 6 May; rape.

William H. Harrison; 69th Infantry, USCT; hanged 12 May; murder of an unidentified person.

Henry Anderson; 9th Michigan Cavalry; shot 13 May; murder of a civilian.

John Willis; 3rd Mississippi Infantry (African Descent), later 52nd Infantry, USCT; hanged 25 May; desertion.

Otto Pierce; 5th Heavy Artillery, USCT; hanged 25 May; desertion.

William Wallace; 52nd Infantry, USCT; hanged 25 May; murder.

Moses Rollins; 52nd Infantry, USCT; hanged 25 May; murder.

Ephraim McDowell; 52nd Infantry, USCT; hanged 25 May; murder.

Peter Moore; 52nd Infantry, USCT; hanged 25 May; murder.

James Morrison; 52nd Infantry, USCT; hanged 25 May; murder.

Henry Johnson; 52nd Infantry, USCT; hanged 25 May; murder.

Thomas Four; 52nd Infantry, USCT; hanged 25 May; murder.

William Cowell; 1st Cavalry, USCT; hanged 26 May; murder, but perhaps another offense.

John Lewis; 13th Heavy Artillery, USCT; hanged 13 June; murder of a civilian.

Frank Hudson; 2nd California Cavalry; hanged 30 June; desertion and murder.

Henry Jay; 5th Infantry, USCT; shot 21 June; rape.

Simon Grant; 21st Infantry, USCT; hanged 23 June; murder of an enlisted man.

Patrick McNamara; 132nd New York; hanged 30 June; murder of an enlisted man.

George Dixon; 79th Infantry, USCT; hanged 21 July; murder of an unidentified person.

William A. Wilson; 12th Illinois Cavalry; shot 28 July; desertion — though doubt exists whether this was the man executed.

William Jackson; 38th Infantry, USCT; hanged 30 July; rape.

Dandridge Brooks; 38th Infantry, USCT; hanged 30 July; rape.

William Kease; 116th Infantry, USCT; shot 11 August; mutiny.

Doctor Moore; 116th Infantry, USCT; shot 11 August; mutiny.

Aaron Collins; 6th Cavalry, USCT; Adjutant General's Office reports he was executed for murder 18 August. That is the only mention.

Alexander McBroone; 1st Arkansas; shot 21 August; desertion.

John W. Hardup; 43rd Ohio; hanged 6 September; desertion.

Hiram Oliver; 43rd Ohio; hanged 6 September; unknown offense, since no file exists.

Juan Madrid; 1st New Mexico Cavalry; hanged 9 September; murder of an enlisted man.

John Sheppard; 38th Infantry, USCT; hanged 13 October; rape, pillage and plunder.

James Gripen; 103rd Infantry, USCT; hanged 20 November; rape.

Benjamin Rudding; 103rd Infantry, USCT; hanged 20 November; unknown offense, due to lack of file.

David Craig; 3rd Infantry, USCT; shot 1 December; mutiny.

Joseph Grien; 3rd Infantry, USCT; hanged 1 December; mutiny.

James Allen; 3rd Infantry, USCT; hanged 1 December; mutiny.

Jacob Plowder; 3rd Infantry, USCT; hanged 1 December; mutiny.

Nathaniel Joseph; 3rd Infantry, USCT; hanged 1 December; mutiny.

Howard Thomas; 3rd Infantry, USCT; hanged 1 December; mutiny.

### 1866

Benjamin McCloud; 37th Infantry, USCT; government acknowledged he was not executed 9 February for mutiny.

Lewis Wilson; 10th Heavy Artillery, USCT; shot 23 March 1866; murder of an enlisted man.

Fortune Wright; 96th Infantry, USCT; shot 23 March; murder.

Robert Rodgers; 77th Ohio; shot 8 June; murder of a civilian.

# ACKNOWLEDGEMENTS . . . and some personal history

*Civil War Justice* began more than a decade ago when I was looking around for a subject for a magazine article for a Sunday supplement. Little did I realize at the time that the small article would become two books, and a doctoral dissertation.

Back in the late Seventies, my main starting point for historical subjects was the Free Library of Philadelphia. I would spend hours on end going through their collection of microfilm newspapers. When I found something that captured my fancy, I would make a copy and file it away for future use. This time, however, I could not put the reference aside.

I came across an article in the *Sunday Dispatch* [ironically I worked for that newspaper as a freelance writer before its demise in 1979] that stated that the civilian who was to cut the body down at a military execution was oblivious to what he was doing. "His attention," *The Dispatch* reported, "was about equally divided between the dullness of his knife and the mouth of bread he was munching at the time . . . ." That quotation stuck in my mind. I could not write about anything else until I finished finding out why any man was treated so miserably.

A year later I finished my research. The result was *Stop the Evil: A Civil War History of Desertion and Murder* [Presidio Press, 1978], and the story of William H. Howe. Even while I was researching that book, I began to pick up bits and pieces about other Union soldiers who had been executed. I realized even then that *Stop the Evil* was not the entire story, and that I had a great deal more work to do before I had even scratched the surface.

When I decided to obtain a master's degree in 1980, and entered the University of Pennsylvania, I used my research, embryonic as it was, for class projects in statistics, with Professor Mel Hammerberg. The research that I conducted at that time was based on the 1885 report of the Office of the Judge Advocate General. It had to be scrapped as I conducted more in-depth research, ignoring the military's figure of 267 men executed. That report, the cornerstone for many historians, was and is false. My research has proven this.

In 1981, after I finished my master's and moved uptown to Temple University, I was lucky to have my dissertation topic accepted. Three years later, my research was turned into my doctoral dissertation. When I went through my oral defense, I was asked if I considered my research complete. I answered honestly: I hadn't scratched the surface in my dissertation. There was a great deal more work that had to be done. I still believe that after days, weeks, and months of continued research. There is much, much more that has to be done before we can ever accurately state how many Union soldiers were actually executed for military offenses . . . and how many men were actually guilty of the crimes for which they were accused. This book was the first step in that direction.

To be very honest, military executions and military justice during the Civil War period has consumed my thinking for longer than I would like to accept. I have very strong reservations about the system employed during that period. I also have lost a great deal of respect for Abraham Lincoln's handling of the cases. And, one thing I can state with certainty: more men died than the military acknowledged. How many? Only God knows.

What *Civil War Justice* attempts to do is introduce the reader to the whole concept of military justice as a separate entity from constitutional law, show how it developed during the war, how it was employed, and the results. This book is really two books in one: the first if on military justice during the Civil War; the second, the heretofore unrecorded history of the "criminals" of the war.

An interesting aspect [the author is also a critic, so he should have some idea about what is interesting or not] of the book is the detailed accounts of the individual cases. The men whose names you will find cannot be located in any general — or specific — work on the period. They were not generals, they were not — at least not many were — noncommissioned personnel. They were mostly private soldiers, the grunts of another era.

I make some observations and develop some conclusions about the cases themselves. Some might be questioned by members of today's legal profession but they must remember this was a time long gone by. Also, they should recognize that if we don't learn from the past, we are doomed to repeat its mistakes in the future.

*Robert I. Alotta, Ph.D.*
*Department of Communication*
*James Madison University*
*November 1987*

Though the title page of this book carries only my name, it would be arrogant on my part not to admit to the help of a large number of people who assisted me.

The following people, listed in alphabetical order by state, provided me with help above and beyond the call of duty.

*California.* W. N. Davis, Jr., chief of archives, California State Archives

*Connecticut.* Kristin Woodbridge, reference librarian, Archives, History and Genealogy Unit, State of Connecticut

*Delaware.* Evelyn Hundley Kuserk, research and reference department, Eleutherian Mills Historical Library; W. Emerson Wilson, chairman, Fort Delaware Society

*District of Columbia.* Mary L. Shaffer, director, The Army Library, US Army Service Center for the Armed Forces, Pentagon; LTC Hugh G. Waite, chief, News Branch, Public Information Office, Department of the Army; Craddock R. Goins, curator, Division of Military History, The Smithsonian Institution; COL Herbert M. Hart, deputy director for Marine Corps history; the entire staff at the National Archives was extremely helpful in producing whatever they had on the individual soldiers' records. Contrary to common practice, they presented me with a truckload of documents and kept them out of circulation for the several days I worked on them. Additional personal attention was given to me by Sarah Dunlap Jackson and Dale Floyd — both of whom have been helpful to me in most of my military history pursuits. Mike Pilgrim came through with my illustrations in the nick of time.

*Illinois.* John Daly, director, Illinois State Archives

*Indiana.* Martha E. Wright, reference librarian, Indiana Division, Indiana State Historical Society

*Kansas.* LTC George C. Dellinger, public affairs officer, Headquarters 1st Infantry Division and Fort Riley; Terry Harmon, Kansas State Historical Society

*Kentucky.* James C. Klotter, assistant editor, Kentucky Historical Society; Nancy D. Baird, librarian, Western Kentucky University

*Louisiana.* Lucas F. Bruno, Jr., corresponding secretary, The Louisiana Historical Society; G. Hammerschmidt, curator, Fort Polk Military Museum; Mary B. Oalmann, military historian, Military Department, State of Louisiana

*Maine.* Sylvia J. Sherman, director, archives services, Maine State Archives

*Maryland.* Martin Gordon and White Mane, for realizing the importance of this book. Without Martin and his cohorts, this book might not have seen the light of day.

*Michigan.* Richard J. Hathaway, head, Michigan Unit, Department of Education, State Library Services; the interlibrary loan staff of Zumberge Library, Grand Valley State College

*Missouri.* Alma Vaughan, newspaper library, The State Historical Society of Missouri

*New Hampshire.* Bill Copeley, assistant librarian, New Hampshire Historical Society

*New Jersey.* William C. Wright, state archivist; E. Richard McKwistry, reference librarian, The New Jersey Historical Society; David C. Munn, historical editor, New Jersey Archives

*Pennsylvania.* LTC James C. Shepard, executive officer, US Army Military History Institute, Carlisle Barracks; Gale Schreiber, map collection, and the interlibrary loan staff, the Free Library of Philadelphia; Professor Warren Hassler, The Pennsylvania State University. Words cannot describe the assistance I received from Professor Russell Frank Weigley, my dissertation supervisor. Professor Weigley has helped change my outlook from that of a journalist to that of an historian. Without his help, I doubt that I would have continued or concluded my doctoral studies. However... The contents of this book do not in any way reflect Weigley's opinions. He read it as a dissertation, not as a book.

Heartfelt thanks for cooperative assistance must go to Michael J. Winey, curator, US Army Military History Institute, Carlisle Barracks, and the staff at the Institute. Through a fellowship grant in 1981, I was able to spend long hours in Upton Hall poring through early editions of manuals of courts-martial.

*Texas.* Joe B. Frantz, the Texas State Historical Association

*Vermont.* Marilyn Blackwell, library staff, Vermont Historical Society

*Virginia.* Gerald W. Barnes, executive assistant, Norfolk District, Corps of Engineers; William P. Bradshaw, of Portsmouth; James N. Haskett, chief park historian, Colonial National Historical Park, Yorktown; George E. Hicks, curator, Fort Monroe Casemate Museum; Reva S. Maxwell, public information officer, Headquarters, US Army Quartermasters Center and Fort Lee; James I. Robertson, Jr., C. P. Miles Professor of History, Virginia Polytechnic Institute and State University; MAJ Brigham S. Shuler, chief of public affairs, US Army Criminal Investigation Command, Falls Church; Louis J. Venuto, historian, Petersburg National Battlefield; George Wead, my department head at JMU.

*West Virginia.* Harold Newman, State of West Virginia Department of Archives and History

*Wisconsin.* Katherine Thompson, reference assistant, The State Historical Society of Wisconsin; James L. Hansen, reference librarian, The State Historical Society of Wisconsin.

I must also applaud the IBM corporation for "Dudley," my PC-XT with MultiMate word processor. He replaced "Waldo," who had a very short memory.

Over the years, I tried to keep records of all the people who were kind to me, but in the past seven years I have moved from Philadelphia, Pennsylvania, to Grand Rapids, Michigan, to Starkville, Mississippi, to Harrisonburg, Virginia. I hope that those whose names I've left out will not blame me — but rather put the blame on forty boxes of material that are still packed.

# BIBLIOGRAPHY

Adams, John G. B. *Reminscences of the Nineteenth Massachusetts Regiment.* Boston: Wright and Potter, 1899.

Adams, John R. *Memorials and Letters of Rev. John R. Adams, D.D.* Cambridge: John Wilson, 1890.

Alotta, Robert I. *Stop the Evil: A Civil War History of Desertion and Murder.* San Rafael, Calif.: Presidio Press, 1978.

Ambrose, D. Leib. *History of the Seventh Regiment Illinois Volunteer Infantry.* Springfield: Illinois Journal Co., 1868.

Anders, Leslie. *The Eighteenth Missouri.* Indianapolis and New York: The Bobbs-Merrill Company, Inc., 1968.

Angle, Paul M., ed. *Three Years in the Army of the Potomac, The Letters and Diary of Major James A. Connolly.* Bloomington: Indiana Press, 1959; New York: Kraus Reprint Company, 1969.

*Antietam to Appomattox with the 118th Penna. Vols. Corn Exchange Regiment.* Philadelphia: J. L. Smith 1892.

Army Times. *Guide to Army Posts.* Harrisburg: The Stackpole Company, 1966.

Ayling, Augustus D. *Revised Register of the Soldiers and Sailors of New Hampshire in the War of the Rebellion, 1861-1866.* Concord: Ira C. Evans, 1895.

Barth, Gunter, ed. *All Quiet on the Yamhill. The Civil War in Oregon, the Journal of Corporal Royal A. Bensell, Company D, Fourth California Infantry.* Eugene: University of Oregon Books, 1959.

Barry, Louise. "Legal Hangings in Kansas," *Kansas Historical Quarterly*, XVIII [August 1950]:279-301.

Bartlctt, Asa W. *History of the Twelfth Regiment, New Hampshire Volunteers in the War of the Rebellion.* Concord: Ira C. Evans, 1897.

Bartlett, John Russell. *Memoirs of Rhode Island Officers Who Were Engaged in the Service of Their Country During the Great Rebellion of the South.* Providence: Sidney S. Rider & Brother, 1867.

Beach, William H. *The First New York [Lincoln] Cavalry, From April 17, 1861 to July 7, 1865.* New York: The Lincoln Cavalry Association, 1902.

Benet, Capt. Stephen Vincent. *A Treatise on Military Law and the Practice of Courts-Martial.* New York: D. Van Nostrand, 1862, [revised edition] 1864.

Benton, Charles E. *As Seen from the Ranks, A Boy in the Civil War.* New York: G. P. Putnam's Sons, 1902.

Berlin, Ira, Barbara J. Field, Joseph P. Reidy, and Leslie S. Rowland. "Writing *Freedom*'s History," *Prologue* [Fall 1982, Vol. 14, No. 13], pp. 129-39.

Berlin, Ira, ed. *Freedom: A Documentary History of Emancipation 1861-1867.* [Series II: The Black Military Experience] Cambridge: Cambridge University Press, 1982.

Becknell, Rev. George W. *History of the Fifth Regiment Maine Volunteers.* Portland: Hall L. Davis, 1871.

Bishop, Joseph Warren. *Justice Under Fire, A Study of Military Law.* New York: Charterhouse, 1974.

Black, Samuel. *A Soldier's Recollections of the Civil War.* Minco, Okla.: Minco Minstrel, 1911-12.

Blake, Henry N. *Three Years in the Army of the Potomac.* Boston: Lee and Shepard, 1865.

Bloodgood, Rev. John D. *Personal Reminiscences of the War*. Chicago: H. W. Bolton, 1892.

Boatner, Mark M. III. *The Civil War Dictionary*. New York: David McKay Co., 1962.

Bolton, Horace W. *Personal Reminiscences of the Late War*. Chicago: H. W. Bolton, 1892.

Borton, Benjamin. *Awhile with the Blue or Memories of War Days*. Passaic: W. Taylor, 1898.

Bridges, Albert Fletcher. "The Execution of Private Robert Gay," *Indiana Magazine of History*, XX [June 1924] 2:174-186.

Bryant, Clifton D. *Khaki-Collar Crime, Deviant Behavior in the Military Context*. New York: The Free Press, 1979.

Butler, Benjamin F. *Butler's Book*. Boston: R. M. Thayer & Co., 1892.

Byrne, Edward M. *Military Law*. Annapolis: Naval Institute Press, 1976.

Caldwell, Charles K. *The Old Sixth Regiment, Its War Record, 1861-5*. New Haven: Tuttle, Morehous and Taylor, 1875.

Callahan, John F. *The Military Laws of the United States*. Philadelphia: George W. Childs, 1863.

Camper, Charles, and J. W. Kirkley, comps. *Historical Record of the First Regiment Maryland Infantry*. Washington: Gibson Bros., 1871.

Cannon, Le Grand B. *Personal Reminiscences of the Rebellion 1861-1866*. New York: Burr Printing House, 1895.

Catton, Bruce. *The Army of the Potomac: Glory Road*. Garden City, New York: Doubleday & Co., Inc., 1952.

Collins, Lewis. *History of Kentucky*. Berea, Kentucky: Kentuckee Imprints, 1975.

Copp, Elbridge J. *Reminiscences of the War of the Rebellion 1861-1865*. Nashua: The Telegraph Publishing Company, 1911.

Corby, Very Rev. William, C.S.C. *Memoirs of Chaplain Life: Three Years Chaplain in the Famous "Irish Brigade," Army of the Potomac*. Notre Dame: Scholastic Press, 1894.

Cooke, Philip St. George. *Scenes and Adventures in the Army; or, Romance of Military Life*. Philadelphia: Lindsay and Blakiston, 1895.

*The Daily Conservative*. Leavenworth, Kansas. [newspaper]

*Daily Oregonian*. Portland, Oregon. [newspaper]

Davis, William C. *The Deep Waters of the Proud: The Imperiled Union, 1861-1865*. Garden City, New York: Doubleday, 1982.

DeHart, William Chetwood. *Observations on Military Law, and the Constitution of Courts-Martial, with a Summary of the Law of Evidence, As Applicable to Military Trials; Adapted to the Laws, Regulations and Customs of the Army and Navy of the United States*. New York: Wiley and Putnam, 1846.

*Delaware Republican*. [newspaper]

Dennett, Tyler, ed. *Lincoln and the Civil War in the Diaries and Letters of John Hay*. New York: Dodd, Mead & Co., 1939.

Dornbusch, C. E., comp. *Regimental Publications & Personal Narratives of the Civil War, A Checklist*. New York: The New York Public Library, 1961-62.

Doster, William E. *Lincoln and Episodes of the Civil War*. New York: G. P. Putnam's Sons, 1915.

Drake, Julia A. *The Mail Goes Through or The Civil War Letters of George Drake [1846-1918], Eighty-Fifth Illinois Vol. August 9, 1862 to May 29, 1865*. San Angelo: Anchor Publishing Co., 1964.

DuChanal, General. "How Soldiers Were Tried," *Civil War Times Illustrated*. VII [February 1969] 10:10-15.

Dwight, Wilder. *Life and Letters of Wilder Dwight*. Boston: Little, Brown and Co., 1891.

Elkins, Vera Dockery. *Letters from a Civil War Soldier*. [Jasper E. James] New York: Vantage Press, 1969.

Emerson, Edward W. *Life and Letters of Charles Russell Lowell*. Cambridge: The Riverside Press, 1907.

Everett, Robinson O. *Military Justice in the Armed Forces of the United States*. Harrisburg: Military Service Publishing Co., 1956.

*Field Records of Officers of the Veteran Reserve Corps, from the Commencement to the Close of the Rebellion*. Washington: Scriver & Swing, undated.

Finn, James. *Conscience and Command*. New York: Random House, 1971.

Ford, Andrew E. *The Story of the Fifteenth Regiment Massachusetts Volunteer Infantry in the Civil War 1861-1864*. Clinton: W. J. Coulter, 1898.

Fox, S. M. *The Seventh Kansas Cavalry: Its Service in the Civil War*. Topeka: State Printing Office, 1908.

Frederick, Gilbert. *The Story of a Regiment, Being a Record of the Military Service of the Fifty-Seventh New York State Volunteer Infantry in the War of the Rebellion*. Chicago: C. H. Morgan Co., 1895.

Friedman, Leon, ed. *The Law of War: A Documentary History*. 2 vols. New York: Random House, 1972.

Fuller, Richard F. *Chaplain Fuller: Being a Life Sketch of A New England Clergyman and Army Chaplain*. Boston: Walker, Wise and Co., 1863.

Generous, William T., Jr. *Swords and Scales: The Development of the Uniform Code of Military Justice*. Port Washington: Kennikat Press, 1973.

Gerrish, Theodore. *Army Life: A Private's Reminiscences in the Civil War*. Portland: Hoyt, Fogg and Dunahan, 1882.

Glover, Edwin A. *Bucktailed Wildcats: A Regiment of Civil War Volunteers*. New York: Thomas Yoseloff, 1960.

Goddard, Henry P. *Fourteenth Connecticut Volunteers: Regimental Reminiscences of the War of the Rebellion*. Middletown: C. W. Church, 1877.

Graham, Stanley Silton. "Life of the Enlisted Soldier on the Western Frontier." M. A. thesis, North Texas State University, 1972.

Gregg, Rev. J. Chandler. *Life in the Army, in the Departments of Virginia, and the Gulf, including Observations in New Orleans, with an Account of the Author's Life and Experience in the Ministry*. Philadelphia: Perkinpim and Higgins, 1866.

Hallowell, Norwood P. *The Negro as a Soldier in the War of the Rebellion*. Boston: Little, Brown and Co., 1897.

Hartpence, William R. *History of the Fifty-First Indiana Veteran Volunteer Infantry*. Cincinnati: The Robert Clarke Co., 1894.

Hicken, Victor. *The American Fighting Man*. New York: The Macmillan Co., 1969.

Higginson, Thomas Wentworth. *Army Life in a Black Regiment*. Boston: Fields, Osgood and Co., 1870.

History Committee. *History of the Eleventh Pennsylvania Volunteer Cavalry*. Philadelphia: Franklin Printing Co., 1902.

Houghton, Edwin B. *The Campaigns of the Seventeenth Maine*. Portland: Short & Loring, 1866.

Humphreys, Charles A. *Field, Camp, Hospital and Prison in the Civil War, 1863-1865*. Freeport, New York: Books for Libraries Press, 1971.

Hunt, Aurora. *The Army of the Pacific. Its Operations in California, Texas, Arizona, New Mexico, Utah, Nevada, Oregon, Washington, Plains Region, Mexico, etc. 1860-1866*. Glendale, California: The Arthur H. Clark Co., 1951.

Hunter, Alf. G. *History of the Eighty-Second Indiana Volunteer Infantry, Its Organizations, Campaigns and Battles*. Indianapolis: Wm. B. Burford, 1893.

Hyman, Harold M. *A More Perfect Union: The Impact of the Civil War and Reconstruction on the Constitution*. New York: Alfred A. Knopf, 1973.

Johnson, E. Polk. *A History of Kentucky and Kentuckians*. 3 vols. Chicago: Lewis Publishing Co., 1912.

*Journal of the Adjourned Session of 1863-4, of the House of Representatives of the Commonwealth of Kentucky*. Frankfort: privately published, 1865.

Kansas Adjutant General. *Official Military History of Kansas Regiments During the War for the Suppression of the Great Rebellion*. Leavenworth: W. S. Burke, 1870.

Klein, Frederic S. "On Trial," *Civil War Times Illustrated.* VII [January 1969] 9:40-46.

Knudten, Richard D. *Crime in a Complex Society: An Introduction to Criminology.* Homewood: Dorsey Press, 1970.

*Lawrence Republican*, Kansas. [newspaper]

Lemke, W. J. *Chaplain Edward Gee Miller of the 20th Wisconsin: His War 1862-1865.* Fayetteville: Washington County Historical Society, 1960.

"List of U. S. Soldiers Executed by United States Military Authorities during the Late War." Washington: Adjutant General's Office, 1 August 1885.

Lonn, Ella. *Desertion during the Civil War.* New York: Century, 1928.

Love, William Deloss. *Wisconsin in the War of the Rebellion: A History of All Regiments and Batteries.* Chicago: Church and Goodman, 1866.

Maine, Adjutant General's Office. *Annual Report of the Adjutant General for the State of Maine for the Year Ending December 31, 1863.* Augusta: Stevens and Sayward, 1863.

*The Manhattan Express.* Kansas. [newspaper]

Matchett, William B. *Maryland and the Glorious Old Third in the War for the Union.* Washington: T. J. Brashears, 1882.

McPherson, James M. *Ordeal by Fire, The Civil War and Reconstruction.* New York: Alfred A. Knopf, 1982.

Meade, George Gordon, ed. *The Life and Letters of George Gordon Meade.* 2 vols. New York: Charles Scribner's Sons, 1913.

Meagher, Thomas Francis. *The Last Days of the 69th in Virginia.* New York: Office of the "Irish-Americans," undated.

Michigan, Adjutant General's Office. *Records of Service of Michigan Volunteers in the Civil War, 1861-1865.* Kalamozoo: Ihling Brothers and Everard, 1903.

Murdock, George Converse. *Patriotism Limited: 1862-1865, The Civil War Draft and the Bounty System.* Kent, Ohio: Kent State University Press, 1967.

National Archives. *RG 94, Records of the Adjutant General's Office, 1780s-1917.* Muster Rolls of Volunteer Organizations, Civil War.

-----. *RG 94, Records of the Adjutant General's Office, 1780s-1917.* Compiled Military Service Records.

Neal, Mary J., ed. *The Journal of Eldress Nancy.* Nashville: The Parthenon Press, 1963.

Nelson, Herbert B., and Preston E. Onstad, eds. *A Webfoot Volunteer, The Diary of William M. Hilleary 1864-1866.* Corvallis: Oregon State University Press, 1965.

*News from Fort Craig, New Mexico, 1863. Civil War Letters of Andrew Ryan, with the First California Volunteers.* Introduction and notes by Ernest Marchand. Sante Fe: Stagecoach Press, 1966.

O'Brien, John. *A Treatise on American Military Laws, and the Practice of Courts-Martial; With Suggestions for Their Improvement.* Philadelphia: Lea and Blanchard, 1846.

O'Brien, Thos. M., and Oliver Diefendorf. *General Orders of the War Department, Embracing the Years 1861, 1862 & 1863.* New York: Derby and Miller, 1864.

Page, Charles A. *Letters of a War Correspondent.* Boston: L. C. Page and Co., Inc., 1899.

Page, Charles Davis. *History of the Fourteenth Regiment, Connecticut Vol. Infantry.* Meriden: Horton Printing Co., 1906.

Peck, Henry T. *Historical Sketch of the 118th Regiment Pennsylvania Volunteers, "Corn Exchange Regt."* "...read at the Ceremonies of Dedicating the Monument on Round Top, Gettysburg, September 8th, 1884." No publisher, 1884.

*Philadelphia Inquirer* [newspaper]

Post, Lydia Minturn, ed. *Soldiers' Letters, From Camp, Battle-Field and Prison.* New York: Bunce and Huntington, 1865.

Price, Isaiah. *History of the Ninety-Seventh Regiment, Pennsylvania Volunteer Infantry, During the War of the Rebellion, 1861-65.* Philadelphia: By the author, 1875.

Prucha, Francis Paul. *A Guide to the Military Posts of the United States 1789-1895.* Madison: The State Historical Society of Wisconsin, 1964.

Pullen, John J. *The Twentieth Maine*. Philadelphia: J. B. Lippincott Co., 1957.

Quarles, Benjamin. *The Negro in the Civil War*. New York: Russell & Russell, 1968.

Quiner, E. B. *The Military History of Wisconsin: A Record of the Civil War and Military Patriotism of the State, in the War for the Union*. Chicago: Clarke & Co., 1866.

Randall, James G. *Constitutional Problem Under Lincoln*. Urbana: University of Illinois Press, 1964.

*Report of the Adjutant General of the State of Kansas, 1861-65*. Topeka, 1896.

Robertson, James I. "Military Executions," *Civil War Times Illustrated* V [May 1966] 2:34-39.

Roe, Alfred S. *The Twenty-Fourth Regiment, Massachusetts Volunteers 1861-1866, "New England Guard Regiment."* Worcester: Twenty-Fourth Veteran Association, 1907.

Roehrenbeck, William J. *The Regiment That Saved the Capital*. New York: Thomas Yoseloff, 1961.

Root, William Francis Stanton. *The Sixty-Ninth Regiment in Peace and War*. New York: Blanchard Press, 1905.

Rowell, John W. *Yankee Artillerymen: Through the Civil War with Eli Lilly's Indiana Battery*. Knoxville: The University of Tennessee Press, 1975.

-----. *Yankee Cavalrymen: Through the Civil War with the 9th Pennsylvania Cavalry*. Knoxville: The University of Tennessee Press, 1971.

Smith, A. P. *History of the Seventy-Sixth Regiment New York Volunteers*. Cortland: Truair, Smith and Miles, Printers, 1867.

Smith, Donald L. *The Twenty-fourth Michigan of the Iron Brigade*. Harrisburg: The Stackpole Co., 1962.

Smith, Page. *Trial by Fire*. New York: McGraw-Hill, 1982.

Sparks, David S., ed. *Inside Lincoln's Army, The Diary of Marsena Rudolph Patrick, Provost Marshall General, Army of the Potomac*. New York: Thomas Yoseloff, 1964.

Sprague, Homer Baxter. *History of the Thirteenth Regiment of Connecticut Volunteers during the Great Rebellion*. Hartford: Case, Lockwood & Co., 1867.

Stansfield, George James. "A History of the Judge Advocate General's Department, United States Army," *Military Affairs*. [Fall 1945] 9:219-237.

Starr, N. D., and T. W. Holman, comps. *The 21st Missouri Regiment Infantry Veteran Volunteers*. Fort Madison: Roberts and Roberts, 1899.

Swinton, William. *History of the Seventh Regiment, National Guard, State of New York, During the War of the Rebellion*. New York: Fields, Osgood and Co., 1870.

Thomas, Benjamin P., and Harold M. Hyman. *Stanton: The Life and Times of Lincoln's Secretary of War*. New York: Alfred A. Knopf, 1962.

Toombs, Samuel. *Reminiscences of the War, Comprising a Detailed Account of the Experiences of the Thirteenth Regiment New Jersey Volunteers in Camp, on the March, and in Battle*. Organe: Journal Office, 1878.

U. S. Judge Advocate General's Office. *Digest of Opinions of the Judge Advocate General of the Army [1862-1868]*. W. Winthrop, ed. 3rd ed. Washington: Government Printing Office, 1868.

U. S. War Department. *War of the Rebellion: A Compilation of the Official Records of the Union and Confederate Armies*. ed. by Robert N. Scott, et al. 70 vols. in 128 parts. Washington: Government Printing Office, 1881-1901.

Waitt, Ernest Linden, comp. *History of the Nineteenth Regiment Massachusetts Volunteer Infantry, 1861-1865*. Salem: Salem Press Co., 1906.

Walkley, Stephen. *History of the Seventh Connecticut Infantry, Hawley's Brigade, Terry's Division, Tenth Army Corps, 1861-1865*. Privately published, 1905.

Walton, Clyde C., ed., Thaddeus C. S. Brown, Samuel J. Murphy, William G. Putney, authors. *Behind the Guns; The History of Battery I, 2nd Regiment, Illinois Light Artillery*. Carbondale and Edwardsville: Southern Illinois Press, 1965.

Weigley, Russell F. *History of the United States Army*. New York: The Macmillan Co., 1967.

West Virginia, Department of Archives and History. Civil War Service Records.

Weygant, Charles H. *History of the One Hundred and Twenty-Fourth Regiment, N.Y.S.V.* Newburgh: Journal Printing House, 1877.

Wright, J. J. *History of the Eighth Regiment Kentucky Volunteer Infantry, During Its Three Years Campaign*. St. Joseph: St. Joseph Steam Printing, 1880.

Zornow, William Frank. "Lincoln and Private Lennan," *Indiana Magazine of History*. XXXXIX [September 1953] 3:267-272.

# Index

## V